RESEARCH ON ACCOUNTING ETHICS

Volume 2 • 1996

RESEARCH ON ACCOUNTING ETHICS

Managing Editor: LAWRENCE A. PONEMON
SUNY Binghamton
and KPMG Peat Marwick, LLP

Associate Editors: TIMOTHY B. BELL
KPMG Peat Marwick, LLP

MARC J. EPSTEIN
Stanford University

JAMES GAA
University of Alberta

ROBERT G. RULAND
The Ruland Management Corporation

VOLUME 2 • 1996

JAI PRESS INC.

Greenwich, Connecticut *London, England*

55 Old Post Road No. 2
Greenwich, Connecticut 06836

JAI PRESS LTD.
The Courtyard
28 High Street
Hampton Hill
Middlesex TW12 1PD
England

ISBN: 1-55938-997-4

Manufactured in the United States of America

This volume is dedicated to the memory of Professor David R.L. Gabhart, a dear friend, colleague, and scholar in the accounting ethics community.

CONTENTS

LIST OF CONTRIBUTORS

C. Richard Baker	Department of Accounting and Financial Management University of Essex
Bonita A. Daly	College of Business and Industry University of Massachusetts, Dartmouth
Ronald A. Davidson	Faculty of Business Administration Simon Fraser University
Martha M. Eining	David Eccles School of Business University of Utah
Craig Emby	Faculty of Business Administration Simon Fraser University
Dann G. Fisher	College of Business Kansas State University
Marshall Geiger	Department of Accounting University of Rhode Island
James R. Hamill	Anderson School of Management University of New Mexico
Sara York Kenny	David Eccles School of Business University of Utah
James Lampe	College of Business Admistration Texas Tech University

Raef A. Lawson	School of Business The University at Albany
Alan G. Mayper	College of Business Administration University of North Texas
Barbara D. Merino	College of Business Administration University of North Texas
Steven M. Mintz	School of Business Southwest Texas State University
Kathy S. Moffeit	School of Business Southwest Texas State University
Bruce L. Oliver	College of Business Rochester Institute of Technology
Richard L. Ott	College of Business Kansas State University
K. Raghunandan	Department of Accounting University of Massachusetts, Dartmouth
Samuel L. Seaman	Hankamer School of Business Baylor University
Rajendra P. Srivastava	Ernst & Young Center for Auditing Research and Advanced Technology School of Business University of Kansas
D.V. Rama	Department of Accounting University of Massachusetts, Dartmouth
Ruth Lesher Taylor	School of Business Southwest Texas State University
C. William Thomas	Hankamer School of Business Baylor University
Tom Tolleson	College of Business Administration University of North Texas

EDITORIAL BOARD

GUIDELINES FOR PUBLICATION FOR *RESEARCH ON ACCOUNTING ETHICS*

Authors may submit manuscripts by sending a hard copy version to:

Professor Lawrence A. Ponemon
School of Management
SUNY Binghamton
Binghamton, NY 13902-6000

Computer files should be submitted on a 3.5-inch IBM compatible diskette. Computer copies may be submitted in any wordprocessing program, although WordPerfect 5.0 or 5.1 is preferable. Computer files should be submitted in as basic a format as possible; font changes should be avoided except where italics or underlining are necessary. All tables should be submitted in the same computer file. *All* pages should be numbered. The order for presentation is as follows: body, appendices, notes, references, tables, figures. Notes should appear at the *end* of the text before the references; notes should *not* appear at the end of each page.

When identifying a reference in text, the last name of the author(s) and the date of the reference should be listed in parentheses, *with no punctuation between the author and date*; a semicolon should separate multiple references.

Example:
... in previous cash flow research (Wilson 1986; Rayburn 1986, 1988; Bernard and Stober 1989), and in other areas ...

When citing a direct quote, the page number of the quote *must* also be provided.

Examples:
"...employment with a firm" (Miceli and Near 1992, 37). Miceli and Near (1992) suggest "... with a firm" (p. 37).

References are listed in alphabetical order with no numbers. Presented below is a sample of the reference format. Please note in particular that the first author is listed last name first; however, each author thereafter is listed with first initials first, followed by last name.

Sample References

Barth, M.E. 1991. Relative measurement errors among alternative pension asset and liability measures. *The Accounting Review* (July): 433-463.

Belsley, D.A., E. Kuh, and R.E. Welsch. 1980. *Regression Diagnostics: Identifying Influential Data and Sources of Collinearity*. New York: Wiley.

Chatterjee, S., and B. Price. 1977. *Regression Analysis by Example*. New York: Wiley.

Financial Accounting Standards Board. 1984. *Statement of Financial Accounting Standard No. 81: Disclosures of Postretirement Health Care and Life Insurance Benefits.* Stamford, CT: FASB.

Harper, R.M., W.G. Mister, and J.R. Strawser. 1991. The effect of recognition versus disclosure of unfunded postretirement benefits on lenders' perception of debt. *Accounting Horizons* (September): 50-56.

Mittelstaedt, F., and M. Warshawsky. 1992. The impact of liabilities for retiree health benefits on share prices. Working paper, Department of Accountancy, University of Notre Dame.

SAS Institute Inc. 1985. *SAS User's Guide: Statistics*. Cary, NC: SAS Institute.

White, H. 1980. Covariance matrix estimator. *Econometrics* 50: 817-838.

SHOULD AUDITORS PROVIDE NONAUDIT SERVICES TO THEIR AUDIT CLIENTS?

Ronald A. Davidson and Craig Emby

ABSTRACT

Public accounting firms are providing an increasing amount of nonaudit services, both to their audit clients and to other companies. Over the years, questions have been raised on the ethics of the provision of nonaudit services to audit clients by auditors and many studies have considered the effects of the provision of such services. Whether or not it is ethically appropriate depends on the potential effects of such activities on auditors' independence.

The purpose of this paper is to summarize the research that considers the effects on perceptions of independence from the point of view of either auditors or users and to provide additional evidence on one of the key issues underlying the ethical questions that surround this question: are auditors' decisions actually affected by the provision of nonaudit services to their audit clients?

Research on Accounting Ethics, Volume 2, pages 1-20.

ISBN: 1-55938-997-4

The studies included in this paper are categorized according to six important questions to be answered in evaluating the ethics of this problem. Published studies using auditor or user subjects that provide empirical evidence on the answers to these questions are reviewed and the overall results are evaluated in terms of the answers they provide to the questions.

The second part of the paper presents the results of an experiment that addresses the question of auditor independence "in fact"—the experiment examines whether an auditor's independence may be compromised in the evaluation of a client's internal control system by bias due to the knowledge that the designer of the system was the auditor's own firm. The results show that the auditors do not act in a manner indicating bias in favor of their own firm. The results indicate that if there are weaknesses in the internal control system designed by their own firm, auditors tend to be more conservative in their audit planning. This evidence does not support the position that the provision of nonaudit services such as systems design compromises the auditor's independence and therefore may be unethical.

INTRODUCTION

Should auditors provide nonaudit services to their audit clients? This question has been asked for at least 30 years, but no consensus has emerged on the answer. Although numerous research studies have been undertaken on this question, their results do not provide clear answers. The controversial nature of the arguments that surround this question is derived, in part, because it involves an ethical question: Given that users of audited financial statements value audit opinions for the credibility added to the financial statements by the opinion of auditors who are independent of management, is it ethical for auditors to conduct any other business with their audit clients? Underlying this question is the concern that auditors will compromise their independence if they have any other relationship with the audit client other than that of auditor.

Loss of independence can be either in appearance or in fact. Loss of independence *in appearance* will result in a loss of credibility for the auditor, with a resulting lack of faith in their audit opinion. Loss of independence *in fact* may lead to audit opinions that are unduly influenced by management or other business considerations rather than by an objective analysis of the accounting information.

The importance of auditor independence is not disputed in the many articles that have appeared in recent years. What is disputed is the effect on independence, both in appearance and in fact, of the provision of services other than auditing to audit clients. The provision by audit firms of a range of services (frequently referred to under the general category of "management advisory services" or "MAS") to audit clients and other companies comprises an important and increasing proportion of the total revenues of public accounting firms (Hillison and Kennelly 1988; Reckers and Stagliano 1981; Scheiner and Kiger 1982).[1] The position of audit firms is that the provision of nonaudit services to audit clients does not impair their audit independence and raises no ethical conflicts. However, an opposing position is taken by others, including regulators, who fear that any additional involvement by auditors with their audit clients may be detrimental to auditor independence. Such involvement may create situations that could result in the auditor as consultant making decisions for the client, becoming too much like an employee of the client, developing too close a relationship with the client, assuming an advocacy role for the client, or possessing a financial stake in the client (Schulte 1966).

One purpose of this paper is to review the published studies that provide empirical evidence of the effect on auditors' independence from the provision of MAS to audit clients and to summarize and integrate these findings. Our approach has been to group the papers into one of six categories, according to the specific aspect of the independence question addressed by the paper. Our review is limited to published studies that use auditors and/or users as subjects.

Following discussion of the last question, which deals with possible impairment of independence "in fact," we present an experiment that provides further evidence on the question of whether ethical concerns are justified. We examine whether the provision of MAS by an audit firm (specifically systems design) biases the judgments of the auditor in the evaluation of the resulting internal control system and subsequently influences their decision as to the appropriate amount of audit work to be done.

THE REVIEW

Question 1: Do Users of Audited Financial Statements Have Ethical Concerns that Auditors are Providing MAS to Their Audit Clients?

One of the earliest studies to address this question was Schulte (1965). Schulte received 635 responses to a mail questionnaire from financial executives (commercial loan officers and financial analysts) who represent important groups of third parties who rely on audited financial statements. Approximately 45% indicated that MAS "possibly could" impair auditor independence and 55% indicated that it did not. Interestingly, a number of respondents (20%) indicated that knowledge that the auditor was providing MAS would actually increase their confidence in audit reports.

Similar results were found by Titard (1971) and Barton (1985). Titard presented 160 bank trust and loan officers and financial analysts from other companies with a list of 33 different types of MAS that are provided by auditors to their audit clients. Subjects were asked to indicate which of these services "might cause a loss of independence." A total of 46% of respondents with an opinion indicated that none of the 33 would cause a loss of independence while 46% indicated that some types would (9% of the 160 subjects had no opinion). Respondents showed little agreement on the sensitive types of MAS as all 33 were selected by at least 11 respondents. None of the 33 was selected by more than 50 respondents. In Barton's (1985) smaller sample (39 usable replies), 72% indicated MAS had no effect on auditor independence, 20% indicate MAS improves independence, and 8% indicated it lessens independence.

In summary, the results indicate a fairly even split—slightly less than half the 841 total respondents (45%) perceive the provision of some forms of MAS as a potential threat to auditor independence and slightly more than half (55%) did not. The results of Schulte (1965) and Barton (1985) indicate that some users actually have more confidence in the audited financial statements if the auditors also provide MAS to the audit client.

Question 2: Do Auditors and Users Have Similar Concerns?

Dykxhoorn and Sinning (1981) asked 108 German auditors if they would maintain their independence in each of ten different situations. The situations covered different types of relationships and services being provided by auditors to audit clients. In nine of the ten scenarios, a majority of the auditors indicated independence would be maintained.

However, a more powerful research design, used in the following four studies, asked the same questions of both auditors and users to determine if there were differences in responses between the two groups. Briloff (1966, 1987) strongly disagrees with the view that auditors and users share the same views on auditor independence when auditors provide MAS to audit clients: Briloff supported his opposition to this contention in a study that compared responses received from 72 financial analysts and 64 auditors. When asked if MAS is detrimental to independence, a majority of the users (53%) said it detracts, but a majority of the auditors (69%) said it has no effect.

Similar results were found by Hartley and Ross (1972) who compared the responses of 474 auditors and 501 financial analysts and financial officers. When asked their opinion on whether the provision of MAS affects independence, a majority of the auditors (56%) indicated that it had no effect but the users were split evenly on the question. Firth (1980) presented 29 different auditor-client relationships to 251 British Chartered Accountants (CAs) and 138 financial analysts and loan officers and asked them for their opinion on the effects on independence. The relationships included the provision of MAS to audit clients. Both the CAs and the users indicated that 15 of the 29 relationships would result in the auditors maintaining their independence and 14 of the 29 would result in loss of independence (although the groups did not choose the identical subsets of items). Lindsay, Rennie, Murphy, and Silvester (1987) used a research design that was similar to Firth (1980), presenting 15 scenarios to 191 Canadian CAs and 265 financial analysts and bank loan officers. The CAs showed consensus in 12 of the 15 cases, with 11 of these agreeing the auditors maintained their independence. The analysts and bankers showed consensus in 12 and 10 scenarios respectively, agreeing that independence was maintained in 9 scenarios each.

A different result was found by Lavin (1976) using a similar research method. Lavin presented 202 auditors and 188 users with a series of 12 scenarios. Auditors stated that independence was maintained in seven cases, while the users indicated eight.

Overall, these studies suggest that the 1,164 external financial statement users are slightly more concerned about auditors' possible loss of independence than the 1,182 auditors themselves (approximately 57% compared to 53%). However, the difference between the two groups is not large, and even within the groups, there is not complete agreement as to circumstances which may lead to impaired independence.

Question 3: What Aspects of the Auditor, the Audit Client and the Relationship Influence These Ethical Concerns?

Five studies attempted to find reasons for the differences in perceptions by manipulating several attributes in the cases presented to subjects. Four of these manipulated the relative size of the MAS fees as a proportion of total audit fees (Reckers and Stagliano 1981; Pany and Reckers 1983; Knapp 1985; Pany and Reckers 1987). Types and numbers of subjects included 50 financial analysts and 50 MBA students (Reckers and Stagliano 1981), 92 members of boards of directors (Pany and Reckers 1983), 43 bank loan officers (Knapp 1985), and 333 bank loan officers and 215 financial analysts (Pany and Reckers 1987). In each of these four studies, auditor independence was perceived to be lessened as the relative size of the MAS fees increased.

Two of these cases manipulated the type of MAS. Reckers and Stagliano (1981) used five types of MAS while Pany and Reckers (1983) used three types. Reckers and Stagliano do not report finding any differences that are consistent with the type of MAS involved but Pany and Reckers do. They ranked systems design as the most sensitive, followed by acquisition review, then tax preparation. This ranking is different from the findings of Titard (1971). In Titard's study mergers and business acquisitions were the most sensitive type of MAS and systems designs were listed as number 13 of the 33 types.

Other variables manipulated included competition for audit clients (Shockley 1981; Knapp 1985). Both studies found that increased competition for audit clients results in perceptions of greater loss of audit independence. Shockley also manipulated the size of the audit firm and its tenure as auditor for the client. He found that larger audit firms are perceived to be able to maintain their independence better than small firms. Length of auditor-client association had no significant effect. Knapp also manipulated the financial condition of the client and found that stronger clients would have more influence over their auditors.

In summary, based on the findings of five studies that included 959 subjects, relative size of the MAS fee expressed as a percentage of the audit fees does appear to be important. The type of MAS also appears to be important based on the findings of three studies.

Question 4: Are the Ethical Perceptions of Auditors Affected by Personal or Cognitive Characteristics?

Two studies attempted to determine if individual characteristics of auditors affect their perceptions of auditors' independence. Gul (1987) assessed cognitive style (field dependence or independence) of 22 Australian CAs and asked them to assess four cases (a two-by-two design manipulating provision of MAS or not and a qualified or unqualified opinion). He found that cognitive style was related to perceptions of independence for the cases used in his study. While all subjects perceived reduced independence with MAS, the reduction was greater for field dependent subjects. Similarly, all subjects perceived greater independence with a qualified report, with field dependent subjects showing the largest increase. Ponemon and Gabhart (1990) related independence judgments made by 119 audit partners and managers with measures of their ethical cognition. They found that independence judgments are related to the stage of development of the ethical cognition displayed by subjects.

In summary, from the limited evidence provided by two studies involving 141 subjects, certain personal cognitive characteristics appear to affect perceptions of auditor independence. These findings are consistent with research in cognitive psychology, which has long known that each individual processes information differently, depending on his or her unique mix of cognitive content (ideas about the world) and cognitive processes (Scott, Osgood, and Peterson 1979; Chen and Olson 1989).

Question 5: Are the Decisions of Financial Statement Users Affected by the Auditor-Client Relationship?

Four papers asked user subjects to make decisions on different versions of the same basic set of facts.[2] Firth (1981) asked 586 British bankers to evaluate two loan applications each. Nine different versions of the case were used with different potential conflicts, two of which involved providing MAS by the auditors. For both situations involving the provision of MAS, subjects made different loan decisions compared to the control case. With MAS, lower loan amounts were recommended.

Dykxhoorn and Sinning (1982) provided 86 German bank loan officers with 27 scenarios each and asked them to rate the independence of the auditors and the effect of the situation on the loan decision. They found that, in general, perceived lack of independence had a significant negative effect on the loan decision.

In two other studies, banker subjects responded to a loan application package that included audited financial statements and indications that the auditor provided management advisory services in varying amounts. McKinley, Pany, and Reckers (1985) used 261 subjects who each received one version of the case. The auditors were described as being either a large or medium sized office of a Big Eight firm or a medium sized local firm. The instrument included two levels of management advisory services, either nil or 30% of audit fees, for each of the last three years. While the financial statements were perceived to be more reliable with large auditors compared to local firms and the provision of MAS resulted in reduced concern that fraud may be present in the financial statements, no significant differences were noted in the loan decisions made from the manipulations of MAS level or CPA firm size.

Pany and Reckers (1988) extended this study by including both loan officers (192) and financial analysts (104). Provision of MAS by the auditor was set at nil, 25%, 60%, or 90% of audit fees. Each subject received only one version of the case. Loan officers' decisions were affected by the level of MAS with the 25% case receiving a significantly higher loan approval rate. The financial analysts' decisions were affected only by the 90% case as they rated the company lower on a 12 month investment safety rating.

In summary, although the evidence provided by the 1895 user subjects is not totally unequivocal, the answer to Question 5 is "yes." Bank loan officers (and financial analysts) evaluate loan applications (or investment decisions) differently depending on the whether or not the auditors of the applicant's financial statements also provide MAS to the applicant. However, the relationship between the perceptions and the loan decision is not clear and may be affected by intervening factors such as a perceived lack of independence reduces the credibility of the audited financial statements, which likely increases the perceived risk of the loan applicant.

Question 6: Are the Decisions Made by Auditors During Audits Affected by the Provision of Other Services?

Perhaps the most interesting aspect of lack of independence is the effect on the auditor's decisions. Although DeAngelo's (1981) definition of auditor independence suggests that the actual discovery of an error is a given before independence becomes involved, it may be possible that lack of independence could lead to auditors not being sensitive to the possible existence of errors in the first place. An example of this type of situation would be when the auditor's firm designs and installs a client's internal control system and the audit staff fails to evaluate it properly. If the answer to this question is "yes," then the ethical concerns are justified and auditors should not be permitted to provide nonaudit services to their audit clients.

This potential problem was considered by Plumlee (1985), although he used internal auditors as subjects. Plumlee asked 39 internal auditors first to design a system either for sales and receivables or purchasing for a hypothetical firm. He then asked the subjects to evaluate either their own or someone else's design. He found that subjects who reviewed their own designs were better able to identify the strengths of their systems. Subjects who evaluated someone else's system were better able to identify the weaknesses of these systems. The implication of this finding is that auditors (at least internal auditors), may not properly evaluate systems they designed and so may fail to detect client errors.

Corless and Parker (1987) also investigated this problem. They asked 181 auditor subjects to analyze an internal control system that was described as being designed either by the client or by the auditor. No significant differences were found in the analysis of the internal control systems when the analyses of the two groups were compared. In fact, there was a slight tendency for auditors to be more critical of systems that were described as being designed by their own firm.

These two studies involving 220 subjects found different results. Plumlee (1985) found that internal auditor involvement in the design of client systems resulted in poorer analysis of the systems, but Corless and Parker (1987) found no differences using external auditors as subjects. This is a critical area as it underlies the concerns raised about auditor provision of MAS to audit clients. Are decisions made by auditors detrimentally affected by their provision of nonaudit services?

SUMMARY

Based on a substantial number of subjects (3,187) included in eight different studies, users and auditors appear to be evenly split in their perceptions as to whether the provision of MAS to audit clients appears to lessen auditor independence. Relative size and type of MAS impact on these concerns (based on six studies involving 1,092 subjects). There is preliminary evidence that personal and cognitive differences also affect these concerns (two studies and 141 subjects). Users' decisions appear to be affected by the provision of MAS (based on findings involving four studies and 1895 subjects), but it is not clear if auditors' decisions are also affected (two studies and 220 subjects).

As a final note, the question of the ethical nature of the provision of MAS to audit clients appears to be an international concern. Of the 21 empirical studies included in this review, data from five countries are included (United States, Canada, United Kingdom, Australia, and Germany). An international review of legal and regulatory prohibitions would be valuable.

The next section of the paper describes an experiment which is designed to provide additional information on Question 6.

THE EXPERIMENT

Rationale and Statement of the Hypothesis

If auditors' decisions are affected by their provision of nonaudit services to audit clients, then this practice could be viewed as being not only unethical, but also unwise as it could eventually lead to a loss of credibility. An area of MAS that would be very sensitive to this potentially negative effect is the design of systems that must be evaluated by auditors for control risk.

The preliminary evaluation of the internal control system plays a critical role in the audit. For example, if the strength of internal controls is overestimated, the extent and types of audit tests selected may not be sufficient for the actual level of risk in the system. Any systematic biases that occur in the evaluation of the internal control system could ultimately lead to significant errors in the final summary opinion. As discussed in Question 6, the results of prior empirical research are inconsistent. As a result we simply state the hypothesis in the null form:

Hypothesis 1. There is no difference in audit assessments between auditors who assess internal control systems designed by their own firm and auditors who assess internal control systems designed by the client.

Subjects

The subjects were 112 practicing auditors from four of the "Big Six" firms in a major Canadian city. There were three juniors, 59 seniors, 36 managers, and 14 partners. The respondents' average auditing experience was 6.5 years (range of 0.5 years to 30.5). They were assigned randomly to one of four experimental conditions. The subjects were asked at the end of the experimental case to indicate the number of audits of inventory systems in which they had been involved—the responses ranged from 0 to 300 with a mean of 28 and a standard deviation of 49.

Experimental Design

The study employed a 2 × 2 factorial between-subjects design requiring before-and-after evaluation of an internal control system that changed during the year. The first experimental manipulation related to the designer of the new system (the audit firm or the client). The second manipulation related to the strength of the new system. Weaker and stronger versions of the case were included to test if there were any differential effects depending on the relative strength of the new system.

On the basis of an initial description of the inventory internal control system (the same for all cases), the auditors were first asked to specify the appropriate level of substantive testing for the inventory area. The purpose of the initial substantive testing decision was twofold—first, to establish the initial equality of the four groups, and second, to provide a covariate for an ANCOVA analysis of the revised substantive testing decision based on the "new" internal control system. They were then given a description of the "new" system. There were four versions of this new system, reflecting the 2 × 2 design. The auditors were asked to evaluate the strength of the new system and to indicate the amount of substantive testing that they now felt was appropriate for the inventory area.

Administration

Copies of the case were provided to contact partners in six offices of four accounting firms who agreed to distribute them to professional staff.[3] Each subject received only one version of the case. A cover letter was included with each case asking for the assistance of subjects in the study, which was described quite generally as a study on internal control. Return envelopes were included so subjects could mail them directly to the researchers.

The initial narrative informed subjects they were evaluating the client's internal control system over inventory to finalize the audit plan for that area. Subsequent to the initial narrative which introduced the client and provided a brief description of the inventory system, the auditors were asked to make a preliminary assessment of the amount of substantive testing (PAAST) they believed necessary for inventory, using a scale ranging from "1-minimal" to "7-exhaustive."

After making a preliminary assessment the auditors read that the client had changed their inventory system from a manual periodic system to a computerized perpetual system. The first manipulation was achieved by having one version state that the client's chief accountant designed the new system and the other version state that the client hired "your firm's systems group" to change the system. This was crossed with the manipulation of the relative strength of the new internal control system. There were seven items of additional information about the changes to the internal control system—three aspects of the internal control system were different between the two treatments. One version of the case contained aspects intended to make the system appear relatively weaker; the other version described a relatively stronger system. The descriptive changes were minimal to reduce the probability of unintentionally introducing other changes to the two versions of the case. An example is: "Receipts of inventory are counted, inspected for damages, completeness, etc., *on a test basis* [italics not in actual case material] and a receiving report, *not prenumbered*, is prepared for all materials crossing the receiving dock" (for the weaker version) and "Receipts of inventory are counted, inspected for damages, completeness, etc. and a receiving report, *prenumbered*, is prepared for all materials crossing the receiving dock" (for the stronger version).

Subjects were then asked to evaluate the new internal control system using a scale that ranged from "1-very weak" to "7-adequate to strong." They then made a revised assessment of the amount of substantive testing (RAAST) that would be appropriate using a scale identical to the first assessment. The last part of the instrument asked for demographic data to determine position level and experience of the subjects.[4]

Results

It was first necessary to ensure that the four groups all started with the same assessment of the old system. As all versions of the case contained the same preliminary descriptive information about the company and the inventory system before the changes (from "the previous year's working paper files"), the preliminary assessment of the amount of substantive testing (PAAST) that would be needed for this area should be the same for each group. Table 1 shows the mean responses of each of the four groups to the "initial assessment" on the amount of substantive testing needed for the system before learning that it had changed during the year. A 2×2 ANOVA on the responses to this "initial assessment" showed no significant main effects or interactions for the initial decisions, indicating that all subjects started from similar assessments.

After reading a description of the new system, subjects evaluated the strength of the internal control system on a scale ranging from 1 for "very weak" to 7 for "adequate to strong." Table 1 shows the internal control evaluation after learning of the change, and the revised assessment on the amount of substantive testing needed for the system (after learning of the change). The differences between the initial and revised assessments are significantly different, using t-tests, for three of the four case versions. The correlation coefficient between the internal control evaluations and the revised substantive testing assessments was, as expected, significantly negative ($\rho = -.75$, $p < .0001$).[5]

Table 2 shows the results of an analysis of covariance for the revised substantive testing assessments. The 2×2 ANCOVA shows that there is a significant main effect for the strength manipulation, that is, the weaker versus stronger case versions ($F = 31.99$, $p < .001$). These results indicate that auditors are sensitive to the effects of changes made to internal control systems (and that they were "paying attention" to the case material). They indicate that, as is normatively

Table 1. Preliminary Decisions About the Appropriate Amount of Substantive Testing (PAAST)

Case Version	*Statistic*	*Initial Assessment*	*Internal Control Assessment*	*Revised Assessment*
Client/ Weaker ($n = 28$)	Mean:	4.518	3.286	4.714
	Std. Dev.:	1.391	1.049	1.272
Client/ Stronger ($n = 37$)	Mean:	4.743	4.473	4.122*
	Std. Dev.:	1.176	1.067	1.063
Audit firm/ Weaker ($n = 25$)	Mean:	4.400	2.980	5.240**
	Std. Dev.:	1.061	1.183	0.779
Audit firm/ Stronger ($n = 22$)	Mean:	4.773	4.773	3.727**
	Std. Dev.:	0.922	1.075	1.298

Notes: * t-test of difference between initial and revised assessments significant at $p < .05$.
** t-test of difference between initial and revised assessments significant at $p < .01$.

appropriate, these auditors judge new systems with weak internal control features to need more substantive testing and new systems with strong internal control features to need less substantive testing. There is no main effect for the designer of the system, that is, the client versus the audit firm ($F = 0.16, p = .69$). It appears that, overall, their assessments were not affected by the identity of the designer of the new system. Thus in an overall analysis, the null hypothesis of no designer effect is not rejected.

However, Table 2 shows that the interaction of the two is significant ($F = 5.74$, $p = .0183$). The significant interaction effects suggest that the auditors were differentially sensitive in their assessments of internal control systems designed by audit clients and audit firms. Auditors appear to react more strongly to changes made by their audit firms than to changes made by the client. When the changes made resulted in a stronger system, the respondents indicated that less substantive testing is required when the changes are designed by the audit firm than the same system would need if designed by the audit client (3.727 versus 4.122). However, when the changes result in a weaker system, the responses indicate that more substantive testing is required when the changes are designed by the audit firm than the same system would need if designed by the audit client (5.240 versus 4.714).

Table 2. ANCOVA Results for the Test of the Bias Hypothesis

Effects	*SS/MS*	*DF*	*F*	*Significance*
Grand Mean:	55.153	1,107	50.02	.0000
Covariate:	16.365	1,107	14.84	.0002
Main effects:				
Designer	0.175	1,107	0.16	.69
Strength	35.272	1,107	31.99	.0000
Interaction:				
Designer × Strength	6.333	1,107	5.74	.0183
Error	117.97	1,103		

In Figure 1, the "fan pattern" of the preliminary and revised substantive testing assessments of the four groups illustrates graphically the more extreme reaction of the auditors to both the positive and negative changes in the internal control system when the changes were made by their own firm as opposed to when they were made by the client. It is noteworthy that when the design of the internal control system was relatively weak the auditors were more critical of their own firm's work than was the case for the client-designed system. This is in fact similar to the findings of Corless and Parker (1987), who also found that their auditor-subjects were somewhat more critical of the system designed by their own firm. It appears that in some circumstances at least, auditors are prepared to be critical of their own firm's work.

Summary

This study provides evidence on the question of whether it is ethical for audit firms to provide nonaudit services to their audit clients. In this case the assumption made is that the question of the ethicality of this practice is correlated with the question of whether auditors' decisions are actually affected in assessing internal control systems that were designed by their audit firm. The results of the study are mixed. The responses indicate that when the system is designed by the auditor's own firm, less substantive testing is needed if the new system is strong, but more substantive testing is needed if the new system is weak, as compared to the amount of substantive testing that would be needed if the new system had been designed by the audit client.

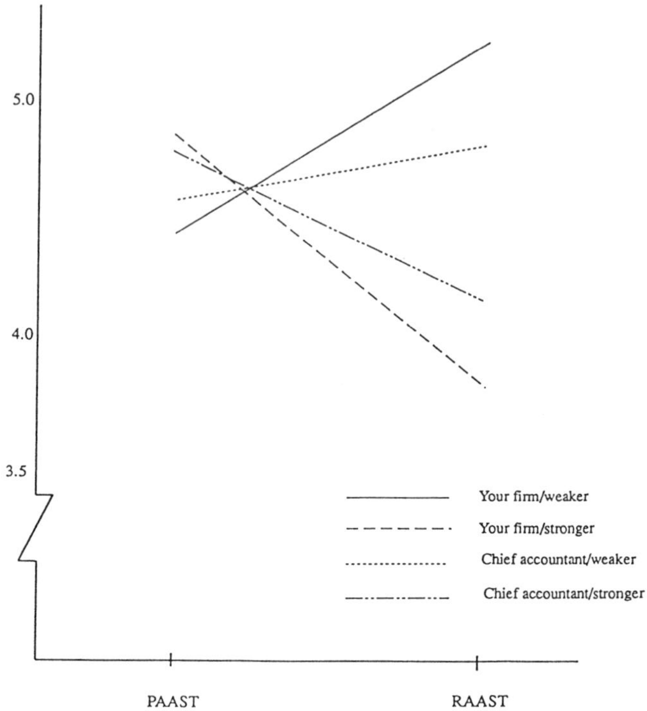

Figure 1. Preliminary and Revised Assessments of the Appropriate Amount of Substantive Testing (PAAST/RAAST)

DISCUSSION AND CONCLUSIONS

One purpose of this paper has been to review the published studies that provide empirical evidence on the effect on auditors' independence from the provision of MAS to audit clients and to summarize and integrate those findings. A number of questions were formulated that appear to summarize some of the concerns with this practice. The empirical research can be divided into two groups, one that considered the perceptions of auditors and users, and one that considered whether the concerns underlying these perceptions may be justified (Are the actual decisions made by users and auditors affected by the provision of nonaudit services to audit clients?). Both types of research are important as auditing involves the perceptions of credibility, but auditing has earned this credibility by its record of accuracy in its audit decisions. Any threat to the accuracy of audit decisions could eventually impact on audit credibility. Thus auditors should be aware that the provision of MAS to their audit clients is a potential threat to their credibility as almost one half of users believe it lessens auditors' independence. The research evidence on this is clear.

In general, the experimental results support the findings of Corless and Parker (1987) rather than those of Plumlee (1985). Auditors do not appear to be consistently biased towards a more favorable assessment when they assess systems designed by their firm's systems group. In fact, in some situations, the results indicate a tendency toward the opposite effect. While all auditors were sensitive to perceived weaknesses in the new internal control system, the auditors appeared to be more sensitive to limitations in the work of their own firm's systems group.

An implication of these findings appears to be that external auditors can maintain their independence when evaluating audit-client systems that were designed by their own firm. Future research could address the question of whether or not this would extend to the evaluation of systems they personally designed.

An obvious limitation of this study is that it involved just one hypothetical case presented to one set of 112 Canadian auditors from the large international accounting firms. Further studies should include different scenarios and auditors from different sizes of firms. Another extension would be to include auditors from different countries as this appears to be an interesting ethical issue in the international setting.

ACKNOWLEDGMENTS

The authors gratefully acknowledge helpful comments by Alec Gelardi, Rob Bahnson, and the participants in the workshop of the Northwest Accounting Research Group.

NOTES

1. Some of the reasons why auditors want to provide nonaudit services are indicated by Carmichael and Swieringa (1968) and Hillison and Kennelly, (1988). Reasons include the role of the auditor as a professional, demand for such services by clients, expansion of business in a maturing audit industry, efficiency, ability to attract and retain better staff, and risk diversification away from auditing. Another stream of research has emerged that emphasizes incentives and possible economies

that may be achievable with the joint production of both audit and nonaudit services (Beck, Frecka, and Solomon 1988a, 1988b; Abdel-Khalik 1990; Dopuch and King 1991; Parkash and Venable 1993; Davis, Ricchiute, and Trompeter 1993).

2. Note that these studies actually required a decision from the subjects (e.g., a planned action), as opposed to the foregoing studies which asked whether subjects *believed* audit independence would be affected.

3. Statistical tests on internal control evaluations and substantive testing decisions showed no significant differences by firm.

4. Statistical tests showed no significant differences in assessments by position or experience.

5. Subjects were also asked how confident they were about their judgments. No relationship was found with their level of confidence and any other variable, so confidence was not used in any tests.

REFERENCES

Abdel-Khalik, A.R. 1990. The jointness of audit fees and demand for MAS: A self-selection analysis. *Contemporary Accounting Research* 6 (2-I): 295-322.

Barton, M.F. 1985. Audit clients' perceptions of the independence of their CPA. *Mid-South Business Journal*: 20-22.

Beck, P.J., T.J. Frecka, and I. Solomon. 1988a. A model of the market for MAS and audit services: Knowledge spillovers and auditor-auditee bonding. *Journal of Accounting Literature* 7: 50-64.

———. 1988b. An empirical analysis of the relationship between MAS involvement and auditor tenure: Implications for auditor independence. *Journal of Accounting Literature* 7: 65-84.

Briloff, A.J. 1966. Old myths and new realities in accountancy. *The Accounting Review* (July): 484-495.

———. 1987. Do management services endanger independence and objectivity? *CPA Journal* (August): 22-29.

Carmichael, D.R., and R.J. Swieringa. The compatibility of auditing independence and management services—an identification of issues. *The Accounting Review* (October): 697-705.

Chen, K.H., and S.K. Olson. 1989. Measuring cognitive complexity in the accounting domain. *Behavioral Research in Accounting*: 160-181.

Corless, J.C., and L.M. Parker. 1987. The impact of MAS on auditor independence: An experiment. *Accounting Horizons* (September): 25-29.

Davis, L.R., D.N. Ricchiute, and G. Trompeter. 1993. Audit effort, audit fees, and the provision of nonaudit services to audit clients. *The Accounting Review* 68 (1): 135-150.

DeAngelo, L.E. 1981. Auditor independence, 'low balling', and disclosure regulation. *Journal of Accounting and Economics*: 113-127.

Dopuch, N., and R. King. 1991. The impact of MAS on auditors' independence: An experimental markets study. *Journal of Accounting Research* 29 (Supplement): 60-98.

Dykxhoorn, H.J., and K.E. Sinning. 1981. Wirtschaftsprufer perception of auditor independence. *The Accounting Review* (January): 97-107.

________. 1982. Perceptions of auditor independence: Its perceived effect on the loan and investment decisions of German financial statement users. *Accounting, Organizations and Society*: 337-347.

Firth, M. 1980. Perceptions of auditor independence and official ethical guidelines. *The Accounting Review* 55 (July): 451-466.

________. 1981. Auditor-client relationships and their impact on lenders' perceived lending decisions. *Accounting and Business Research* 55 (Summer): 179-188.

Gul, F.A. 1987. Field dependence cognitive style as a moderating factor in subjects' perceptions of auditor independence. *Accounting and Finance* 27 (May): 37-48.

Hartley, R.V., and T.L. Ross. 1972. MAS and audit independence: An image problem. *The Journal of Accountancy* 134 (November): 42-51.

Hillison, W., and M. Kennelly. 1988. The economics of nonaudit services. *Accounting Horizons* (September): 32-40.

Knapp, M.C. 1985. Audit conflict: An empirical study of the perceived ability of auditors to resist management pressure. *The Accounting Review* (April): 202-211.

Lavin, D. 1976. Perceptions of the independence of the auditor. *The Accounting Review* (January): 41-50.

Lindsay, D., M. Rennie, G. Murphy, and H. Silvester. 1987. Independence of external auditors: A Canadian perspective. *Advances in International Accounting*: 169-189.

McKinley, S., K. Pany, and P.M.J. Reckers. 1985. An examination of the influence of CPA firm type, size, and MAS provision on loan officer decisions and perceptions. *Journal of Accounting Research* (Autumn): 887-896.

Pany, K., and P.M.J. Reckers. 1983. Auditor independence and nonaudit services. *Journal of Accounting and Public Policy*: 43-62.

________. 1987. Within-vs. between-subjects experimental designs: A study of demand effects. *Auditing: A Journal of Practice & Theory* (Fall): 39-53.

________. 1988. Auditor performance of MAS: A study of its effects on decisions and perceptions. *Accounting Horizons* (June): 31-38.

Parkash, M., and C.F. Venable. 1993. Auditee incentives for auditor independence: The case of nonaudit services. *The Accounting Review* 68 (1): 113-133.

Plumlee, R.D. 1985. The standard of objectivity for internal auditors: Memory and bias effects. *Journal of Accounting Research* (Autumn): 683-699.

Ponemon, L.A., and D.R.L. Gabhart. 1990. Auditor independence judgments: A cognitive-developmental model and experimental evidence. *Contemporary Accounting Research* (Fall): 227-251.

Reckers, P.M.J., and A.J. Stagliano. 1981. Non-audit services and perceived independence: Some new evidence. *Auditing: A Journal of Practice & Theory* 1 (Summer): 23-37.

Scheiner, J.H., and J.E. Kiger. 1982. An empirical investigation of auditor involvement in non-audit services. *Journal of Accounting Research* (Autumn): 482-496.

Schulte, A.A. 1965. Compatibility of management consulting and auditing. *The Accounting Review* 40 (July): 587-593.

———. 1966. Management services: A challenge to audit independence? *The Accounting Review* (October): 721-728.

Scott, W.A., D.W. Osgood, and C. Peterson. 1979. *Cognitive Structure: Theory and Measurement of Individual Differences*. New York: Wiley.

Shockley, R.A. 1981. Perceptions of auditors' independence: An empirical analysis. *The Accounting Review* (October): 785-800.

Titard, P.L. 1971. Independence and MAS—opinions of financial statement users. *The Journal of Accountancy* (July): 47-52.

APPLYING BEHAVIORAL MODELS AS PRESCRIPTIONS FOR ETHICS IN ACCOUNTING PRACTICE AND EDUCATION:

REVISITING FISH OUT OF WATER AND AN EXPERIMENT

Tom Tolleson, Barbara D. Merino, and
Alan G. Mayper

ABSTRACT

Recently, accounting ethics researchers have used a Kohlbergian framework to measure accountants' moral reasoning abilities. Using these results, they advocate that we educate accountants so as to increase their ethical reasoning abilities as defined by Kohlberg's (1971) stage model. Feminists have critiqued Kohlberg's model, arguing that it contains a moral "gender gap." This paper

Research on Accounting Ethics, Volume 2, pages 21-49.

ISBN: 1-55938-997-4

examines Gilligan's (1982) criticisms of the Kohlberg model to show why it may be dysfunctional from a feminist perspective. We conducted an experiment to determine if the simplicity and moral minimalization of the Kohlberg model dilemmas alienate women.

Findings suggest that subjects were significantly impacted by dilemma context, socialization processes, and remoteness to a dilemma. We suggest that before we uncritically accept Kohlberg's model as single prescription for accounting education, more research is needed.

PRELUDE

Critiquing behavioral research in the early 1970s, Robert Jensen warned us that our research frequently extends into other disciplines looking for easy answers to our perceived problems. We look to others "for answers in order to avoid the dirty and painstakingly slow, expensive, and methodical means by which empirical evidence can be conceived and nurtured in their own studies." (Jensen 1970, 508) This outside influence "often flounders like a fish out of water when plucked from the environment in which it was generated" (p. 508).

Today, efforts to use Kohlberg's (1971) model of moral development to "remedy" the moral reasoning capacities of students and practitioners may be another example of "floundering fish." We are inundated with studies and prescriptions on how to include ethics in the classroom and to evaluate the ethical being of accountants. Our search for the golden fleece is a search for the universal truth of what is moral and how to be moral. We are, like Francis (1990, 1993), rather skeptical of the prescriptions being offered as principles and universal rules of human moral behavior.

Our concern with accountants' examination of ethics is not the advocation of a single prescription nor is it our intent to argue that the problem is too complex for consideration; rather, we believe deliberation is needed before advocacy. We need to ask ourselves what we are committing ourselves to if we unquestioningly accept Kohlberg's (1971) cognitive model of moral development and judgment.

For example, Ponemon and his associates (Ponemon 1990, 1992; Ponemon and Gabhart 1990, 1992) have reported that accountants are at a low "conventional" level of ethical reasoning with few obtaining the "postconventional" level as their careers advance. These studies indicate that accountants with lower ethical reasoning abilities remain in the profession while those with higher levels are not promoted. The measures of ethical reasoning are based on Kohlberg's model and use either Kohlberg's Moral Judgment Interview (MJI) instrument or Rest's (1988) Defining Issues Test (DIT) to categorize individuals at the various stage levels within Kohlberg's model. Based on these results, they advocate that we educate accountants to help them increase their ethical reasoning abilities as defined by Kohlberg's stage model. This represents an unquestioning commitment to Kohlberg's model.

Nevertheless, there is extensive criticism, outside of accounting, of the Kohlbergian morality framework. Feminists have justifiably critiqued Kohlberg's model, showing that the model's stages of development contain a moral "gender gap" (Gilligan 1982; Friedman 1987). The model and subsequent empirical applications of the model have ignored the moralities of "care" and "responsibility" in favor of a morality of "justice and rights" (Gilligan 1982). The stories used in moral reasoning measurements ignore the contextual richness and complexity actors would bring with them in making moral assessments (Friedman 1987). This allows for a narrow and minimalist approach to moral development. Others have criticized it for its utilitarian overtones and its implicit assumption of rationality (including extensions into economic rationality). Kohlberg's model represents an intersection of Kantian and utilititarian philosophies; moral reasoning and behavior represent autonomy (not community), universalizability (not contextuality), and moral equality of all persons (individualistic not communal).[1] This assumes as nonproblematic the connection between the ability to reason "morally" and better moral behavior—for example, to act morally.

Kohlberg's studies of moral development are empirically interesting from a cognitive psychology point of view; however, as a theory of morality (as many interpret it) it is, as Kohlberg (quoted in Friedman 1987, 193) acknowledges, not a theory of moral reasoning but a theory of "justice" reasoning. As R.S. Peters states:

> His [Kohlberg's] findings are of unquestionable importance, but there is a grave danger that they may become exalted into a general theory of moral development. Any such general theory presupposes a general ethical theory, and Kohlberg himself surely would be the first to admit that he has done

> little to develop the details of such a general ethical theory. Yet without such a theory the notion of "moral development" is pretty insubstantial (Peters 1971, 264).

This criticism and danger have appeared to come true in the accounting literature. Kohlberg's stages of ethical development have become a mantra for ethical education. Ponemon (1992) advocates that "traditional ethics education in accounting should be replaced by formal courses and programs that foster the highest order of ethical reasoning," based on the Kohlberg stage model. Will this allow us to make better moral decisions? We doubt it. We believe that it will cause stress on female students and practitioners and narrow the decision process to an economic rational model. This training prioritizes individual interests over community interests, relegating relationships and care perspectives to secondary status.[2] It is only valid as an input into the process of moral deliberation not as the end of the process. Accounting is a moral practice (Francis 1990), and, as such a practice, what should be taught is not a particular method of "justice" reasoning or adherence to particular laws but, rather, teaching should attempt to develop judgment with respect to carrying out the practice. As MacIntyre writes:

> The educated moral agent must of course know what he is doing when he judges or acts virtuously. Thus he does what is virtuous *because* it is virtuous. It is this fact which distinguishes the exercise of virtues from the exercise of certain qualities which are not virtues, but rather simulacra of virtues. The well-trained soldier, for instance, may do what courage would have demanded in a particular situation, not because he is courageous but because he is *well-trained* (1984, 149-150, as quoted in Francis 1990, 13; latter emphasis added).

Moral reasoning may include both a justice/rights analysis (Kohlberg) as well as a care/relationship analysis. One should not be prioritized over the other. Accounting practice represents a socially cooperative human activity; feminine reasoning based on relationships and context should not be discarded.

The next section of this paper gives an overview of the Kohlberg model of moral development; then, we examine Gilligan's criticism of that model to show why it may be dysfunctional from a feminist perspective. We then examine Ponemon's prescriptions for assessing moral reasoning (more accurately, "justice reasoning") to highlight the danger these measurement techniques represent for assessing a person's "moral reasoning capacity." In doing this, we adapt Kohlberg's famous Heinz dilemma, demonstrating its simplicity and minimalization of moral reasoning that might alienate a female respondent and not be invariant over alternative contexts.

THE KOHLBERG MODEL

Kohlberg (1971) posits that an understanding of moral judgments and values can only be understood by orienting the psychology of morality to morality's philosophic concepts. Lickona (1976) notes that Kohlberg's approach to morality is one of the few that attempts to integrate psychological and philosophical theory. Kohlberg believes that active programs of moral education demand that the psychological explanation of why children move from one stage to another stage of moral reasoning be coupled with an explanation of why higher stages hold superior moral solutions to lower stages.

Kohlberg based his model on a cognitive-developmental theory of morality. This theory holds that morality, like cognition, develops in a sequence of stages (see Table 1 for a description of the six stages). Kohlberg's ideas were influenced by Piaget's (1932) work in the areas of cognitive and moral development; however, Kohlberg (1971) argues that his theory of moralization is more inclusive than that of Piaget's. As envisaged by Kohlberg, the cognitive-developmental model is an interactive model: human actors do not simply reflect on either external facts and/or internal emotions; rather, the moral judgments of these actors are the products of social interaction. According to Kohlberg (1969), the general quality and extent of an individual's cognitive and social stimulation define the environmental influences in moral development, not specific individual actions that are rewarded or punished. Kohlberg (1971) posits that when children have opportunities to role take, they experience moral conflict; he suggests that a stage's basic principles of justice provide the necessary integration to resolve the moral conflict.

Kohlberg based his moral development model on a 15-year study that recorded at three-year intervals the individual changes in the moral judgment and character of a sample of 75 boys. The study began when the boys were in their early adolescent years (ages 10-16) and continued through young manhood (ages 22-28).

Table 1. Definition of Moral Stages

I. Preconventional level

At this level the child is responsive to cultural rules and labels of good and bad, right or wrong, but interprets these labels in terms of either the physical or the hedonistic consequences of action (punishment, reward, exchange of favors) or in terms of the physical power of those who enunciate the rules and labels. The level is divided into the following two stages:

Stage 1: *The punishment and obedience orientation.* The physical consequences of action determine its goodness or badness regardless of the human meaning or value of these consequences. Avoidance of punishment and unquestioning deference to power are valued in their own right, not in terms of respect for an underlying moral order supported by punishment and authority (the latter being Stage 4).

Stage 2: *The instrumental relativist orientation.* Right action consists of that which instrumentally satisfies one's own needs and occasionally the needs of others. Human relations are viewed in terms like those of the marketplace. Elements of fairness, of reciprocity, and of equal sharing are present, but they are always interpreted in a physical pragmatic way. Reciprocity is a matter of "you scratch my back and I'll scratch yours," not of loyalty, gratitude, or justice.

II. Conventional level

At this level, maintaining the expectations of the individual's family, group, or nation is perceived as valuable in its own right, regardless of immediate and obvious consequences. The attitude is one not only of conformity to personal expectations and social order, but of loyalty to it; of actively maintaining, supporting, and justifying the order; and of identifying with the persons or groups involved in it. At this level, there are the following two stages:

Stage 3: *The interpersonal concordance or "good boy—nice girl" orientation.* Good behavior is that which pleases or helps others and is approved by them. There is much conformity to stereotypical images of what is majority or "natural" behavior. Behavior is frequently judged by intention—"he or she means well" becomes important for the first time. One earns approval by being "nice."

Stage 4: *The "law and order" orientation.* There is orientation toward authority fixed rules, and the maintenance of the social order. Right behavior consists of doing one's duty, showing respect for authority, and maintaining the given social order for its own sake.

III. Postconventional, autonomus, or principled level

At this level, there is a clear effort to define moral values and principles which have validity and application apart from the authority of the groups or persons holding these principles and apart from the individual's own identification with these groups. This level again has two stages:

Stage 5: *The social-contract legalistic orientation.* This generally has utilitarian overtones. Right action tends to be defined in terms of general individual rights and of standards which have been critically examined and agreed upon by the whole society. There is a clear awareness of the relativism of personal values and opinions and a corresponding emphasis upon procedural rules for reaching consensus. Aside from what is constitutionally and democratically agreed upon, right is seem as a matter of personal "values" and "opinion," The result is an emphasis upon the "legal point of view," but with an emphasis upon the possibility of changing law in terms of rational considerations of social utility (rather than freezing it in terms of Stage 4 "law and order"). Outside the legal realm, free agreement and contract is the binding element of obligation. This is the "official" morality of the U.S. government and constitution.

(*continued*)

Table 1. (Continued)

Stage 6: *The universal ethical principle orientation.* Right is defined by the decision of conscience in accord with self-chosen ethical principles appealing to logical comprehensiveness, universality, and consistency. These principles are abstract and ethical (the Golden Rule, the categorical imperative); they are not concrete moral rules like the Ten Commandments. At this stage, these are universal principles of justice, of the reciprocity and equality of human rights, and of respect for the dignity of human beings as individual persons.

Source: Colby and Kohlberg (1987).

Kohlberg supplemented this study by a series of studies which examined moral development in other cultures. From the subjects' responses to hypothetical moral dilemmas, Kohlberg (1971) concluded that the distinctive form of a subject's moral thought is universal—according to Kohlberg, all cultures that he observed exhibited the same categories of moral judgment and valuing.

The universal moral categories of Kohlberg are: modes, elements, and issues (see Table 2). Although Kohlberg's use of moral categories was influenced by the writings of Piaget and Kant, Dewey's (1903) discussion of categories as the object of an ethical science closely resembles Kohlberg's treatment of moral categories. Kohlberg's scheme of moral categories allows a respondent's moral judgment to be classified into a mode, an element, and an issue.

Kohlberg (1971) notes that the results of the longitudinal study involving U.S. boys suggest the following:

1. Although the rate of development may vary for children, the progression through the states is invariant (i.e., a child must move step by step), with the possibility of a child becoming fixated in a given stage.
2. Each stage represents a way of thinking rather than just an attitude toward the context of a situation. However, it is unusual for an individual to be entirely at one stage. Although individuals rarely use stages nonadjacent to their majority stage, it is not uncommon for them to reason partly from the stage above and/or below their majority stage. Therefore, the stages are also hierarchical integrations—higher stages include lower stages. A person at a higher stage is capable of comprehending a lower stage; however, a person at a lower stage cannot comprehend fully a higher stage. Individuals at higher stages prefer those stages to lower stages. Rest, Turiel, and Kohlberg (1969) seem to confirm these conditions.

Table 2. Aspects of Moral Judgment

I. The modes of judgment of obligation and value

A. Judgment of right
B. Judgment of having a right
C. Judgment of duty and obligation
D. Judgments of responsibility—conceptions of consequences of action or of the demands or opinions of others one should consider over and above strict duties or strict regard for the rights of others
E. Judgment of praise or blame
F. Judgments of punishability and reward
G. Justification and explanation
H. Judgments of nonmoral value or goodness

II. The elements of obligation and value

A. Prudence—consequences desirable or undesirable to the self
B. Social welfare—consequences desirable to others
C. Love
D. Respect
E. Justice as liberty
F. Justice as equality
G. Justice as reciprocity and contract

III. The issues or institutions

A. Social norms
B. Personal conscience
C. Roles and issues of affection
D. Roles and issues of authority and democracy, of division of labor between roles relative to social control
E. Civil liberties—rights to liberty and equality to persons as human beings, citizens, or as members of groups
F. Justice of actions apart from fixed rights—reciprocity, contract, trust, and equity in the actions or reactions of one perso
G. Punitive justice
H. Life
I. Property
J. Truth
K. Sex

Source: Colby and Kohlberg (1987).

Kohlberg (1966, 1968) reasons that because his moral stages and Piaget's cognitive (logical) stages meet the above criteria, the two sets of stages are isomorphic. Higher moral stages encompass lower moral stages. The reason for this conclusion is that higher moral stages involve higher logical structures which encompass lower logical structures. This rationale provides the argument that moral thought is usually progressive (upward movement through the model's six stages). Kohlberg (1971) acknowledges that the correlation between cognitive and moral stages is not perfect. Children at a given moral stage of the model will perform adequately on a task from Piaget's equivalent cognitive stage; however, children at a given cognitive stage will not necessarily pass the equivalent moral stage task. Studies show that cognitive maturity is a necessary but not sufficient condition for moral reasoning (see Selman 1971; Kuhn, Langer, and Kohlberg 1971).

When the results of the U.S. study are combined with those conducted in other countries, the implications are as follows:

3. Stages are universal in their development; therefore, moral development occurs in any culture and in the same order.
4. Children's religious and general moral values seem to follow the same stage-sequence order.

Common Core of Each Stage: Justice

The common core of each stage of Kohlberg's model is a justice structure. Each stage reveals a more integrated form of justice, with the justice of Stage 6 implying that all persons should be treated morally as equals. Kohlberg argues that the only principle that is universal is justice; although he acknowledges that other principles such as welfare and law are present at the birth of morality, he reasons that only justice is capable of taking on the character of a principle at the highest levels of moral development. From Kohlberg's viewpoint, efforts using other principles to transcend Stage 4 or Stage 5 are doomed to failure, either because such principles are incapable of resolving moral conflicts or because the resolution seems intuitively wrong.

Revisions to the Model

During the 1970s and 1980s, Kohlberg and his associates refined and clarified his general theory of moral development. As more data became available, Kutnick (1986) notes that the result in scoring refinement of the Moral Judgment Interview instrument depressed the higher stage scores, with Stage 6 becoming an abstraction. Researchers using refined structural insights concluded that individuals in previous studies who regressed from Stage 4 to Stage

2 (recall that the proposed stages are invariant) retained more complex moral reasoning than the researchers had first concluded. The researchers viewed the regression as an incomplete progression from Stage 4 to Stage 5; the differentiation of each stage into Substages A and B provided additional refinement. Kutnick (1986) suggests that these refinements enhanced the Kohlbergian claim that postconventional morality follows a "monotonic judgment-action relationship"—that is, individuals at higher levels of moral reasoning are more likely to take moral action.

In addition, Kohlberg (1986) notes that in recent years, he and others have attempted to incorporate Habermas' theory of the development of communicative competence into his stages of moral reasoning. Kohlberg has also acknowledged Gilligan's criticisms of his model; however, he continues to believe that the justice perspective incorporates the basic elements of the care perspective.

GILLIGAN'S FEMINIST CRITICISM

The Care Perspective and Moral Reasoning

Carol Gilligan (1982) is one of the leading feminist critics of Kohlberg's work. Gilligan charges that Kohlberg's methodology excludes women's perspective of morality; she believes that the care perspective of women will also lead to universal moral judgments. For Gilligan, Kohlberg's use of a rights-based morality results in an inadequate measure of women's levels of moral development. From the results of her study, Gilligan (1982) asserts that the moral orientation of individuals is related to their gender. The moral orientation of an individual is, in turn, a product of the socialization process.

Gilligan and Wiggins (1988) charge that psychologists tend to avoid the relationship between moral reasoning and gender for different reasons: they wish to avoid the negatives associated with stereotyping; they are cognizant of the intimations that may be associated with biological determinism; and the topic of sex differences usually does not generate "disinterested" discussants. However, Gilligan and Wiggins note that the stereotypical aggressive male and nurturing female do have some empirical basis. They reason that the large majority of males in the prison population and the role of females in caring for the young should not be excluded when we form our models of moral reasoning.

Mothering and the Socialization Process

In those societies where the mother of an infant provides most of its care, the infant develops a sense of itself through the relationship with its mother (Chodorow 1978). Chodorow notes that this relationship is critical in determining the object-relationships of subsequent developmental periods. The mothering process creates specific expectations, either conscious or unconscious, in girls and boys: women are seen as having the unique capacity to sacrifice, care, and mother; men are viewed as possessing power and growth. As children mature, Chodorow writes that mothers view their daughters as more like themselves. Thus, the mother-child relationship between mother and daughter usually lasts longer than the one between mother and son. Girls emerge from this relationship with a different concept of "self" than do boys.

These relational asymmetries are products of the mothering process and have an impact on the personality of the child. The masculine personality tends to repress relational issues; males view themselves as more separate and differentiated individuals. The feminine personality tends to define itself in terms of external relationships, their retention, and continuity; females view themselves as connected to the world. Chodorow's work seems to add credence to Gilligan's argument that moral orientation is related to gender. From Chodorow's (1978) analysis, girls do not have the same drive or need to develop morality from a rights perspective.

Chodorow's findings, however, do not imply that the female concern with relationships is monolithic. Hill (1987) suggests that other socialization processes within and outside of the home influence the formation of the male and female personality. For example, many mothers work outside the home; their role models may provide an unconventional socialization process for their children. Such circumstances may explain why Gilligan found some women characterized by a care perspective while other women identified with a justice (rights) perspective; however, Gilligan found very few men who were characterized by a care perspective, in spite of their ability to reason with it.

Women and the Kohlberg Model

Gilligan (1982) charges that although Kohlberg claims universality for the stages of his model, those groups not included in his original sample are usually absent from the upper-level stages. The absence of women from Stages 5 or 6 is especially conspicuous. Women seem to perform no better than Stage 3, especially those women who lead their lives within the home. Morality at Stage 3 is described in interpersonal terms; helping and pleasing others is synonymous with goodness. To Gilligan, this is a paradox—the very traits that have conventionally characterized women as "good" result in women being measured as developmentally morally deficient on the Kohlberg scale.

Gilligan (1982, 22) conjectures, however, that a morality based on rights and noninterference may be frightening to women because of its "potential justification of indifference and unconcern." At the same time, men may question the moral judgments reasoned from a care perspective because such judgments appear to be more contextually relativistic. Gilligan (1987) believes that a shift in moral perspective causes a person to redefine what constitutes a moral problem. She posits that all human relationships can be framed in terms of a justice and care perspective. In other words, individuals can think of human relationships both in terms of equality and attachment. Both inequality and detachment are grounds for moral concerns—not to treat someone unfairly or not to turn from someone in need.

Although Kohlberg has acknowledged the existence of a care perspective in the moral reasoning of individuals, Gilligan (1987) posits that the widespread use of Kohlberg's Moral Judgment Interview test and his propensity to equate moral reasoning with moral judgment leaves the moral perspective issue unresolved. After examining men's and women's responses to real and hypothetical dilemmas, Gilligan (1987) writes that the image of the self is different for the two perspectives of morality. When using a justice perspective, individuals see the self as a moral agent against a web of relationships. These individuals judge conflicting claims of self and others against the standard of equality. In contrast, when using a care perspective, relationships become the central focus for defining self and others. These relationships provide the context for the self's perceptions of needs.

Thus, according to Gilligan, these two moral perspectives are not opposites of each other. The justice perspective is not uncaring; nor is the caring perspective unjust. Within a particular moral perspective, terms and words take on new meanings. A shift from a justice perspective to a caring one results in a metamorphosis. Relationships change from equalities to attachments, from hierarchies to social webs. Gilligan posits that within the justice perspective, care is seen as the mercy that tempers justice; however, care is less understood within its own moral perspective. No moral terms exist within the moral vocabulary to elaborate the term "care." The assumption underlying care is that self and other are interdependent. Therefore, action is viewed as arising from a relationship rather than from within self. Gilligan suggests that this responsive self is connected to others and is governed by the activity associated with human interaction and human language. Detachment is the moral problem associated with this perspective—detachment births moral indifference which results in individuals ignoring needs.

PONEMON'S ADVOCATION OF JUSTICE REASONING AND A RESPONSE

Ethical studies by Ponemon and his associates,[3] based on Kohlberg's model, are an important contribution to the accounting literature. These studies raise important questions that need to be addressed by academics. Our focus, however, is not on the questions that are implied by Ponemon's work but rather on the underpinnings of his work and his prescriptions, which we believe are over-generalized. Ponemon (1993) writes that his work suggests:

> that cognitive-developmental psychology and theory of ethical reasoning and moral development advanced by Lawrence Kohlberg (1984), James Rest (1986) and others provide an important framework for studying the human decision process prior to ethical behavior. It is concerned with the psychological and epistemological processes that cause individuals to develop higher and more sophisticated cognitive abilities for identifying, dealing with and resolving ethical conflict, including the wide array of ethical issues found every day in professional practice (p. 5).

The methods used in all the studies have been Kohlberg's Moral Judgment Interview instrument and Rest's Defining Issues Test. Both these instruments, using hypothetical dilemmas such as the Heinz story, categorize subjects on Kohlberg's stage model. Principled reasoning is based on a justice/rights framework. Ponemon (1992, 254) advocates:

> A prerequisite to ethical development is more effective educational interventions at both the university and the firm level.... Therefore, traditional ethics education in accounting should be replaced by formal courses and programs that foster the highest order of ethical reasoning (cf. Ponemon and Glazer 1990).

Should we train students and practitioners to actually apply the justice reasoning and advere this to be the one and only universal ethic? No, for this would be a minimalist approach which would ignore context and the true complexity of ethical reasoning that could be applied in ethical behavior (Friedman 1987).

Ponemon and Gabhart (1990) have also attempted to transfer Kohlberg's theoretical stages to a theory of auditor independence. They propose preconventional, conventional, and postconventional stages of independence. Is this a "fish out of water" problem? They state that the postconventional auditor is independent if his or her state of mind "conforms to the rules of the profession, and such beliefs are themselves independent of societal norms or conventions" (Ponemon and Gabhart 1990, 234). Does this highest level of independence allow for ethical reasoning on any basis? Is there really a need for a stage development model which has these structuralist definitions? This model assumes a justice/*integrity* reasoning process and implies that if a person does not always exemplify integrity, he or she cannot be independent.

Moral Dilemma Applications and Moral Reasoning

To evaluate the problems associated with the above prescriptions,[4] we examine the Heinz dilemma, the famous dilemma used by both Kohlberg for the MJI and Rest for the DIT in measuring the level of moral reasoning of individuals. The original dilemma is as follows:

> In Europe, a woman was near death from cancer. One drug might save her, a form of radium that a druggist in the same town had recently discovered. The druggist was charging $2000, ten times what the drug cost him to make. The sick woman's husband, Heinz, went to everyone he knew to borrow the money, but he could only get together about half of what it cost. He told the druggist that his wife was dying and asked him to sell it cheaper or let him pay later. But the druggist said, "No." The husband got desperate and broke into the man's store to steal the drug for his wife. Should the husband have done that? Why? (Kohlberg 1969, 379).[5]

Gilligan's research found that women tend to be uncomfortable in responding to this dilemma. Friedman (1987) points out that the "forced choice" of to steal or not to steal or to let the wife die or not let the wife die does not appear reasonable to most women. Women will seek more details, as compared to male subjects, clearly showing their affinity for compassion and care as compared to justice (in Kohlberg's model, a Stage 3 response). Friedman argues convincingly that care and relationship are more important to moral reasoning than Kohlberg is willing to credit. One of her major concerns (that we concur with) is that Kohlberg's framework is biased toward only the narrow justice consideration of moral reasoning, and this consideration only represents "part of the whole range of our moral reasonings" (Friedman 1987, 192). According to Kohlberg's interpretation of the Heinz dilemma, "Heinz's care for his wife would be regarded as supplementing the obligation that he has to respect her right to life... an ethic of care is, and of itself, not well adapted to resolve justice problems" (Freidman 1987, 193). This subordination of care and special relationships to justice is somewhat consistent with Western thought. As Friedman states:

> the world of personal relationships, of the family, and of family ties and loyalties—the traditional world of women—is a world of lesser moral importance than the public world of government and of the marketplace—the male-dominated world outside the home (Friedman 1987, 194).

Does the above really represent our behavior and actions? Would moral reasonings always give primacy to the justice perspective? Friedman's point is that at times, justice reasonings may prevail over care; however, "sometimes considerations of justice and rights *are* legitimately overridden by considerations of special relationships." Friedman demonstrates her perspectives through various modifications of the Heinz dilemma.

First, she personalizes the Heinz dilemma and performs a sex-change operation on the characters to remove some of the heroism and villainy aspects of the male actors. This is done as follows:

> In Europe, a man was near death from cancer. One drug might save him, a form of radium that a druggist in the same town, a woman named Hilda, had recently discovered. The druggist was charging $2000, ten times what the drug cost her to make. The sick man's wife, Heidi, went to everyone she knew to borrow the money, but she could only get together about half of what it

> cost. She told Hilda, the druggist, that her husband was dying and asked Hilda to sell it cheaper or let her, Heidi, pay later. But Hilda said, "No." Heidi got desperate and broke into the woman's store to steal the drug for her husband. Should the wife have done that? Why? (Friedman 1987, 197-198).

Would the same responses be given to this dilemma as the original? Based on Gilligan's research, would not the women show more of a care perspective? Would they not try to work something out so neither party got hurt? As Friedman points out, this reformulation of the story makes the forced choice of steal/don't steal more ambiguous.

Next, Friedman adds a degree of remoteness to the story. She no longer portrays Heidi (Heinz) as man and wife but rather as strangers. In this scenario, Heidi reads of the man's plight in the newspaper and is moved to act but cannot raise the money to buy the drug. Therefore, she breaks into the store to steal the drug for someone she does not even know. According to Kohlberg, the original dilemma with a special relationship and the above changes should not make any difference on moral reasoning or behavior. We suspect, as Friedman does, that many individuals would change their moral reasoning and not say "that a serious personal risk should be taken to steal the drug, break the law, and harm the druggist—even to save a life" (p. 198).

Finally, directly confronting our own moral reasonings, Friedman further modifies the dilemma to where "*you are*" the perfect stranger who happens to read about a man dying of cancer and the availability of the drug which the man cannot afford. "Will *you* take the risk of stealing the drug to save the life of someone you don't know?" (Friedman 1987, 199). We may aspire to be this "heroic," but would we truly act on this aspiration? We suggest that we have all had the chance to do this but have not.

Friedman then goes on to stress the contextualization of moral dilemmas. She stresses that we normally know more about the human aspects of the individuals involved in a moral context. What if the individual who is dying of cancer has an exceptional low quality of life—is bedridden and dependent on others for daily functioning? The individual begs us to let him or her die in peace. What about the druggist? What if the druggist is a single parent, barely making ends meet? Real-life dilemmas are complex, not simple. After a decision is made, the status quo will change. Kohlberg makes no mention

Figure 1. Experimental Scenarios

SCENARIO 1

Heinz and the Drug

In Europe, a woman was near death from a special kind of cancer. There was one drug that the doctors thought might save her. It was a form of radium that the druggist in the same town had recently discovered. The drug was expensive to make, and the druggist was charging ten times what the drug cost to make. He paid $2,000 for the radium and charged $20,000 for a small dose of the drug. The sick woman's husband, Heinz, went to everyone he knew to borrow the money, but he could get together only about $10,000, which is half of what it cost. He told the druggist that his wife was dying and asked him to sell it cheaper or let him pay later. But the druggist said, "No., I discovered the drug and I'm going to make money from it." So Heinz became desperate and began to think about breaking into the man's store to steal the drug for his wife.

Should Heinz steal the drug? (check one)

______ Should Steal It ______ Can't Decide ______ Should Not Steal It

SCENARIO 2

Heidi and the Drug

In Europe, a man was near death from a special kind of cancer. There was one drug that the doctors thought might save him. It was a form of radium that the druggist in the same town, a woman named Hilda, had recently discovered. The drug was expensive to make, and the druggist was charging 10 times what the drug cost to make. Hilda paid $2,000 for the radium and charged $20,000 for a small dose of the drug. The sick man's wife, Heidi, went to everyone she knew to borrow the money, but she could get together only about $10,000, which is half of what it cost. She told the druggist that her husband was dying and asked her to sell it cheaper or let her pay later. But Hilda, the druggist, said, "No, I discovered the drug and I'm going to make money from it." So Heidi became desperate and began to think about breaking into the woman's store to steal the drug for her husband.

Should Heidi steal the drug? (check one)

______ Should Steal It ______ Can't Decide ______ Should Not Steal It

SCENARIO 3

Hilda and the Stranger, Heidi

In Europe, a man was near death from a special kind of cancer. There was one drug that the doctors thought might save him. It was a form of radium that the druggist in the same town, a woman named Hilda, had recently discovered. The drug was expensive to make, and the druggist was charging 10 times what the drug cost to make. Hilda paid $2,000 for the radium and charged $20,000 for a small dose of the drug. A perfect stranger, a women named Heidi, chanced to read about the sick man's plight in the local newspaper. She was moved to act. She went to everyone she knew to borrow the money, but she could get together only about $10,000, which is half of what it cost. She asked the druggist to sell it cheaper or let her, Heidi, pay later. But Hilda, the druggist, said, "No, I discovered the drug and I'm going to make money from it." So Heidi became desperate and began to think about breaking into the woman's store to steal the drug for a man she did not know.

Should Heidi steal the drug? (check one)

______ Should Steal It ______ Can't Decide ______ Should Not Steal It

SCENARIO 4

YOU and Hilda

In Europe, a man was near death from a special kind of cancer. There was one drug that the doctors thought might save him. It was a form of radium that the druggist in the same town, a woman named Hilda, had recently discovered. The drug was expensive to make, and the druggist was charging 10 times what the drug cost to make. Hilda paid $2,000 for the radium and charged $20,000 for a small dose of the drug. YOU chanced to read about the sick man's plight in the Dallas newspaper. YOU decide you must act. YOU go to everyone you know to borrow the money, but you could get together only about $10,000, which is half of what it cost. You fax the druggist and request her to sell it cheaper or let YOU pay later. But Hilda faxes you back and says, "No, I discovered the drug and I'm going to make money from it." So YOU became desperate and began to think about going to Europe and breaking into the woman's store to steal the drug for this sick man, someone you do not know.

Should YOU steal the drug? (check one)

______ Should Steal It ______ Can't Decide ______ Should Not Steal It of this. "[C]ontextual detail matters overridingly to matters of justice as well as matters of care and relationships" (Friedman 1987, 203).

BEHAVIORAL EXPERIMENT

Overview

The purpose of the experiment was to examine the impact of context, care relationships, socialization, and perceived behavioral action on individuals' moral dilemma judgments. The experimental design represents a 2×2×4 design, where the independent variables are: (1) gender; (2) socialization, distinguished by first year accounting/business students as compared to accounting graduate students; and (3) context manipulation of the famous "Heinz" dilemma where in four different scenarios, the individual relationship of the primary actor to the cancer victim becomes more remote. In addition, to highlight the care perspective, in two of the scenarios all the primary actors are female.

The primary instrument used was a slightly modified version of Rest's DIT short instrument. We modified the instrument in two respects: first, we used the original plus three manipulated versions of the Heinz dilemma (see Figure 1); second, we deleted the one "antiestablishment" response in the Heinz case and substituted a more direct care/relationship response which would normally be viewed as a Stage 3 type response.[6]

We used three variables from Rest's DIT instrument as our dependent variables: (1) the "P" score, which is a measure of how much weight an individual places on a postconventional reasoning process; (2) the percentage of weight given to the conventional Stage 3 (interpersonal concordance) responses; and (3) the decision response being: Steal, Don't Steal, or Can't Decide. We measured these variables for the Heinz case by itself, as well as for the other two cases of the short version together (the Newspaper and Escaped Prisoner cases). The latter measure of the two cases was used as a covariate in our model.[7] Our analysis used a regular multivariate analysis of covariance (MANCOVA) model (or an appropriate regression model) as well as limited dependent variable version of MANCOVA or regression. We included appropriate covariates that might impact the responses, such as age and work experiences.

Hypotheses

Hypothesis 1. In both Scenarios 1 and 2, female P-scores will be less than male P-scores.

In both these cases, where the actors portray a close relationship, we believe Gilligan's arguments that females will tend to show a greater care perspective as compared to a justice orientation and, hence, respond less frequently to the postconventional level responses. We do not predict response for Scenarios 3 and 4, although we tend to think that there will not be a gender difference due to the remoteness of the context and no clear relationships developed in the case.

Hypothesis 2. Females will have a greater Stage 3 percentage than males.

Hypothesis 3. Undergraduates will have a greater Stage 3 percentage than graduate students.

Hypothesis 4. Female undergraduate students will have a greater Stage 3 percentage than female graduate students.

Hypothesis 5. Male undergraduate students will not differ on Stage 3 percentage than male graduate students.

The above hypotheses indicate that the primary difference in Stage 3 responses (a caring response) is primarily due to female responses. This is consistent with Gilligan and, in general, we agree with her. On the other hand, as Friedman points out, the accounting education process will begin to socialize the females into responding as the "norm," and this will lean toward the justice orientation. This is the basis for the difference in our beliefs about undergraduate and graduate females.

Hypothesis 6. Scenario 2 will have a greater Stage 3 percentage than Scenarios 1, 3, and 4.

Hypothesis 7. Female undergraduates in the Scenario 2 group will have a greater Stage 3 percentage than female graduate students in the Scenario 2 group.

Scenario 2 allows for the greatest care perspective since it involves both close relationships and females working with each other. We believe this scenario is closest in line with Gilligan's arguments and this group will use a care perspective more frequently modified for the socialization process.

Hypothesis 8. Percentage responses to stealing will be the least for Scenario 4, followed by Scenario 3, with the most in Scenarios 2 and 1.

Hypothesis 9. Undergraduates' responses to stealing will be less than graduates' responses to stealing.

Hypothesis 10. Females assigned to Scenario 2 will respond less to stealing than females assigned to Scenario 1, and there will be no difference between males in these scenarios.

Hypothesis 11. Undergraduate students in Scenarios 1, 2, and 3 will respond less to stealing than graduate students assigned to the same scenarios.

Hypothesis 12. Percentage responses to "can't decide" will be the least for Scenarios 1 and 2 as compared to Scenarios 3 and 4.

Hypothesis 13. Male responses to "can't decide" will be less than female responses to "can't decide."

Hypothesis 14. Percentage responses to "don't steal" will be less for males as compared to females.

Hypothesis 15. Percentage responses to "don't steal" will be greater for Scenario 4 as compared to Scenario 3 and least for Scenarios 2 and 1.

The basis for these hypotheses is primarily that when the decision is to steal or not to steal, then females will view the situation as "let's try to work it out before we commit to a final decision" and, therefore, will say "can't decide" or "not steal" more frequently than males. This, again, is an example of a care/relationship perspective. The socialization process may modify this and cause graduate students to more frequently take the narrow justice perspective of the Heinz case and say "steal" to save a life. Finally, as the actors in the scenarios become more remote to each other and the respondent is brought closer to being in the case (Scenario 4), there will be a lesser tendency to steal and a greater tendency to say either "don't steal" or "can't decide."

Procedures

Participation in the experiment was voluntary. The original sample consisted of 257 students enrolled in either the introductory accounting course or graduate accounting courses. Forty-five participants were eliminated from the sample after applying the reliability/consistency checks as suggested by Rest (1986). The final sample consisted of 212 subjects as follows: 51 undergraduate females, 72 undergraduate males, 37 graduate females, and 52 graduate males.[8] The experiment was administered using class groups over a two-week period. Standardized instructions (as suggested by Rest 1986) were read and reviewed with the participants. The administration of the complete experiment took approximately 25 minutes. Subjects were randomly assigned to the experimental scenarios based on random distribution of the instrument.

Results and Discussion

Tables 3 through 5 summarize the mean or percentage responses to each of the dependent variables by the individual independent variables (gender, class, and scenario) and each cell of the combined independent variables. All reported means and analyses are adjusted for the controlling covariates (individual *P*-scores and Stage 3 percentages derived from the two nonexperimental dilemmas). The MANCOVA model for *P*-score and Stage 3 and the logistic regression model for the decision response variables was statistically significant.[9,10]

Table 3 reports the adjusted mean results of the *P*-score, our surrogate for a "justice"-oriented justification. Gender effects were not significant. There was no significant difference between males' and females' justification for the combined effects of Scenarios 1 and 2 (which involved close relations), as we predicted in Hypothesis 1. Directionally, the hypothesis was consistent with Scenario 2, in which females relied less on a justice orientation than males. In terms of the ANOVA significance, the primary effects were between graduate (mean = 35.1) and undergraduate (mean = 28.7) and between Scenario 3 (mean = 36.6) and Scenario 1 (mean = 28.1). This implies

Table 3. P-Scores—Adjusted Means (Std. Dev.) (N = 212)

	Male n = 124 m = 32.1 (1.8)		*Female* n = 88 m = 31.7 (2.2)		
	Undergraduate	*Graduate*	*Undergraduate*	*Graduate*	*Total*
Scenario					
S1	n = 19 m = 18.6 (4.7)	n = 11 m = 36.4 (6.1)	n = 10 m = 19.8 (6.4)	n = 10 m = 37.7 (6.4)	n = 50 m =28.1 (3.0)
S2	n = 18 m = 28.5 (4.7)	n = 13 m = 35.0 (5.6)	n = 14 m = 25.8 (5.4)	n = 8 m = 31.3 (7.1)	n = 53 m = 30.1 (2.9)
S3	n = 16 m = 40.4 (5.1)	n = 13 m = 40.8 (5.6)	n = 15 m = 26.0 (5.2)	n = 8 m = 39.1 (7.1)	n = 52 m = 36.6 (2.9)
S4	n = 19 m = 31.0 (4.7)	n = 15 m = 26.1 (5.2)	n = 12 m = 39.8 (5.8)	n = 11 m = 34.1 (6.2)	n = 57 m = 32.7 (2.7)
	Undergraduates n = 123 m = 28.7 (1.9)		*Graduates* n = 89 m = 35.1 (2.2)		*Overall* n = 212 m = 31.9 (1.4)

that a socialization process may take place in justifying an attitude using a justice orientation; interestingly, when the context of the dilemma becomes very remote to the respondent (as in Scenario 3) as compared to the Heinz dilemma, a justice orientation is dominant. [Table 4 shows that the care orientation dominates when the husband/wife relationship is a focus (Scenarios 1 and 2 compared to 3 and 4).]

Table 4 reports the adjusted mean results of the Stage 3 percentage, our surrogate for a "care"-oriented justification. At best, gender differences were marginal. Hypothesis 2 cannot be supported (male mean = 28.1 versus female mean = 27.1). Hypotheses 3 and 4 are supported whereas Hypothesis 5 is not. These related primarily to differences in undergraduate/graduate with consideration of female (Hypothesis 4) and male (Hypothesis 5). It appears that a socialization process does take place which reduces the use of the care justification (UG mean = 31.6 versus G mean = 23.6). It is slightly stronger for females as compared to males and we did not anticipate the male difference. The most interesting results are related

Table 4. Stage 3 Percentages—Adjusted Means (Std. Dev.) (N = 212)

	Male *n = 124* *m = 28.1* *(1.9)*		*Female* *n = 88* *m = 27.1* *(2.3)*		
	Undergraduate	*Graduate*	*Undergraduate*	*Graduate*	*Total*
Scenario					
S1	n = 19 m = 46.7 (4.8)	n = 11 m = 30.3 (6.3)	n = 10 m = 32.3 (6.6)	n = 10 m = 26.4 (6.6)	n =50 m =33.9 (3.0)
S2	n = 18 m = 35.2 (4.9)	n = 13 m = 21.6 (5.8)	n = 14 m = 32.9 (5.5)	n = 8 m = 30.7 (7.5)	n = 53 m = 30.1 (3.0)
S3	n = 16 m = 22.7 (5.2)	n = 13 m = 18.6 (5.8)	n = 15 m = 26.8 (5.4)	n = 8 m = 20.0 (7.3)	n = 52 m = 22.0 (3.0)
S4	n = 19 m = 26.2 (4.8)	n = 15 m = 23.6 (5.4)	n = 12 m = 30.2 (6.0)	n = 11 m = 17.5 (6.3)	n = 57 m = 24.4 (2.8)
	Undergraduates n = 123 m = 31.6 (1.9)		*Graduates* n = 89 m = 23.6 (2.3)		*Overall* n = 212 m = 27.6 (1.5)

to Hypotheses 6 and 7. Both are partially supported. A care orientation was not different between Scenario 1 (mean = 33.9) and Scenario 2 (mean = 30.1), although we expected that Scenario 2 would evoke the greatest care orientation. However, both scenarios were significantly more dominated by a care orientation when compared to Scenario 3 (mean = 22.0) and Scenario 4 (mean = 24.4). This implies that when the dilemma becomes very remote from relationships (a stranger helping in Scenario 3) or becomes close in context (YOU help a person in Europe), a care justification appears to decrease. Also, as the socialization process takes place, the care justification tends to decrease. This was directionally true for females in Scenario 2 as our Hypothesis 7 states, but the change was not significant.

Table 5 reports the percentage decision responses to the dilemma ("steal," "can't decide," or "don't steal"). Context of the dilemma and remoteness to the dilemma did have a significant impact on this

Table 5. Decision Responses
(N = 211)

	Male						Female						Total		
	Undergraduate			Graduate			Undergraduate			Graduate					
	ST. % N	CAN'T DEC. % N	DON'T ST. % N	ST. % N	CAN'T DEC. % N	DON'T ST. % N	ST. % N	CAN'T DEC. % N	DON'T ST. % N	ST. % N	CAN'T DEC % N	DON'T ST. % N	ST. %	CAN'T DEC. %	DON'T ST. %
Scenario 1															
	12	3	4	4	1	6	6	1	3	3	1	6			
	63	16	21	36	9	55	60	10	30	30	10	60	50	12	38
Scenario 2															
	7	0	10	0	0	13	5	2	7	1	3	4			
	41	0	59	0	0	100	36	14	50	12	38	50	25	10	65
Scenario 3															
	1	2	13	2	2	9	3	1	11	1	0	7			
	6	13	81	15	15	70	20	7	73	12	0	88	13	10	77
Scenario 4															
	2	3	14	2	1	12	0	2	12	0	1	10			
	10	16	74	13	7	80	0	17	83	0	9	91	7	12	81

	Undergraduate (%)	Graduate (%)
Steal	30	15
Can't Decide	11	10
Don't Steal	59	75

	Male (%)	Female (%)
Steal	24	22
Can't Decide	10	12
Don't Steal	66	66

	Overall (%)
Steal	23
Can't Decide	11
Don't Steal	66

Notes: ST. = Steal; CAN'T DEC. = Can't Decide; DON'T ST. = Don't Steal.

decision. When "you" was the respondent in helping a stranger in Europe (Scenario 4), only 7% of the respondents would steal, compared to 13% when the context was a stranger helping someone else (Scenario 3) and 38% when close relations were involved (Scenarios 1 and 2). Hypothesis 8 was clearly supported. Hypothesis 15 was not as strongly supported in that the percent of respondents saying "don't steal" was not significantly different between Scenario 4 (81%) and Scenario 3 (77%) but, as expected, both were significantly different from Scenarios 1 and 2 (52%). We also expected that respondents would consider the "can't decide" option more frequently when relationships were not involved, but this was not supported (Hypothesis 12). Nevertheless, it appears that when context and remoteness from the dilemma change, the decision behavior changes.

We anticipated that undergraduates would be less likely to steal than graduate students (Hypothesis 9) and this would be amplified in Scenarios 1, 2, and 3, with no difference in Scenario 4 if "you" were directly involved (Hypothesis 11). Just the opposite happened for Hypothesis 9. Graduate students were significantly less likely to steal than undergraduates. This is interesting because we initially accepted the Kohlberg/Rest implication that stealing was the outcome of a "principled" justice justification. The socialization process did influence graduate students to use more of a justice orientation and less of a care orientation (see Tables 3 and 4), but the outcome choice was the opposite of the Kohlberg/Rest implication. These results also appear to be driven by the original Heinz dilemma (Scenario 1) where stealing was the dominate choice (especially for undergraduates); this scenario had the lowest use of the justice orientation (Table 3) and the highest use of the care orientation (Table 4).

As with the prior results, there appear to be only marginal gender effects. Partial, but not significant, support was shown for Hypotheses 10 and 13. Females were less likely to choose stealing in Scenario 2 compared to Scenario 1, but this was the same for the males, which was not predicted. Males were less likely to choose "can't decide" but not at a significant level. Finally, it was equally likely that females and males would choose the "don't steal" response, and this does not provide support for Hypothesis 14.

CONCLUSION

Our behavioral study probably raises more questions than it answers. That may be the normal case when trying to study ethics and morality. Although we did not find significant gender effects as expected, there were significant impacts of dilemma context, remoteness to a dilemma, and socialization processes. This study, however, should influence us to stop and pause to consider the uncritical acceptance of an individualistic morality model such as Kohlberg's cognitive model. Can it be a "universalistic" model when simple scenario changes in a dilemma lead to different justification reasoning and decision choices?

The Kohlberg model may be viewed as an extension of the reification of reason—that is, an extension of Kantian rationalistic ethics. Humans no longer simply obeyed God's law; they had the capacity (free will) and the ability (reason) to determine first principles. Gilligan correctly noted that the Kohlberg model relegated the "care" perspective, more closely associated with women, to secondary status. We believe it is important to take note of those criticisms to question the appropriateness of using a model based on a single invariant sequence of moral development in accounting ethics research (Pierce 1990; Moody-Adams 1990). Our focus on Gilligan's criticisms should not be taken to mean that we find her model adequate for future accounting research. We do not. Gilligan, like Kohlberg, found unity rather than the diversity that we would expect to find given the focus on diversity in feminist theory (Pierce 1990). We also have great concern for the dichotomy of the "rights" versus the "care" perspective; we share recent critics' skepticism about reducing women to the role of an "angel in the house" rather than relevant actors in our economic life (Moody-Adams 1990, 198). We view this paper as a quest to open up the agenda on ethics research and to begin to question some of the basic underlying presuppositions of that research.

Evaluating morality at an individual level is difficult at best. An individual is influenced by various institutions and cultures. How do the institutions influence us and what societal concerns do we need to take into account? The relevant questions may be: What do society and our communities expect morality/ethics to be? How do we as individuals then become accountable to these expectations? It may be difficult at best to "prescribe" ethics/morality going from an individual-oriented model up to a societal-model as compared to the other direction.

NOTES

1. See Adler (1987, 206) for an elaboration of these elements.

2. See Jack and Jack (1988) for a discussion of the stress felt by women lawyers who attempt to subordinate their care/relationships perspectives in favor of a justice orientation.

3. See Ponemon (1993) for capsule summaries of the many studies performed by Ponemon and associates.

4. This section draws heavily from Friedman (1987) and, where appropriate, page number references are shown.

5. Rest, in the Defining Issues Test, modifies the dilemma by asking "Should Heinz steal the drug? and states in the story that Heinz begins to think about stealing the drug. This modification is partially due to the "objective" nature of the DIT, for it is not an interview instrument but a behavioral rating instrument. However, this modification is minor since the underlying evaluation of both instruments is made on a justice/rights perspective.

6. This deletion should not be considered radical since in all formal analysis of the DIT instrument, this response variable is essentially ignored. The additional response allows for a more care-oriented response and it states: Don't steal, for [Heinz] and the druggist should be able to develop a relationship allowing for a cooperative solution to the dilemma. This response is included in our analysis as if it were a Stage 3 level response.

7. We realize that the DIT measures are meant to be taken for all three cases; however, this does not suit our experimental purpose. Our concern is with a comparison between groups and not within an individual; therefore, it is our belief that these measures, albeit rough, will allow for an assessment of justice and care orientations.

8. The reduction of sample for consistency checks appears to be in line with prior studies using the short version of the DIT. Complete information was received from the remaining 212 subjects, except for one subject who did not give a decision response reply ("steal," "can't decide," "don't steal"). Therefore, only 211 responses are used in examining hypotheses 8-15.

9. Rather than report individual significant levels, we imply when using the word significant that the significance level will be $\leq .075$. In most of these instances, the level is actually less than .05.

10. We initially included additional covariates related to job experience and age; however, these were insignificant and we excluded them from the reported results.

REFERENCES

Adler, J. 1987. Moral development and the personal point of view. In *Women and Moral Theory*, eds. E. Kittay and D. Meyers, 205-234. Totowa, NJ: Rowman & Littlefield Publishers.

Chodorow, N. 1978. *The Reproduction of Mothering: Psychoanalysis and the Sociology of Gender*. Berkeley, CA.: University of California Press.
Colby, A., and L. Kohlberg. 1987. *The Measurement of Moral Judgment*. Cambridge, MA: Cambridge University Press.
Dewey, J. 1903. *The Logical Conditions of a Scientific Treatment of Morality*. Chicago, IL: University of Chicago Press.
Francis, J.R. 1990. After virtue? Accounting as a moral and discursive practice. *Accounting, Auditing and Accountability Journal* 3(3): 5-17.
________. 1993. Aristotle's practical ethics. *Ethics in Accounting–Newsletter of The Public Interest Section American Accounting Association* 18(March): 13.
Friedman, M. 1987. Care and context in moral reasoning. In *Women and Moral Theory*, eds. E. Kittay and D. Meyers, 190-204. Totowa, NJ: Rowman & Littlefield.
Gilligan, C. 1982. *In a Different Voice: Psychological Theory and Women's Development*. Cambridge, MA: Harvard University Press.
________. 1987. Moral orientation and moral development. In *Women and Moral Theory*, eds. E. Kittay and D. Meyers, 19-33. Totowa, NJ: Rowman & Littlefield.
________ and G. Wiggins. 1988. The origins of morality in early childhood relationships. In *Mapping the Moral Domain*, eds. C. Gilligan, J. Ward, and J. Taylor, with B. Bardige, 111-138. Cambridge, MA: Harvard University Press.
Hill, T., Jr. 1987. The importance of autonomy. In *Women and Moral Theory*, eds. E. Kittay and D. Meyers, 129-138. Totowa, NJ: Rowman & Littlefield.
Jack, D., and Jack, R. 1988. Women lawyers: Archtype and alternatives. In *Mapping the Moral Domain*, eds. C. Gilligan, J. Ward, and J. Taylor, with B. Bardige, 263-288. Cambridge, MA: Harvard University Press.
Jensen, R.E. 1970. Empirical evidence from the behavioral sciences: Fish out of water. *The Accounting Review* (July): 502-509.
Kohlberg, L. 1966. A cognitive developmental analysis of children's sex-role concepts and attitudes. In *The Development of Sex Differences*, ed. E. Maccoby. Stanford, CA.: Stanford University Press.
________. 1968. Early education: A cognitive-developmental approach. *Child Development* 39: 1013-1062.
________. 1969. Stage and sequence: The cognitive-developmental approach to socialization. In *Handbook of Socialization Theory and Research*, ed. D. Goslin, 347-380. New York: Rand McNally.
________. 1971. From is to ought: How to commit naturalistic fallacy and get away with it in the study of moral development. In *Cognitive Development and Epistemology*, ed. T. Mischel, 151-235. New York: Academic Press.
________. 1986. A current standing on some theoretical issues. In *Lawrence Kohlberg: Consensus and Controversy*, eds. S. Modgil and C. Modgil. Philadelphia, PA: The Falmer Press.
Kuhn, D., J. Langer, and L. Kohlberg. 1971. Relations between logical and moral development. In *Recent Research in Moral Development*, eds. L. Kohlberg and E. Turiel. New York: Holt.
Kutnick, P. 1986. Kohlberg's theory, criticism and revision. In *Lawrence Kohlberg: Consensus and Controversy*, eds. S. Modgil and C. Modgil. Philadelphia: The Falmer Press.

Lickona, T. 1976. Critical issues in the study of moral development and behaviour. *In Moral Development and Behaviour*, ed. T. Lickona. New York: Holt, Rinehart, and Wilson.

MacIntyre, A. 1984. *After Virtue*. Notre Dame, IN: University of Notre Dame Press.

Moody-Adams, M. 1990. "Gender and the Complexity of Modern Voices. In *Feminist Ethics*, ed. C. Card, 195-212. Lawrence, KS: University of Kansas Press.

Moreland, K. 1985. The defining issues test. In *The Ninth Mental Measurements Yearbook*, ed. J. Mitchell. Lincoln, NE: Buros Institute of Mental Measurements of the University of Nebraska-Lincoln.

Peters, R.S. 1971. Moral developments: A plea for pluralism. In *Cognitive Development and Epistemology*, ed. T. Mischel, 237-267. New York: Academic Press.

Piaget, J. 1932. *The Moral Judgment of the Child*. New York: Harcourt, Brace and Company.

Pierce, C. 1990. Postmodernism and Other Skepticisms. In *Feminist Ethics*, ed. C. Card, 60-77. Lawrence, KS: University of Kansas Press.

Ponemon, L. 1990. Ethical judgments in accounting: A cognitive-developmental perspective. *Critical Perspectives on Accounting* (March): 191-215.

________. 1992. Ethical reasoning and selection-socialization in accounting. *Accounting Organizations and Society* 17(3/4): 239-258.

________. 1993. Commentary on ethical reasoning research in accounting. *Ethics in Accounting–Newsletter of The Public Interest Section American Accounting Association* 18(March): 5-7.

Ponemon, L., and D. Gabhart. 1990. Auditor independence judgments: A cognitive developmental model and experimental evidence. *Contemporary Accounting Research*: 227-251.

Ponemon, L., and A. Glazer. 1990. Accounting education and ethical development: The influence of liberal learning on students and alumni in accounting practice. *Issues in Accounting Education* 5(Fall): 195-208.

Rawls, J. 1971. *A Theory of Justice*. Cambridge, MA: Harvard University Press.

Rest, J. 1986. *Manual for the Defining Issues Test*. 3rd ed. Minneapolis: University of Minnesota Press.

Rest, J., E. Turiel, and L. Kohlberg. 1969. Relations between level of moral judgment and preference and comprehension of the moral judgment of others. *Journal of Personality* 37: 225-252.

Selman, R. 1971. The importance of reciprocal role-taking for the development of conventional moral thought. In *Recent Research in Moral Development*, eds. L. Kohlberg and E. Turiel. New York: Holt.

A STUDY OF THE RELATIONSHIP BETWEEN ACCOUNTING STUDENTS' MORAL REASONING AND COGNITIVE STYLES

Dann G. Fisher and Richard L. Ott

ABSTRACT

Empirical studies suggest a deficiency in the development of the moral reasoning abilities of accounting students and accountants. This finding has been attributed to the failure of the traditional accounting curriculum to foster moral growth but also seems to imply that persons attracted to a traditional accounting curriculum have similar individual attributes that quell their moral growth. One such attribute appears to be cognitive style. The purpose of this study is to determine whether a relationship exists between the cognitive styles of accounting students, as measured by the Myers-Briggs Type Indicator, and their moral reasoning abilities, as measured by the Defining Issues Test.

Research on Accounting Ethics, Volume 2, pages 51-71.

ISBN: 1-55938-997-4

The results indicate that persons with the sensing/thinking cognitive style, the predominant style among accounting students, display levels of moral reasoning lower than the norm for college students and consistent with the level of moral reasoning displayed in previous accounting studies. In contrast, persons with the intuition/thinking cognitive style, who comprise a small percentage of accounting students, display the highest mean level of moral reasoning. The results suggest that changes in pedagogy and course materials aimed at strengthening and balancing the cognitive styles of accounting students may be necessary if moral reasoning abilities are to be improved.

INTRODUCTION

Empirical studies suggest a deficiency in the development of the moral reasoning abilities of accounting students and accountants (Armstrong 1984, 1987; Arnold and Ponemon 1991; Lampe and Finn 1992; Ponemon 1988, 1990, 1992a, 1992b; Shaub 1994). Because the study of moral reasoning abilities of persons choosing a career in accounting is still in the formative stages, an understanding of the causes for this finding is currently being sought.

The findings of this research have been attributed to the traditionally technical focus of the accounting curriculum and its failure to foster the "general intellectual stimulation" (Rest and Narvaez 1991, 239) that is considered so critical to the development of moral reasoning (Armstrong 1987; Ponemon and Glazer 1990). The research findings also seem to imply that persons attracted to a traditional, technically oriented accounting curriculum have similar individual attributes.

One such attribute appears to be cognitive style—the preferences a person holds for gathering information and making decisions (Fleming 1985; Frisbie 1988; McIntyre and Capen 1993). Fleming (1985) and McIntyre and Capen (1993) assert that persons use their preferred cognitive style when reasoning about ethical problems. Research in accounting, employing the Myers-Briggs Type Indicator (MBTI), indicates that accountants tend to display a similar cognitive style preference and suggests that certain cognitive styles are well suited and attracted to accounting (Barrett 1969; Descouzis 1989; Geary and Rooney 1993; Jacoby 1981; Keirsey and

Bates 1978; Myers 1985; Myers and McCaulley 1986; Stricker and Ross 1962). These results suggest that the cognitive style prevalent among persons attracted to accounting and fostered by accounting education influences the level of moral reasoning displayed. The purpose of this study is to determine whether a relationship exists between the cognitive styles of accounting students and their moral reasoning abilities.

The results obtained in the current study indicate that cognitive style and the level of moral reasoning are related. In particular, persons who prefer to use sensing and thinking—the predominant preference among accounting students and accounting practitioners—to gather information and make judgments (Geary and Rooney 1993; Jacoby 1981; Myers and McCaulley 1986), display levels of moral reasoning lower than the norm for college students and consistent with the level of moral reasoning displayed in previous accounting studies (Lampe and Finn 1992; Ponemon 1993; Ponemon and Glazer 1990; Shaub 1994). In contrast, persons who use intuition and thinking to gather information and make judgments, comprising a small percentage of the current sample and previous samples of accountants (Geary and Rooney 1993; Jacoby 1981; Myers and McCaulley 1986), displayed the highest mean level of moral reasoning.

These results have implications for accounting education. Identification of the cognitive styles associated with higher levels of moral reasoning may aid in the development of pedagogy and course materials aimed at strengthening these processes. Although a person prefers one cognitive style to the others, theory suggests that he or she can adopt, develop, and strengthen the other styles (Frisbie 1988; Geary and Rooney 1993). Thus, education should encourage use of all styles in an attempt to balance the student's perception and judgment abilities (Frisbie 1988; Geary and Rooney 1993).

Curriculum and pedagogical changes suggested by the profession (Bedford Committee 1986; Arthur Andersen & Co. et al. 1989) and supported by the Accounting Education Change Commission (AECC) seem consistent with this objective. Movement from strict reliance on the lecture pedagogy and highly structured problem solving activities to more diverse pedagogies (e.g., cooperative learning, group work, written cases, and oral presentations) and less-structured problem solving activities should lead to greater balance in the cognitive styles of accounting graduates and greater diversity in the cognitive styles of persons attracted to accounting (Geary and Rooney 1993; Lawrence 1982; Myers 1985). A product of strengthened and balanced cognitive styles should be an improvement in the cognitive exercise of moral reasoning. If this is true, assertions that the AECC erred by funding curriculum change projects that fail to specifically integrate ethics into the curriculum (Mintz 1993) may be overstated.[1]

The remainder of this paper is organized as follows. First, the theory and measurement of moral reasoning is reviewed. Second, the theory and measurement of cognitive styles is presented. Third, the research hypotheses are advanced. Fourth, the empirical methods are described and the results reported. Finally, the implications of the results, the limitations of the study, and suggestions for future research are discussed.

THEORY AND MEASUREMENT OF MORAL REASONING

Cognitive moral development—associated with Piaget (1965 [1932]), Kohlberg (1969, 1976; Colby and Kohlberg 1987) and Rest (1979, 1986a, 1986b)—offers a description of the cognitive processes used to identify and frame possible courses of action to a moral dilemma. When faced with a moral dilemma, a person must ascertain how possible courses of action may affect not only his or her welfare but also the welfare of others. The individual then must resolve the conflict by choosing the course of action that would best fulfill the moral ideal. According to the moral developmental approach, differences exist among people in the complex cognitive processes they use to make such moral judgments.

Proponents of the cognitive developmental approach characterize development in moral reasoning not as the learning of additional specific norms but as a "progressive understanding of the purpose, function, and nature of social cooperation" (Rest 1983, 562). Social experiences are posited to increase understanding of the need for cooperative arrangements, the cooperative arrangements that are possible, and the benefits and obligations that may result from cooperative arrangements (Rest 1983, 1986a, 1986b). The lasting effects of social experiences are stored in long-term memory in the form of general concepts of justice or "schemes of cooperation" (Rest 1985). The various schemes of cooperation are called stages.

Table 1. Six Stages of Moral Reasoning

Stage 1	*Obedience:* Do what you are told to avoid being punished.
Stage 2	*Instrumental egoism and simple exchange:* Let's make a deal. Considers only the costs and benefits to oneself.
Stage 3	*Interpersonal concordance:* Be considerate, nice and kind and you will get along with people. System of cooperation is limited to friends.
Stage 4	*Law and duty to social order:* Everyone in society is obligated and protected by law. Society-wide system of cooperation in which roles have been formally organized.
Stage 5	*Societal consensus:* You are obligated by whatever arrangements are agreed to by due process procedures. With each person having a say in the decision process, each will see that his or her interests are maximized while at the same time having a basis for making claims on others.
Stage 6	*Non-arbitrary social cooperation:* How rational and impartial people would organize cooperation is moral. Focus is on fairness of the law or rules derived from general principles of what is just and right.

Note: Adapted from Rest (1979) and Ponemon (1992b, 1993).

Each stage is characterized by distinct notions of fairness and justice. Table 1 presents the brief characterization of the stages of moral reasoning originally derived by Kohlberg (1964, 1969) and modified by Rest (1979). The model asserts that there are six complex, cognitive processes or stages that people use in making moral judgments. Progression through the stages is from logically simple to more complex as moral development occurs.

A person reasoning at the early stages (Stages 1 and 2) complies with rules and social expectations only when a personal benefit is derived or a personal consequence is avoided. A person reasoning at the intermediate stages (Stages 3 and 4) views compliance with rules as necessary for the furtherance of a system of social cooperation and maintenance of an organized society. A person reasoning at the advanced stages (Stages 5 and 6) relies on personally held principles, rather than categorical rules, as a means for choosing among the alternative social systems and developing new laws and arrangements.

The most commonly used measure of moral reasoning is Rest's (1979, 1987) Defining Issues Test (DIT). The DIT is an objective questionnaire requiring a subject to select prototypic responses that are aligned with his or her point of view on several standard dilemmas. The ease of administration of the DIT has led to its use in more than 1,000 studies (Rest 1987). The large resulting database has allowed group standards to be developed.

The DIT produces a quantitative measure of moral development, in contrast to the qualitative measure developed and employed by Kohlberg (see Colby and Kohlberg 1987). In contrast to Kohlberg, who claims that a person exhibits moral reasoning consistent with only one stage (unless in momentary transition between stages), Rest (1979, 1983) conceptualizes development as inherently probabilistic, claiming that a person may exhibit reasoning at different stages simultaneously. Thus, Rest views development as a shifting distribution of responses rather than as a step-by-step progression through the stages.

The P score, the sum of scores for Stages 5 and 6, has shown the best internal consistency reliability, test-retest stability, presence of longitudinal trends, and convergent-divergent validity among potential DIT indices (Rest 1979, 1983). The P score, a continuous variable presented as a percentage, is a useful index because it reflects the increased use of principled reasoning (Stages 5 and 6) and the decreased use of lower stage reasoning (Stages 1 through 4) that occurs over time. Thus, the P score is thought to be the best measurement for locating a person along the developmental continuum.

THE THEORY AND MEASUREMENT OF COGNITIVE STYLE

Cognitive style, assessed using the Myers-Briggs Type Indicator (Myers and McCaulley 1986), refers to a person's preferred manner of perception and judgment. Perception refers to the way a person determines what a problem or situation entails and analyzes alternative methods of action. Judgment refers to the way that a person decides what action will be taken to solve the problem or resolve the situation. According to Jung (1977 [1921]), a person is capable of using two distinct, contrasting ways of perceiving: sensing (S) and intuition (N). Sensing or direct perception, requires utilization of the senses—sight, hearing, smell, taste, and touch—to gather the facts of a situation. Intuition, or indirect perception, shows meanings, relationships, and possibilities far beyond the reach of the senses. Theory suggests a person develops a preference for either sensing or intuition at an early age (Myers 1985). The preferred process of perception is exercised and strengthened, while the contrasting form of perception is neglected. Although a person is capable of using sensing or intuition, he or she prefers and trusts one process more than the other and his or her interests and energies are directed toward activities that allow him or her to use the preferred process.

Jung (1977 [1921]) also asserts that a person is capable of using two distinct, contrasting ways of judging or developing conclusions: thinking (T) and feeling (F). Thinking involves the use of logical processes to predict the result of any decision made or action taken. Thinkers judge alternatives impersonally, considering whether they are logical and consistent (Myers 1985). Feeling involves making decisions based on personal values. Feelers judge alternatives as to whether they "are pleasing or displeasing, supporting or threatening ideas already prized" (Myers 1985, p. 3). Theory suggests a person develops a preference for either thinking or feeling at an early age (Myers 1985). The preferred process of judgment is exercised and strengthened, while the contrasting form of judgment is neglected. Although a person is capable of using thinking and feeling, he or she prefers one process more than the other and his or her interests and energies are directed toward activities that allow them to use the preferred process. For this reason, the person who prefers thinking grows more adroit at organizing facts and ideas, while the person who prefers feeling grows more proficient in managing human relationships (Myers 1985).

The combination of perception and judgment preferences forms a person's cognitive style (Frisbie 1988). The cognitive styles include ST (sensing/thinkers), SF (sensing/feelers), NT (intuitive/thinkers), and NF (intuitive/feelers). Although the MBTI (Myers and McCaulley 1986) includes two other preferences relating to how a person interacts with his or her environment (Extrovert (E)/Introvert (I) and Judging (J)/Perceptive (P)), the concept of cognitive styles focuses on the core of Jung's typology (Frisbie 1988). Because the DIT measures a person's moral cognitions, not his or her moral action, focus on preferences for perceiving and judging—the cognitive processes—appears conceptually warranted.

RELATIONSHIP BETWEEN MORAL REASONING AND COGNITIVE STYLES

Because cognitive style is composed of two functions (S/N and T/F), the expected relationships between each function and the level of moral reasoning is examined in turn. From this discussion, hypothesized relationships between each of the four cognitive styles (i.e., SF, ST, NF, and NT) and the level of moral reasoning is developed.

The Perception Function

The theory of cognitive styles posits that an individual uses his or her senses (S) or intuition (N) for gathering information. Sensors focus on actualities (Lawrence 1982; Myers 1985). Because they do not like to make inferences, sensors consider information that is explicitly stated to be the most reliable (Myers 1985). Sensors crave enjoyment and possession, displaying a reluctance to sacrifice present enjoyment for future gain or good (Myers 1985). This suggests that sensors give careful consideration to the personal costs and benefits of an act, considering an act to be right if it serves their desires and interests (Stage 2 reasoning). In addition, sensors are imitative, wanting to have what other people have and do what other people do (Myers 1985), implying that they pay close attention to group norms when deliberating the moral course of action (Stage 3 reasoning).

Intuitors, on the other hand, are more interested in possibilities than they are in actualities (Lawrence 1982; Myers 1985). Intuitors are concerned with seeing the "big picture" and possess the ability to determine and project possibilities for action (Lawrence 1982; Myers 1985). Because moral development involves a growing awareness of the possibilities and requirements for arranging cooperation among the various stakeholders, intuitors display a preference for gathering information in a manner conducive to moral growth. Moreover, intuitors tend to be indifferent to what other people have and do and tend to be very independent of their physical surroundings (Myers 1985). This suggests that intuitors would be moved less by group norms than by personally held principles. Thus, theory suggests that intuitors (N) will display greater moral reasoning skills than sensors (S).

The Judgment Function

In choosing among alternatives (judgment), thinkers (T) prefer to use logical analysis in the pursuit of objective truth (Lawrence 1982; Myers 1985; Myers and McCaulley 1986). Thinkers are skilled at organizing facts and ideas into logical sequences to posit cause-and-effect relationships (Lawrence 1982; Myers 1985). Less interested in personal relationships than feelers (F), thinkers tend to be impersonal, preferring truthfulness to tactfulness (Lawrence 1982; Myers 1985). Assuming that persons who do not agree with them are wrong, thinkers are likely to question the conclusions of others on principle (Myers 1985). Concerned with principles of justice and fairness (Lawrence 1982; Myers and McCaulley 1986), thinkers are expected to display a high level of moral reasoning.

The theory of cognitive styles suggests that feelers (F) display a lower level of moral reasoning than thinkers (T). Although they base decisions on their own personal values and principles (Lawrence 1982; Myers 1985), feelers value relationships and prize harmony (Lawrence 1982; Myers 1985). They are likely to agree with persons around them (Myers 1985), connoting that feelers may yield to group norms when facing a moral dilemma (Stage 3 reasoning). Moreover, feelers contribute to the welfare of society "by their loyal support of good works and those movements, generally regarded as good by the community" (Myers 1985, p. 68), denoting a tendency toward Stage 4 reasoning. Thus, theory suggests that thinkers (T) will display higher levels of moral reasoning than feelers (F).

Research Hypotheses

Table 2 summarizes the characteristics of the four cognitive styles and presents expectations, based on the previous discussion, for the level of moral reasoning. Theory suggests that persons preferring intuition (N) for gathering information and thinking (T) for making judgments will display the most advanced moral reasoning abilities. Based on this discussion, intuitive/thinkers (NT) are posited to display the highest level of moral reasoning among the four cognitive styles.

Hypothesis 1. Persons with the NT cognitive style will display the highest mean level of moral reasoning.

Conversely, theory suggests that persons preferring sensing (S) for gathering information and feeling (F) for making judgments will display the least advanced moral reasoning abilities. Based on the previous discussion, sensing/feelers (SF) are posited to display the lowest level of moral reasoning among the four cognitive styles.

Table 2. Characteristics of Cognitive Styles

	SF	*ST*	*NF*	*NT*
Focus on	Facts	Facts	Possibilities	Possibilities
Handle these with	Personal warmth	Impersonal Analysis	Personal warmth	Impersonal Analysis
Tend to become	Sympathetic and friendly	Practical and matter-of-fact	Enthusiastic and insightful	Logical and ingenious
Good at	Empathizing; cooperating personalizing	Observing and ordering; filing and recalling; sequencing and categorizing	Imagining; forming hypotheses; making new combinations	Discovery and inquiry; problem solving; comparing and contrasting
Important issues in moral reasoning and judgments	Personal cost/ benefit and group norms	Conform to laws and codes of conduct	Harmony based on personal values and values of others close to them	Justice and fairness leading to objective decision making
Expected level of moral reasoning	Low	Moderate	Moderate	High

Sources: Frisbie (1988); Lawrence (1982); McIntyre and Capen (1993); Myers and McCaulley (1986)

Hypothesis 2. Persons with the SF cognitive style will display the lowest mean level of moral reasoning.

Predictions for the remaining two cognitive styles, ST and NF, are less clear. For the ST and NF cognitive styles, the expected relationships between the perception (S/N) and judgment (T/F) functions and the level of moral reasoning are incongruent and potentially offsetting. For the sensing/thinker (ST), preference for sensing (S) is expected to be related to lower levels of moral reasoning, while preference for thinking (T) is thought to be related to higher levels of moral reasoning. For the intuitive/feeler (NF), preference for intuition (N) is expected to be related to higher levels of moral reasoning, while preference for feeling (F) is thought to be related to lower levels of moral reasoning. A priori, there is no reason to expect that one function will dominate the other when forming moral cognitions. Thus, sensing/thinkers (ST) and intuitive/feelers (NF) are expected to display similar levels of moral reasoning.

Hypothesis 3. Persons with the ST and NF cognitive styles will display equivalent mean levels of moral reasoning.

When compared to persons who exhibit preferences for NT and SF, persons with the ST and NF cognitive styles are expected to display moderate levels of moral reasoning. For the NT and SF cognitive styles, the expected relationship between the level of moral reasoning and the perception (S/N) function and the expected relationship between the level of moral reasoning and the judgment (T/F) function are congruent. For the NT cognitive style, both functions point toward advancement in moral reasoning abilities. For the SF cognitive style, both functions point toward lack of growth in moral reasoning abilities.

In contrast, for the ST and NF cognitive styles, the expected relationship between the level of moral reasoning and the perception (S/N) function and the expected relationship between the level of moral reasoning and the judgment (T/F) function are incongruent. In each case, one function suggests advancement in moral reasoning abilities while the other function is believed to quell growth in moral reasoning capacities. Because the relationships between the two cognitive style functions and the level of moral reasoning are incongruent and potentially offsetting, persons displaying the ST and NF cognitive styles are posited to display levels of moral reasoning that are less than that displayed by persons exhibiting the NT cognitive style but greater than that displayed by persons exhibiting the SF cognitive style.

Hypothesis 4. Persons with the ST and NF cognitive styles will display moderate mean levels of moral reasoning compared to the mean levels of moral reasoning for persons with the NT and SF cognitive styles.

Hypothesis 4A. Persons with the ST and NF cognitive styles will display lower mean levels of moral reasoning than persons with the NT cognitive style.

Hypothesis 4B. Persons with the ST and NF cognitive styles will display greater mean levels of moral reasoning than persons with the SF cognitive style.

METHODS

The subjects were 195 accounting students, constituting more than 90% of the senior class, at a large state university located in the midwest region of the United States. The subjects were administered Form G of the MBTI during class time. The six-story DIT was completed outside of class at the subjects' leisure. In an attempt to ensure that the subjects understood the task, instructions for the DIT were read to the subjects by one of the researchers during the class period. Given an approximation of the amount of time needed to complete the task and instructed not to discuss the task with any other students, the subjects were given one week to complete the DIT. In order to provide an incentive, subjects were given course credit upon completing and returning the DIT. Grade-point averages (GPAs) were obtained from the university registrar.

The responses of six subjects were eliminated because they failed the DIT consistency and manipulation checks (Rest 1987).[2] Four of the remaining 189 subjects did not complete the MBTI. GPAs were not obtainable for an additional three subjects,[3] leaving 182 usable responses.

The MBTI was hand-scored using the scoring stencils provided by Consulting Psychologists Press. Reported test-retest, split-half, and coefficient alpha reliability have been high for both of the MBTI's dichotomous function scores (i.e., S/N and T/F), especially among samples of college students (Myers and McCaulley 1986).

The DIT forms were acquired from and scored by the Center for the Study of Ethical Development at the University of Minnesota. Reported test-retest reliability of the six-story version of the DIT have been in the high .70s or .80s (Rest 1979, 1987) and coefficient alpha reliability has been reported to be in the high .70s (Davison and Robbins 1978; Rest 1987). However, low reliability has been found in recent accounting samples (Bernardi 1992), raising concern about the use of the DIT (Jones 1993). When reliability is low, significant relationships between variables may be hidden by random errors of measurement (Nunnally 1978).

For the current sample, coefficient alpha for the DIT P score is .50.[4] Because the scenarios used are factorially complex and do not parallel each other, coefficient alpha provides a lower bound, rather than an estimate of, reliability (Davison and Robbins 1978), suggesting that a coefficient alpha of .50 for the current sample is tolerable.

RESULTS

The mean DIT P score for the sample is 37.5 ($m = 36.7$; $s.d. = 11.9$), consistent with many of the studies employing accounting students (Lampe and Finn forthcoming; Ponemon 1993; Ponemon and Glazer 1990; Shaub 1994),[5] but substantially below the norm, approximately 43, for college seniors in general (Rest 1987). The distribution of cognitive styles is: SFs 25.3% (46); STs 50.5% (92); NFs 9.9% (18); and NTs 14.3% (26). Consistent with previous studies using accountants (Barrett 1969; Descouzis 1989; Jacoby 1981; Keirsey and Bates 1978; Myers 1985; Myers and McCaulley 1986; Stricker and Ross 1962) and accounting/business students (Geary and Rooney 1993; McIntyre and Capen 1993; Myers 1985), ST is the predominate cognitive style in the sample.

Table 3. DIT P by Cognitive Style

	Count	*Mean*	*Std. Dev.*	*Minimum*	*Maximum*
SF	46	35.36	10.22	11.67	63.33
ST	92	36.18	12.02	10.00	63.33
NF	18	39.44	14.38	11.67	60.00
NT	26	44.55	9.86	23.33	58.33

Dependent Variable: DIT P Scores

Source	*Sum of Squares*	*DF*	*Mean Square*	*F*	*Significance*
Covariates					
GPA	*1043.8*	1	1043.8	8.019	.005
Main Effect					
Cognitive Styles*	*1435.0*	3	478.3	3.675	.013
Explained	*2478.8*	4	619.7	4.761	.001
Residual	*23039.5*	177	130.2		
Total	*25518.3*	181	141.0		

Bonferroni Multiple Comparison Tests

	Differences Between Means	*Significance*
SF-ST	-0.82	n.s.
SF-NF	-4.08	n.s.
SF-NT	-9.19	$p < .05$
ST-NF	-3.26	n.s.
ST-NT	-8.38	$p < .05$
NF-NT	-5.11	n.s.

Note: *Cognitive styles: 1=SF; 2=ST; 3=NF; 4=NT.

Analysis of variance (ANOVA) was used to test for potential differences in the level of moral reasoning across the four cognitive styles. Because the cell sizes are unequal and disproportionate, a generalized least squares approach was used to perform the ANOVA (Berenson et al. 1983; Tabachnick and Fidell 1989). The dependent variable was the continuous DIT P score. The independent variable was cognitive style. GPA was entered as a covariate designed to partial out other differences in abilities among the subjects. The results, as shown in Table 3, indicate that the covariate for GPA is significant ($p = .005$), implying that individual differences other than cognitive styles are related to the DIT P scores in this sample.[6] After adjustment for the covariate, the main effect for cognitive style is significant ($p = .013$). This result suggests that how a person gathers information and makes judgments is significantly related to the level of moral reasoning.

A one-way ANOVA employing Bonferroni multiple comparison tests was performed to determine differences in mean DIT P scores by cognitive styles. The DIT P score was the dependent variable and cognitive style was the independent variable. The results of the multiple comparisons, as reported in Table 3, suggest that the mean DIT P score for persons preferring the NT cognitive style (44.6) is significantly greater than the mean DIT P scores of the SF (35.4) and ST (36.2) cognitive styles at $p = .05$, providing some support for Hypothesis 1. Contrary to Hypotheses 1 and 4a, the mean DIT P score for persons preferring the NT cognitive style does not differ significantly from the mean DIT P score of persons preferring the NF cognitive style (39.4). Contrary to Hypotheses 2 and H4b, the mean DIT P score of persons preferring the SF cognitive style was not significantly lower than the mean DIT P scores of persons preferring the ST or NF cognitive styles. In support of H3, the mean DIT P scores for persons preferring the NF and ST cognitive styles do not differ significantly.

The limited support for the research hypotheses appears to imply that the perception function (i.e., S/N), and not the judgment function (i.e., T/F), is influencing the relationship between cognitive style and the level of moral reasoning. In order to explore this presumption, the cognitive style variable was split into two variables—S/N and T/F—representing the two functions. An ANOVA was performed using the DIT P score as the dependent variable. Two factors—the S/N and T/F dichotomous variables—were employed. GPA again was used as a covariate.

Table 4. DIT P by Cognitive Function

	Count	*Mean*	*Std. Dev.*	*Minimum*	*Maximum*
Sensing (S)	138	35.9	11.4	10.0	63.3
Intuition (N)	44	42.5	12.0	11.7	60.0
Thinking (T)	118	38.0	12.1	10.0	63.0
Feeling (F)	64	36.5	11.6	11.7	63.3

Dependent Variable: DIT P Scores

Source	*Sum of Squares*	*DF*	*Mean Square*	*F*	*Significance of F*
Covariates					
GPA	1043.8	1	1043.8	8.019	.005
Main Effects					
S-N*	1269.1	1	1269.1	9.750	.002
T-F**	122.3	1	122.3	0.940	.334
Interaction					
S-N by T-F	93.3	1	93.3	0.717	.398
Explained	2478.8	4	619.7	4.761	.001
Residual	23039.4	177	130.2		
Total	25518.3	181	141.0		

Notes: * S-N: 1 = sensing; 2 = intuition.
**T-F: 1 = thinking; 2 = feeling.

The results, as reported in Table 4, reveal a significant main effect for the S/N variable ($p = .002$). Neither the main effect for the T/F variable ($p = .334$) nor the S/N-T/F interaction ($p = .398$) were significant. Thus, the results support the presumption that a person's preference for gathering information is significantly related to the level of moral reasoning. In particular, persons who prefer to use intuition (mean = 42.5) to gather information and analyze alternatives outperformed persons who prefer to use sensing (mean = 35.9).

DISCUSSION, LIMITATIONS, AND SUGGESTIONS FOR FUTURE RESEARCH

The results of this study suggest cognitive style is related to a person's level of moral reasoning. Intuitive/thinkers (NT), comprising only 14.3% of the sample and rarely comprising more than 20% of previous samples of accounting practitioners (Barrett 1969; Descouzis 1989; Jacoby 1981; Keirsey and Bates 1978; Myers 1985; Myers and McCaulley 1986; Stricker and Ross 1962), displayed the highest mean level of moral reasoning. In contrast, sensing/thinkers (ST), who predominated in the current sample and previous samples of practicing accountants, displayed a mean DIT P score substantially below the norm for college seniors. Thus, the results shed some light on why accounting students and practicing accountants often fail to demonstrate moral reasoning abilities consistent with adults of similar educational and socioeconomic backgrounds.

Further examination reveals that, of the two functions (perception and judgment) that combine to form a person's cognitive style, only perception is significantly related to the level of moral reasoning. Persons who gather information and analyze alternatives by intuition (N) display a higher level of moral reasoning than do persons who use their senses (S) for gathering data.

The lack of an observed significant relationship between the judgment (T/F) preference and the level of moral reasoning underscores the importance of perception in moral reasoning. Although thinkers (T) may be concerned with justice and fairness (Myers and McCaulley 1986), the judgments they make will only be as good as the information acquired through the perception process. Myers (1985) emphasizes this possibility, stating that "thinking is not always first-class thinking. Its product is no better than the facts it started with (and they were acquired by perception of unknown quality) and no better than the logic employed" (p. 67).

Earlier studies (Armstrong 1987; Ponemon and Glazer 1990) suggest the deficiency in the development of the moral reasoning capacities of accounting students (and, subsequently, accounting practitioners) results from the technical nature of accounting education programs. The results of this study indicate that previous findings also may be attributable to the cognitive styles of persons attracted to the profession. In particular, sensors (STs and SFs) may be drawn to or supported by the traditionally technical, lecture-oriented curriculum. If so, the findings of this study suggest that the development of pedagogy and course materials aimed at strengthening the intuitive abilities of accounting students as well as changes in the education environment aimed at attracting students who prefer the intuitive cognitive styles (NTs and NFs) may be necessary if the moral reasoning abilities of accountants are to be improved.

Curriculum and pedagogical changes suggested by the profession (Bedford Committee 1986; Arthur Andersen & Co. et al. 1989) and supported by the AECC seem consistent with this endeavor. Pedagogies that involve cooperative learning techniques, group work, written cases, and oral presentations (including debates) and that stress searching for and understanding relationships and implications should help to strengthen students' intuitive abilities (Geary and Rooney 1993). If this is true, assertions that the AECC erred by funding curriculum change projects that fail to specifically integrate ethics into the curriculum (Mintz 1993) may be overstated, since greater balance in perception abilities also should translate into improved moral reasoning abilities.

As with all research studies, the results are limited by restrictions to external validity. First, the sample consisted of students from only one university. Although the DIT and MBTI scores for this sample are consistent with other accounting studies using these instruments, the results of this study are generalizable only to the extent that other institutions are similar to the major midwestern university that participated in this study. Second, because the sample consisted of accounting students, any references to how the findings relate to practicing accountants is speculative at present and should be viewed with some caution. The purpose of this exploratory study was merely to determine if a relationship exists between cognitive styles and the moral reasoning abilities of accounting students. Having found such a relationship, it is hoped that the findings in this study will stimulate research, particularly longitudinal research, aimed at understanding how pedagogical interventions affect cognitive styles and influence the cognitive styles of persons attracted to accounting, as well as the impact this has on moral reasoning abilities of persons choosing to pursue careers in accounting.

ACKNOWLEDGMENTS

The authors are grateful for the very helpful comments and assistance provided by Penne Ainsworth, David Donnelly, Larry Ponemon, Kay Stewart, and John Sweeney. The authors are indebted to Jan Benson for her research assistance. An earlier version of this paper was presented at the 1993 meeting of the Western Region of the American Accounting Association.

NOTES

1. This is not to suggest that ethics should not be incorporated into the curriculum. The issue of whether ethics should be taught has been sufficiently addressed elsewhere (Loeb 1988; Langenderfer and Rockness 1989; Ponemon 1992b), and, with the exception of Ponemon (1993), ethics education interventions have been shown to have a positive effect on moral reasoning abilities (Armstrong 1993; Reimer et al. 1983; Rest 1986b, 1988).

2. A consistency check between the ratings and rankings is used to identify subjects who may be randomly marking items. If an issue statement is ranked as most important, then it must be rated at least as high as all other issue statements. Also, meaningless but sophisticated-sounding items (M items) are interspersed throughout the DIT as a manipulation check, identifying subjects who are picking issue statements because they sound complex. If too many of these items are selected, the questionnaire will be discarded too. Rest (1987) indicates that it is not unusual for 5% to 15% of the sample to be invalidated.

3. This was the first semester at the university for two of the subjects. In addition, one of the identification numbers provided by the students produced no match with university registrar records.

4. Coefficient alpha for a particular sample is not a statistic included in the scoring report provided by the Center for the Study of Ethical Development at Minnesota. Coefficient alpha was calculated by taking the raw P score for each scenario and examining the consistency across all the scenarios (see Rest 1987).

5. Notable exceptions are Armstrong (1993) and Jeffrey (1993). The mean DIT P scores in these samples were at or above the norm for college students (Rest 1987).

6. GPA generally has not been used as an explanation for the variance in DIT scores. Research in psychology attempting to explain why formal education is strongly associated with increases in the level of moral reasoning, however, has found measures of academic success to be positively correlated with DIT P scores (Deemer 1987; Spickelmier 1983), providing some support for the significant finding obtained in this study.

REFERENCES

Armstrong, M.B. 1984. Internalization of the professional ethic by certified public accountants: A multidimensional scaling approach. Unpublished Ph.D. dissertation, University of Southern California.

Armstrong, M.B. 1987. Moral development and accounting education. *Journal of Accounting Education* (Spring): 27-43.

Armstrong, M.B. 1993. Ethics and professionalism in accounting education: A sample course. *Journal of Accounting Education* (Spring): 77-92.

Arnold, D.F., and L.A. Ponemon. 1991. Internal auditors' perceptions of whistle-blowing and the influence of moral reasoning: An experiment. *Auditing: A Journal of Practice and Theory* (Fall): 1-15.

Arthur Andersen & Co., Arthur Young, Coopers & Lybrand, Deloitte Haskins & Sells, Ernst & Whinney, Peat Marwick Main & Co., Price Waterhouse, and Touche Ross. 1989. *Perspectives on Education: Capabilities for Success in the Accounting Profession*. New York: Authors.

Barrett, M.J. 1969. Some behavioral attributes of professional audit independence. Unpublished Ph.D. dissertation, University of Colorado.

Bedford Committee, American Accounting Association. 1986. Committee on the future structure, content, and scope of accounting education. *Issues in Accounting Education* (Spring): 168-195.

Berenson, M.L., D.M. Levine, and M. Goldstein. 1983. *Intermediate Statistical Method and Applications: A Computer Package Approach*. Englewood Cliffs, NJ: Prentice Hall.

Bernardi, R. 1992. A reliability check for psychometric research. *The ABO Reporter* (Summer): 7-8.

Colby, A., and L. Kohlberg. 1987. *The Measurement of Moral Judgment*. New York: Cambridge University Press.

Davison, M.L., and S. Robbins. 1978. The reliability and validity of objective indices of moral development. *Applied Psychological Measurement* (Summer): 391-403.

Deemer, D.K. 1987. Moral judgment and life experiences. Unpublished Ph.D. dissertation, University of Minnesota.

Descouzis, D. 1989. Psychological types of tax preparers. *Journal of Psychological Type* 17: 36-38.

Fleming, J.E. 1985. A suggested approach to linking decision styles with business ethics. *Journal of Business Ethics* (April): 137-144.

Frisbie, G.R. 1988. Cognitive styles: An alternative to Keirsey's temperaments. *Journal of Psychological Types* 16: 13-21.

Geary, W.T., and C.J. Rooney. 1993. Designing accounting education to achieve balanced intellectual development. *Issues in Accounting Education* (Spring): 60-70.

Jacoby, P.F. 1981. Psychological types and career success in the accounting profession. *Research in Psychological Type* 4: 24-37.

Jeffrey, C. 1993. Ethical development of accounting students, non-accounting business students, liberal arts students. *Issues in Accounting Education* (Spring): 86-96.

Jones, S.K. 1993. On the coefficient of reliability in studies of ethical behavior of CPAs. *The ABO Reporter* (Winter): 8.

Jung, C.G. 1977. *Psychological Types*. Princeton, NJ: Princeton University Press. (Originally published 1921.)

Keirsey, D., and M. Bates. 1978. *Please Understand Me*. Del Mar, CA: Promethean.

Kohlberg, l. 1964. Development of moral character and moral ideology. In *Review of Child Development Research*, eds. M.L. Hoffman and L. Hoffman, 383-481. New York: Russell Sage Foundation.

Kohlberg, L. 1969. State and sequence: The cognitive development approach to socialization. In *Handbook of Socialization Theory and Research*, ed. D. Goslin, 347-480. Chicago, IL: Rand McNally.

Kohlberg, L. 1976. Moral stages and moralization. In *Moral Development and Behavior*, ed. T. Lickona, 29-53. New York: Holt, Rinehart, and Winston.

Lampe, J., and D. Finn. 1992. A model of auditors' ethical decision process. Auditing: A Journal of Practice and Theory (Supplement).

Langenderfer, H.Q., and J.W. Rockness. 1989. Integrating ethics into the accounting curriculum: Issues, problems, and solutions. *Issues in Accounting Education* (Spring): 58-69.

Lawrence, G. 1982. *People Types & Tiger Stripes: A Practical Guide to Learning Styles*. Gainesville, FL: Center for the Applications of Psychological Type, Inc.

Loeb, S.E. 1988. Teaching students accounting ethics: Some crucial issues. *Issues in Accounting Education* (Fall): 316-329.

McIntyre, R.P., and M.M. Capen. 1993. A cognitive style perspective on ethical questions. *Journal of Business Ethics* (August): 629-634.

Mintz, S.M. 1993. Concerns about the generalizability of results of the AECC grant program. *Journal of Accounting Education* (Spring): 93-100.

Myers, I.B. 1985. *Gifts Differing*. Palo Alto: CA: Consulting Psychologists Press.

Myers, I.B., and M.H. McCaulley. 1986. *Manual: A Guide to the Development and Use of the Myers-Briggs Type Indicator*. Palo Alto, CA: Consulting Psychologists Press.

Nunnally, J. 1978. *Psychometric Theory*. New York: The Free Press.

Piaget, J. 1965. *The Moral Development of the Child.* New York: The Free Press. (Originally published 1932.)

Ponemon, L.A. 1988. A cognitive-developmental approach to the analysis of certified public accountants' ethical judgments. Unpublished Ph.D. dissertation, Union College of Union University.

Ponemon, L.A. 1990. Ethical judgments in accounting: A cognitive-developmental perspective. *Critical Perspectives on Accounting* 1: 191-215.

Ponemon, L.A. 1992a. Auditor underreporting of time and moral reasoning: An experimental-lab study. *Contemporary Accounting Research* (Fall): 171-189.

Ponemon, L.A. 1992b. Ethical reasoning and selection-socialization in accounting. *Accounting, Organizations and Society* (April/May): 239-258.

Ponemon, L.A. 1993. Can ethics be taught in accounting. *Journal of Accounting Education* (Fall): 185-209.

Ponemon, L.A., and A. Glazer. 1990. Accounting education and ethical development: The influence of liberal learning on students and alumni in accounting practice. *Issues in Accounting Education* (Fall): 21-34.

Reimer, J., D.P. Paolitto, and R.H. Hersh. 1983. *Promoting Moral Growth: From Piaget to Kohlberg*. Prospect Heights, IL: Waveland Press.

Rest, J.R. 1979. *Development in Judging Moral Issues.* Minneapolis, MN: University of Minnesota Press.

Rest, J.R. 1983. Morality. In *Manual of Child Psychology,* Vol. 3: *Cognitive Development*, eds. J. Flavell and E. Markman, 556-629. New York: John Wiley & Sons.

Rest, J.R. 1985. An interdisciplinary approach to moral education. In *Moral Education: Theory and Application*, eds. M.W. Berkowitz and F. Oser, 9-25. Hillsdale, NJ: Lawrence Erlbaum Associates.

Rest, J.R. 1986a. *DIT Manual.* 3rd, revised edition. Minneapolis, MN: The Center for the Study of Ethical Development.

Rest, J.R. 1986b. *Moral Development: Advances in Research and Theory.* New York: Praeger.

Rest, J.R. 1987. *Guide for the Defining Issues Test: How to Use the Optical Scan Forms and the Center's Scoring Service*, version 1.2. Minneapolis, MN: Center for the Study of Ethical Development.

Rest, J.R. 1988. Why does college promote development in moral judgment? *Journal of Moral Education* (October): 183-194.

Rest, J.R., and D. Narvaez. 1991. The college experience and moral development. In *Handbook of Moral Behavior and Development*, eds. W.M. Kurtines and J.L. Gewirtz, 229-245. Hillsdale, NJ: Lawrence Earlbaum Associates.

Shaub, M. 1994. An analysis of the association of traditional demographic variables with the moral reasoning of auditing students and auditors. *Journal of Accounting Education* (January): 1-26.

Spickelmier, J.L. 1983. College experience and moral judgment development. Unpublished Ph.D. dissertation, University of Minnesota.

Stricker, L.J., and J. Ross. 1962. *A Description and Evaluation of the Myers-Briggs Type Indicator.* Princeton, NJ: Educational Testing Services.

Tabachnick, B.G., and L.S. Fidell. 1989. *Using Multivariate Statistics.* New York: Harper Collins.

ACCOUNTING ETHICS:
THE SEARCH FOR TRUTH IN AN AGE OF MORAL RELATIVISM

C. Richard Baker

ABSTRACT

This paper addresses a fundamental issue regarding research on accounting ethics, that is, whether there is such a thing as moral truth upon which ethics in general, and accounting ethics in particular, may be based. If there is no such thing as moral truth, then it seems incredible to argue that there is or ought to be a normative code of ethical conduct that should be obeyed. Arguments for normative ethical conduct tend to dissolve in the face of moral relativism. While the focus of this paper might well be on accountants in general and the many roles that accountants play, it is perhaps more manageable to place a boundary on the scope of the inquiry and limit the focus to the ethical dilemmas facing Certified Public Accountants (CPAs) in the practice of auditing financial statements of public companies. The pressures placed on CPAs in their roles as auditors of public

Research on Accounting Ethics, Volume 2, pages 73-86.

ISBN: 1-55938-997-4

companies are strong and growing with increasing legal liability, growing gaps in expectations, and increasing technical change and complexity. Perhaps it is not unexpected that there may be a certain lack of moral focus in this changing environment. Previous research on accounting ethics has focused on how the ethics of accountants may be maintained and improved. Other research has taken the perspective of exposing the ethical credibility of accountants. This paper attempts to understand the difficulty of acting morally in what is perhaps an amoral world.

INTRODUCTION

This paper addresses a fundamental issue regarding research on accounting ethics, that is, whether there is such a thing as moral truth upon which ethics in general, and accounting ethics in particular, may be based. If there is no such thing as moral truth, then it seems incredible to argue that there is or ought to be a normative code of ethical conduct that should be obeyed. Arguments for normative ethical conduct tend to dissolve in the face of moral relativism.

Accountants, as members of society and as members of a profession, are frequently confronted with ethical dilemmas. How the individual accountant and how accountants in general solve ethical dilemmas is of growing interest to accounting researchers and to the larger society (see, e.g., Ponemon 1990; Ponemon and Gabhardt 1990; Arnold and Ponemon 1987; Preston et al. 1990; Puxty et al. 1987; Lehman and Tinker 1987; Neimark and Tinker 1986; Loeb 1972, 1978; Baker 1976). While the focus of this paper might well be on accountants in general and the many roles that accountants play, it is perhaps more manageable to place a boundary on the scope of the inquiry and limit the focus to the ethical dilemmas facing certified public accountants in the practice of auditing financial statements of public companies. The pressures placed on CPAs in their roles as auditors of public companies are strong and growing with increasing legal liability, growing gaps in expectations, and increasing technical change and complexity (Baker 1993). Perhaps it is not unexpected that there may be a certain lack of moral focus in this changing environment. Previous research on accounting ethics has focused on how the ethics of accountants may be maintained and improved (Loeb 1972, 1978; Carey 1966). Other research has taken the perspective of exposing the ethical credibility of accountants

(Preston et al. 1990; Puxty et al. 1987; Lehman and Tinker 1987). This paper intends neither to expose nor to improve but, rather, to attempt to understand the difficulty of acting morally in what is perhaps an amoral world.

CPAs are regarded as professionals because they satisfy the general requirements of a profession in the sociological sense (Greenwood 1966; Abbott 1983; Burns and Haga 1977). One commonality among most professions is that professions subscribe to a code of ethical conduct which is said to be in some sense superior to that of the ethical or moral conduct expected of ordinary persons acting in their daily lives. However, CPAs differ from other professionals in that while they receive fees for services rendered to persons and entities whom they refer to as clients, CPAs also assume other responsibilities to third parties and to the public generally. While other professionals such as doctors and lawyers are expected to perform their services at the maximum possible level of professional competence, CPAs are at times expected by their "clients" to perform their professional services at a level less than the maximum vis-à-vis the interests of third parties who are the implicit beneficiaries of the contractual arrangements between CPAs and their clients. This unusual arrangement poses an ethical dilemma for CPAs. There has been an attempt to resolve this ethical dilemma through the promulgation of a Code of Conduct by the American Institute of CPAs (AICPA), a central tenet of which is to maintain independence from clients in fact and in appearance (AICPA 1993). Whether CPAs can in fact maintain their independence from clients in the face of fee and other pressures is open to discussion, as is the issue of whether the Code of Conduct is an adequate mechanism to assure the independence of CPAs. The sections that follow explore whether anyone is sufficiently free to claim that he or she is an independent actor in the realm of ethical dilemmas.

THEORETICAL DISCUSSION

In general, there are two approaches to the study of ethics: the deontological and the teleological. The deontological, or act-oriented, approach holds that there are certain ethical axioms that dictate what actions a person should take regardless of the circumstances (Frankena 1963). Pursuant to the deontological approach, actions are seen as intrinsically right or wrong. Opposed to the deontological approach is the teleological or results-oriented approach which holds that the rightness or wrongness of an act is determined by its consequences. The teleological approach is sometimes referred to as consequentialism (Frankena 1963).

The study of ethics may also be approached from a perspective that takes into consideration both the deontological and teleological aspects of ethical acts. In other words, in their actual lives, persons evaluate the inherent rightness or wrongness of their acts and/or those of others, and, in addition, they evaluate the consequences of their acts and/or those of others. Thus, a blend of deontological and teleological factors affects the actual behavior of persons. Furthermore, organizational and cultural factors have an impact on ethical behavior, regardless of the deontological or teleological views held by the actors. This means that the organizational settings in which the actors find themselves are often determinative of behavior regardless of their ethical beliefs (Hunt and Vitell 1986; Ajzen and Fishbein 1973; Frankena 1963). There have been studies in the accounting literature which have looked at the impact of organizational factors on ethical behavior (see, e.g., Schilit 1984; Loeb 1971, 1972).

Psychological Views of Ethics

Even though they are investigating actual behaviors, positivistic studies of ethics are usually grounded in normative psychological or sociological models. The ethical or moral development paradigm is well established in psychology (Kohlberg 1981). The ethical development paradigm tends to finesse the question of moral truth by focusing on a person's ethical beliefs and how the person's belief system controls conflict resolution and ethical problem solving in actual life. Nonetheless, these studies of ethical beliefs in relation to behavior are generally founded on a psychological model derived from Piaget. According to Piaget, a person's moral sense develops in a series of stages over time as a result of social interactions. Kohlberg (1958) elaborated upon the stages of moral development as postulated by Piaget in order to explain the processes that appear to cause a particular individual to act according to a certain set of chosen ethical principles. Kohlberg postulated a model of ethical development as a series of cognitive steps. According to this model, a person's ethical judgment develops over time through a series of stages. At any given point in time, a person is at one particular stage in the development of ethical judgment and then proceeds to the next stage depending upon the person's belief system. Ponemon (1990) and others have employed the Kohlberg model in a number of empirical studies in the accounting literature (see Ponemon and Gabhart 1990; Arnold and Ponemon 1987) with the interesting result that persons in higher level positions in public accounting firms do not necessarily demonstrate higher levels of ethical and moral development as measured by the Defining Issues Test (Ponemon 1990; Rest 1979).

Sociological and Postmodernist Views of Ethics

Ethical studies from a sociological perspective are often embroiled in the definition and meaning of professionalism (Abbott 1983; Freedman 1978; Greenwood 1966; Burns and Haga 1977). However, there have been a number of studies which have approached the subject of CPA ethical behavior from a sociological perspective, particularly with regard to independence from clients (see, e.g., Baker 1977, 1993; Gaa and Smith 1985; Knapp 1985; Lightner et al. 1982; Aranya et al. 1981). These studies recognize the ethical dilemmas faced by CPAs and discuss how organizational and structural factors act to ameliorate or exacerbate these dilemmas; however, for the most part, these studies avoid the issue of moral truth.

More recently, a postmodernist perspective has gained influence in accounting research and in the investigation of the ethics in accounting (Macintosh 1993; Preston et al. 1990). Postmodernism is generally defined as a set of beliefs regarding the outmoded nature of modernity. Several claims are made by postmodernism. The first claim is that the metanarratives that constitute the underlying premises of modernity have lost their effectiveness and no longer represent reality. These metanarratives concern the reality of truth, God, nature, progress, freedom, and so forth. The postmodernist stance is one of incredulity with respect to these metanarratives. Second, postmodernism argues that modernity has not been progressive and emancipatory. Instead, it has produced a mechanized social order which has reduced freedom. Third, the modern era spanning the 19th century and most of the 20th century has been a period marked by intense warfare and increased manufacture of weaponry. The ideals of progress and humanity are seen as being suppressed by the actualities of the modern era. Fourth, postmodernism claims that a new political order is emerging which seeks to provide space for those who have been previously marginalized (e.g., women, minorities, gays, etc.). Such groups resist the normalizing tendencies of modernism. Finally, postmodernism argues that the development of new information technologies may open up new opportunities to truly democratize political and social life, or they may become new instruments of coercion for the powerful (Macintosh 1993). Postmodernism essentially rejects the notion that there is such thing as moral truth and may, in fact, see arguments in favor of moral truth as merely another means of controlling the less powerful in society and forcing them to behave in a certain manner.

The Archeology of Ethics

Within the postmodernist perspective, Michel Foucault (1986) has addressed the issues of morality and ethics by proposing various definitions concerning these concepts. Foucault views morality as a type of meta-concept which incorporates various subconcepts. These subconcepts include moral codes, moral behavior, and ethics (see Figure 1). The moral code refers to the set of laws, values, and rules of action that are specified for individuals by entities such as religious authorities, families, and schools.

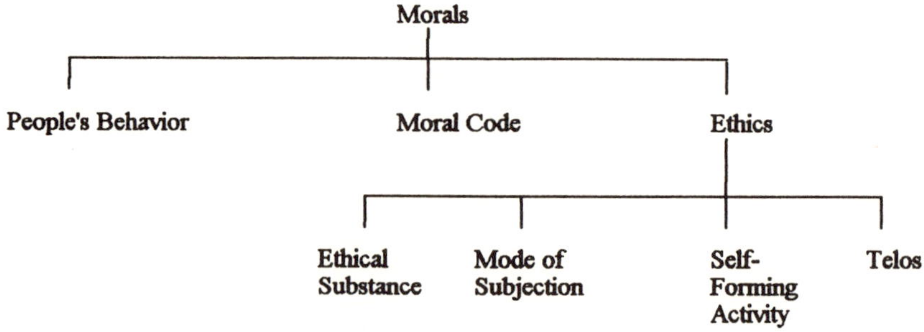

Figure 1. Foucault's Conception of Morality and Ethics

The moral code specifies laws and rules that must be followed on pain of sanction. However, these rules exist within a "complex interplay of elements that counterbalance and correct one another, and cancel each other out on certain points, thus providing for compromises and loopholes" (Foucault 1986, 52). In this sense, the moral code as defined by Foucault may be compared to the deontological approach to ethics discussed previously. However, because Foucault does not subscribe to the belief that the moral code is immutable, nor is it necessarily the same moral code in all places at the same time, there is a distinct difference between Foucault's definition of the moral code and the deontological approach to the study of ethics.

Moral behavior, according to Foucault, consists of the actual behavior of individuals in relation to their moral code. The question here is whether individuals comply more or less fully with a standard of conduct, in what manner they obey or resist an interdiction or a prescription, and in what manner they respect or disregard a set of values (Foucault 1986). Foucault's view of moral behavior may be compared to the positivistic studies of ethical behavior discussed previously. Ethics, from Foucault's perspective, consists in the kind of relationship you ought to have with yourself or the manner in which the individual is supposed to constitute him or herself as a moral subject of his or her own actions (Rajchman 1986). Thus, ethics is distinguished from moral behavior and the moral code. Ethics concerns the manner in which a person ought to conduct him or herself in order to become the right kind of person (Rajchman 1986). Ethics is concerned with practices of the self or self-formation as an ethical subject (Foucault 1986).

Foucault argues that the ethical aspects of morality, at least as he defines ethics, has been insufficiently studied. He further divides ethics into four subparts: ethical substance, mode of subjection, self-forming activity, and telos. Ethical substance refers to those aspects of behavior which in a general sense are subject to moral judgment as opposed to those which are the subject only of technical judgment or opinion. Thus, a CPA's independence is subject to moral judgment and, therefore, is an aspect of ethical substance, whereas the CPA's ability to prepare a worksheet properly is a matter of technical judgment. The second subpart of ethics is the mode of subjection or the way in which an individual recognizes his or her duty to act ethically. Foucault describes the mode of subjection as "the way in which people are invited or incited to recognize their moral obligations. Is it for instance, divine law, which has been revealed in a text? Is it natural law, a cosmological order, in each case the same for every living being? Is it a rational rule?" (quoted in Dreyfus and Rabinow 1982). The mode of subjection is distinguished from the disciplinary mechanisms used to compel compliance with moral codes. In accounting, the mode of subjection may be thought of as the Code of Conduct of the AICPA as well as the rules and laws of the various state societies of CPAs and the state boards of public accountancy. However, what may confuse the practicing CPA is that, while there are relatively clear-cut rules spelled out in the Codes of Conduct, there are also many unwritten rules of how one should behave toward clients, which may in fact take precedence over the written rules.

The third aspect of ethics as defined by Foucault concerns the means by which a person changes or elaborates himself in order to become an ethical subject. This aspect of ethics deals with self-forming activities or asceticism in a broad sense. For example, in various religions, self-examination practices have given rise to a set of techniques that help to change a person into the kind of being who can behave ethically. This aspect of ethics has been evident in recent years in the form of self-help books and diet books, health clubs, psychotherapy, and cult religions. From an accounting perspective, the self-forming aspect of ethics is evident not so much in regard to the Code of Conduct but rather in respect to the various self-disciplining practices that commence early in the career of a prospective professional accountant, ranging from difficult multiple choice and other kinds of tests in the elementary and intermediate accounting courses, to the social rituals associated with Beta Alpha Psi and other accounting clubs, and to the recruitment rituals of public accounting firms. These ritualized activities constitute self-forming and disciplinary practices which form the prospective CPA into an idealized ethical being—not an ethical being who conforms to the AICPA Code of Conduct, but rather an ethical being who is disciplined and self-formed into the idealized CPA of the Big Six public accounting firm. The disciplinary and self-forming practices of the public accounting profession are closely associated with the fourth aspect of ethics, which is referred to as telos and represents the kind of being to which a person aspires when he or she behaves in a moral manner (Davidson 1986). The telos of public accounting is the ideal partner in the Big Six firm, who is an ethical being not is the sense of conforming closely to the Code of Conduct but in being able to satisfy clients, bring in new business, and be technically astute, all while simultaneously giving the impression of acting in the highest ethical manner (Baker 1977, 1993).

Most contemporary moral philosophy is focused on discussions and elaborations of moral codes. Virtually nothing concerning a person's relationship to him or herself is thought to be relevant to studies of ethics. If such questions do arise, it is usually in regard to the question of whether there are such duties. Foucault suggests that the study of ethics should be focused on the person's relationship to him or herself and the manner in which a person is self-disciplined into an ethical being. Although Foucault's analysis of morality and ethics is informative for research on accounting ethics, we are still faced with the problem of moral truth. Perhaps Foucault would say that there is no such thing as moral truth, or that, if there is, it is not knowable. Furthermore, the most important thing is to investigate how persons discipline themselves into ethical beings, regardless of what their moral code may be. In other words, ethics may be a process rather than a normative statement. Nevertheless, it seems clear that in the absence of a moral code which is representative of moral truth in some sense, the self-forming processes employed to turn oneself into an ethical being are lost in a compass-less sea of moral relativity. Thus, we turn to an argument for moral truth as a basis for ethical self-forming practices.

THE METAPHYSICAL BASIS OF MORAL TRUTH

If the deontological approach to ethics is to be accepted, then the question arises as to the origin of moral truth. It is not credible to suggest that there is moral truth without postulating what the origin of this truth might be. Historically, the discussion of moral truth has been founded on metaphysical or religious principles. Unfortunately, because there are various religions, it is difficult for any one religion to claim a monopoly on moral truth. Nevertheless, it may be useful to reflect on a view of moral truth as expressed by one particular religion in the form of the Catholic Church. The following discussion is based on a review of *Veritatis Splendor* (The Splendor of Truth) an encyclical written by Pope John Paul II in 1993 (Neuhaus 1993).

In *Veritatis Splendor*, the pope offered not so much an analysis of the world's moral condition as an examination of why the world no longer makes moral sense (Neuhaus 1993). Making moral sense assumes that there is some truth about the matter in dispute. However, when it comes to morality, it is often assumed that there is no such thing as truth. In fact, moral truth is thought to be an oxymoron. You have your values and I have mine, and there the discussion comes to an end. "What is truth?" This could be viewed as a rhetorical discussion stopper. However, it may be argued that the question of moral truth ought to be the starting point of the discussion.

The modern era stressed the development and expansion of human freedom. In the postmodern era, freedom has been separated from truth. When freedom is separated from truth, it tends to become license. License, in turn, is the undoing of freedom for, as Nietzsche recognized, all personal and social life becomes simply the assertion of power. If freedom is to be maintained and increased, then power—and freedom itself—must be accountable to truth. Historically, it has been believed that there is a necessary connection between freedom and truth. However, the postmodernist position is that freedom can exist without truth. Relativism and subjectivism have marginalized the notion of truth. In an individualistic culture, persons do not discern and obey what is morally true. Rather, each person decides what is true for him or herself. Individuals create truth. The postmodernist view of moral relativism is that all morality is created by culture. We are socially constructed. Freedom may be high among our values, but that is only because we are the products of a culture that values freedom. However, freedom is a delusion. In fact, persons in a free society are as captive to their culture as those who are the product of a culture that values collectivism.

In contrast, the deontological view holds that human beings are truly free. Human beings are created for freedom and, although hindered by difficulties, they are capable of freedom. Without freedom, all discussions about morality make no sense. While it is important to acknowledge the insights of the behavioral sciences into the ways we are conditioned by culture, it is also important to realize that within each person is an aspiration toward moral truth that the person either follows or defies.

Some would say that this is overly metaphysical and that, furthermore, it is not possible to return to a previous era when it may have been possible to assert that: "We hold these truths to be self-evident," as though there actually were some truths to hold evident. We live in a pluralistic society. There is no agreement on what truths we hold. But from another perspective, that is exactly why we need to engage in an argument about the truths that define human freedom and dignity. Differences notwithstanding, we can make sense to one another because we have in common our human nature and the capacity to reason, and these are universal. It may be admitted that to argue for reason and truth is to go against the findings of much previous research. However, as freedom has turned against itself, so also has reason turned against itself, with the result that confidence in what is distinctively human has been undermined. True humanism is directed toward the ultimate good, which is founded in moral truth.

In the intellectual and cultural drift of our time, we should welcome the argument of ultimate moral truth as a call to reaffirm reason and human dignity in the face of nihilism both theoretical and practical. Human rights and duties should be viewed as universal and immutable. That is the position which should be taken toward those who claim that the idea of universal human rights reflects the cultural imperialism of the western world. Some have argued that the human rights agenda is no more than an ideological imposition. This argument can be accepted only if freedom is divorced from truth. The contention that there is no objective moral truth has unfortunately achieved a measure of official status in intellectual circles. Many, if not most, declare that it is up to each individual to determine the concept of existence, of meaning, of the universe, and of the mystery of human life. However, when truth is democratized, when truth becomes no more than the will of each individual or a majority of individuals, democracy, deprived of the claim to truth, stands undefended before its enemies.

Moral truth includes commands that are both positive and negative. It is important to note that religious commandments are usually framed in the negative. We cannot always do the good that we would like to, but we can always refuse to do evil. Some acts are intrinsically wrong, such as homicide, genocide, and slavery. Though it is true that sometimes it is appropriate to tolerate a lesser moral evil in order to avoid a greater one or in order to promote a greater good, it is not appropriate to do wrong just because some good may come of it. Arguments that a morally repugnant act may be justified by the end to which it is directed or by weighing the other goods at stake should be rejected. It is never appropriate to do wrong in order to achieve good. Intentions may be noble; people may claim that they are acting in good conscience; circumstances may mitigate personal responsibility—but the act remains morally wrong.

SUMMARY AND CONCLUSION

This paper has addressed a fundamental issue regarding research on accounting ethics, that is, whether there is such a thing as moral truth upon which ethics in general and accounting ethics in particular may be based. If there is no such thing as moral truth, then it is incredible to argue that there is or ought to be a normative code of ethical conduct that should be obeyed. Arguments for normative ethical conduct tend to dissolve in the face of moral relativism.

Accountants, as members of society and as members of a profession, are frequently confronted with ethical dilemmas. How the individual accountant and how accountants in general solve their ethical dilemmas is of growing interest to accounting researchers and to the larger society. While the focus of this paper might well have been on accountants in general and the many roles that accountants play, it was more manageable to place a boundary on the scope of the inquiry and limit the focus to the ethical dilemmas facing CPAs in the practice of auditing financial statements of public companies. The pressures placed on CPAs in their roles as auditors of public companies are strong and growing, with increasing legal liability, growing gaps in expectations, and increasing technical change and complexity. Perhaps it is not unexpected that there may be a certain lack of moral focus in this changing environment. Previous research on accounting ethics has focused on how the ethics of accountants may be maintained and improved. Other research has taken the perspective of exposing the ethical credibility of accountants. This paper has also looked at various positivistic psychological and sociological studies of ethics, including those of Foucault, who suggests that ethics is a process rather than a normative statement. While this is informative with respect to studies on accounting ethics, it does not resolve the dilemma of what the practicing CPA is supposed to do when faced with an ethical dilemma. It may predict what he or she will do, but it will not answer the question of what he or she should do. Only a deontological perspective on ethics will help the CPA to understand what he or she should do. This paper intended neither to expose nor to improve but, rather, to attempt to understand the difficulty of acting morally in what is perhaps an amoral world.

REFERENCES

Abbott, A. 1983. Professional ethics. *American Journal of Sociology* 88: 855-885.

Ajzen, I., and M. Fishbein. 1973. Attitudinal and normative variables as predictors of specific behaviors. *Journal of Personality and Social Psychology* 27: 41-57.

American Institute of Certified Public Accountants (AICPA). 1993. *Professional Standards*, Vol. 2. New York: AICPA.

Aranya, N., J. Pollock, and J. Amernic. 1981. An examination of professional commitment in public accounting. *Accounting, Organizations and Society* 6: 271-280.

Arnold, D., and L. Ponemon. 1987. Moral judgment prospective for the various auditing judgment issues. *Proceedings of the British Accounting Associations's Annual Meeting*. University of Scotland, Glasgow, April 15.

Baker, C.R. 1976. An investigation of differences in values: Accounting majors vs. non-accounting majors. *The Accounting Review* 51(4, October): 886-893.

________. 1977. Management strategy in a large accounting firm. *The Accounting Review* 52(3, July): 576-586.

________. 1993. Self-regulation in the public accounting profession: The response of the large, international public accounting firms to a changing environment. *Accounting, Auditing, Accountability Journal* 6(2): 68-80.

Burns, D., and W. Haga. 1977. Much ado about professionalism: A second look at accounting. *The Accounting Review* (July): 705-715.

Carey, J. 1966. *The Ethical Standards of the Accounting Profession*. New York: AICPA.

Davidson, A. 1986. Archeology, genealogy, ethics. In *Foucault: A Critical Reader*, ed. D. Hoy, 221-234. New York: Basil Blackwell.

Dreyfus, H., and P. Rabinow. 1982. *Michel Foucault*. Brighton, UK: The Harvester Press.

Frankena, W. 1963. *Ethics*. Englewood Cliffs, NJ: Prentice-Hall.

Freedman, B. 1978. A meta-ethics for professional morality. *Ethics*: 1-19.

Foucault, M. 1986. *The Use of Pleasure: The History of Sexuality*, Vol. 2. New York: Vintage Books.

Gaa, J., and C. Smith. 1985. Auditors and deceptive financial statements: Assigning responsibility and blame. *Contemporary Accounting Research* 1(2): 219-241.

Greenwood, E. 1966. The elements of professionalization. In *Professionalization*, eds. H. Vollmer and D. Mills, 118-135. Englewood Cliffs, NJ: Prentice-Hall.

Hunt, S., and S. Vitell. 1986. A general theory of marketing ethics. *Journal of Macromarketing* 6(2): 5-16.

John Paul II. 1993. *Veritatis Splendor*. Vatican City: Vatican Press.

Knapp, M. 1985 Audit conflict: An empirical study of the perceived ability of auditors to resist management pressure. *The Accounting Review* (April): 202-211.

Kohlberg, L. 1958. The development of modes of moral thinking and choice in the years ten to sixteen. Unpublished Ph.D. dissertation, University of Chicago.

________. 1981. *The Meaning and Measurement of Moral Development*. Worcester, MA: Clark University Press.

Lehman, C., and T. Tinker. 1987. The real cultural significance of accounts. *Accounting, Organizations and Society* 12: 503-522.

Lightner, S., S. Adams, and K. Lightner. 1982. The influence of situational, ethical, and expectancy theory variables on accountants' underreporting behavior. *Auditing: A Journal of Practice and Theory* 2(1): 1-12.

Loeb, S. 1971. A survey of ethical behavior in the accounting profession. *Journal of Accounting Research* (Autumn): 287-306.

________. 1972. Enforcement of the code of ethics: A survey. *The Accounting Review* (January): 1-10.

________. 1978. *Ethics in the Accounting Profession*. New York: John Wiley & Sons.

MacIntosh, N. 1993. A proposal for a post-modernist accounting. Working paper, Queens University, Kingston, Ontario, Canada.

Neimark, M., and T. Tinker. 1986. The social construction of management control systems. *Accounting, Organizations and Society* 11: 369-396.

Neuhaus, R. 1993. The truth about freedom. *The Wall Street Journal.* (October 8): A14.

Ponemon, L. 1990. Ethical judgments in accounting: A cognitive-development perspective. *Critical Perspectives on Accounting* 1(2): 191-215.

Ponemon, L., and D. Gabhart. 1990. Auditor independence judgments: A cognitive-developmental model and experimental evidence. *Contemporary Accounting Research* 7(1, Fall): 227-251.

Preston, A., D. Scarbrough, and R. Chilton. 1990. Transformation in the moral code and ethics of the u.s. accounting profession, 1960-1988: A tale of changing narratives of legitimation. Working Paper No. 90-01, School of Management, Boston University, January.

Puxty, A., H. Willmott, D. Cooper, and T. Lowe. 1987. Modes of regulation in advanced capitalism: Locating accountancy in four countries. *Accounting, Organizations and Society* 12: 273-292.

Rajchman, J. 1986. Ethics after Foucault. *Social Text* (Winter/Spring): 166-167.

Rest, J. 1979. *Development in Judging Moral Issues*. Minneapolis, MN: University of Minnesota Press.

Schilit, H. 1984. Deviant behavior and misconduct of professionals. *The Woman CPA* (April): 20-24.

THE LITIGATION CRISIS:
AUDITOR RESPONSIBILITY TO THE PUBLIC

Bonita A. Daly and James R. Hamill

ABSTRACT

Led by the heads of the Big Six accounting firms and the AICPA, the accounting profession is seeking regulatory relief from what it refers to as the "liability crisis" facing the profession. Many of the relief efforts are directed toward changing federal and state laws to reduce the exposure of the profession to suits brought by investors claiming reliance on audited financial statements. We argue that if courts adopt the California Supreme Court approach in the recent *Bily* decision to defining the responsibilities of an auditor, the profession can adequately deal with auditor liability through self-regulation. In addition, investors and courts need to recognize the inherent limitations of auditors to evaluate management ability and honesty and to predict business failure. By clearly defining the scope of an auditor's responsibilities to the investing public and improving self-regulation, the need for changes to federal and state laws is significantly mitigated.

Research on Accounting Ethics, Volume 2, pages 87-107.

ISBN: 1-55938-997-4

INTRODUCTION

In August of 1992, the Big Six accounting firms joined to issue a position statement titled, "The Liability Crisis in the United States: Impact on the Accounting Profession" (Cook et al.). In this statement, the firms argue that the principal causes of the liability crisis are unwarranted litigation and coerced settlements. Joint-and-several liability and the inability to recover costs of defending against suits of questionable merit are said to encourage investor suits against "deep pockets" auditors. It is necessary to identify what is meant by the litigation crisis before any regulatory solutions can be discussed. It is no crisis that auditors are sued for damages. Auditors receive large fees in exchange for the assurances provided by audit reports and must accept responsibility for their actions. It is also no crisis that companies and audits often fail. Investing in the capital markets necessarily entails risk, and auditors are humans who will, on occasion, fail in meeting their responsibilities. However, the risk of failure can be managed, and who bears the risk of such failure can be specified. The "crisis" arises when the auditor is required to bear risk beyond that appropriate for the assurances provided by an audit.

In this paper, we argue that the optimal solution to the liability crisis facing the accounting profession is to more clearly define the responsibility that an auditor bears to third-party investors and enhance self-regulation by the profession in the practice of auditing. We suggest that a 1992 decision by the California Supreme Court, *Bily v. Arthur Young & Co.*,[1] coincidentally issued within three weeks of the Big Six position statement, should become the standard for evaluating auditor liability to third parties. The *Bily* decision holds the auditor liable for general negligence only to the client. Intended beneficiaries of the audit report can recover for negligent misrepresentation. The *Bily* standard for auditor liability is not as broad as the *foreseeability* standard adopted by some other courts, which holds the auditor liable to any party that the auditor could reasonably foresee as a recipient of audited financial statements. If other courts adopt the California standard, the scope of accountants' liabilities to third parties will be manageable. Elimination of joint-and-several liability is not likely to occur because it would result in the indefensible outcome that a blameless investor or creditor would be forced to bear the loss arising from the negligent actions of guilty codefendants, some of whom are financially capable of satisfying the damages awarded by a court of law. The profession can significantly address the liability crisis through efforts to expand peer reviews and to more accurately assess the risk that management fraud will result in material misstatements to financial statements.

The Big Six position statement documents the financial impact of litigation on the accounting profession. In 1991, the costs of settling and defending lawsuits totalled $477 million, representing 9% of the U.S. accounting and auditing revenues of the Big Six firms (Cook et al. 1992). The prospective costs of defense and the potential exposure to litigation were among the reasons for the $400 million settlement reached in November 1992 by Ernst & Young with federal bank and thrift regulators ("Hard-hit Accountants" 1992). Among firms with 50 or more CPAs, the cost of liability insurance was reported to have increased by 300% from 1985 to 1991 (Cook et al. 1992). Liability exposure was cited as the overriding reason for the failure of Laventhol & Horwath in 1990 and for the 1992 reorganization of approximately 90% of the offices of Pannell Kerr Forster into individual professional corporations. Among California CPAs, almost half are unwilling to undertake audit work, and approximately one-third are discontinuing audit work in high-risk sectors. Society suffers when small and medium-size businesses do not have access to capital markets because of their inability to obtain independent audits at reasonable costs. High technology businesses contribute to U.S. competitiveness in world markets. If the litigation system leads to higher costs of funds for such firms, growth in the high-technology sector will be slowed and the U.S. economy will suffer (Kothari et al. 1988). In addition to the impact on practicing CPAs, the position statement suggests that the liability crisis makes it difficult to attract and retain promising young people to the profession.

The position statement proposes that joint-and-several liability be replaced with proportionate liability, in which each defendant would be liable only for the portion of any damages caused by that defendant. Also included in the statement is a proposal that, when meritless claims are filed, defendants should be entitled to recover litigation costs. The elimination of joint-and-several liability, except in cases of fraud, and sanctions for frivolous suits are both included in the Private Securities Litigation Reform Act of 1995 ("Securities Litigation" 1996).

In many cases, auditor liability arises when a company fails. Without joint-and-several liability, an investor who has suffered financial damages due to the fault of others could be forced to bear a loss because one or more of the codefendants was unable to pay damages, a result we believe is inequitable. Nonetheless, we believe that without a clear standard for when and to whom an auditor bears financial responsibility, the current explosion of suits against auditors will not abate, even if a system of proportionate liability is adopted. Adoption of the California standard would provide a more equitable rule for auditor responsibility to the investing public. Together with refinements to the profession's standards of practice, the fears expressed in the Big Six position statement can, in large measure, be relieved. Our approach is consistent with comments made by John Burton, former chief accountant for the SEC, who stated that the profession should not receive legislative relief until it takes its own responsibilities more seriously (Cowan 1993).

ALTERNATIVE JUDICIAL VIEWS OF AUDITOR LIABILITY

Our discussion does not deal with liability arising from services performed in connection with the registration or sale of publicly traded securities. The 1933 and 1934 Securities Acts regulate services performed in connection with such offerings. Defendants who can show due diligence (absence of negligence) are not liable under Section 11(a) of the 1933 act (Roddy 1993). Section 10(b) of the 1934 act requires the plaintiff to prove an intent to deceive.[2] These acts cover behavior that is much more deliberate (fraud, gross negligence) than is required to prove damages under common law. In fact, most suits alleging violation of the SEC 1933 and 1934 laws also allege auditor negligence under common law.

Auditor liability for negligence is decided under common law standards that vary across jurisdictions (Liebman and Kelly 1992).[3] A strict standard of *privity* holds the auditor liable only to those parties with whom the auditor has contracted.[4] At the other extreme, the auditor may be liable for losses incurred by any party who could be *foreseen* to be a user of the auditor's work product. In between these two positions, the auditor may be liable for negligent misrepresentation to any party who is an *intended beneficiary* of the auditor's work product.[5]

Privity generally holds that only parties to a contract have enforceable rights under that contract. In connection with claims for economic loss, the *Glanzer* case permitted recovery by a third party that lacked contractual privity because the third party's reliance was the end and aim of the transaction.[6] In connection with claims against an auditor, general negligence liability has been extended to relationships that are the equivalent to privity, requiring that the third party be known or foreseen by the auditor.[7] This standard has been justified because to permit otherwise would "expose accountants to a liability in an indeterminate amount for an indeterminate time to an indeterminate class."[8]

At the other extreme from the *privity* standard, certain courts have applied a standard of *foreseeability*.[9] This standard holds the auditor liable to any party that the auditor could reasonably foresee as a recipient of the audited financial statements that is damaged from justifiable reliance on those financial statements. This standard exposes auditors to liability from an indeterminate number of parties and in an indeterminate amount. In contrast to the *privity* standard, because there are parties that cannot be identified at the time the contract is drafted to whom the auditor may nonetheless be held liable, there is no way for the accountant to draft a contract to specify the potential risk of loss. *Foreseeability* has been defended as providing a mechanism for compensation to parties who have been damaged and a deterrent to negligent conduct by the auditor (Wiener 1983). In *Rosenblum v. Adler*, the New Jersey Supreme Court stated that a *foreseeability* standard "may cause accounting firms to engage in more thorough reviews. This might entail setting up stricter standards and applying closer supervision, which should tend to reduce the number of instances in which liability would ensue. Much of the additional costs incurred either because of a more thorough auditing review or increased insurance premiums would be borne by the business entity and its stockholders or customers."[10]

The assumption that "much" of the additional cost of an audit would be borne by the business, and not the auditors, is not supported by any evidence. Arguably, theory might support such a contention, but there would have to be some method of estimating risks in order for the audit fee to compensate the auditor for the risk assumed. Melumad and Thoman (1990) model an equilibrium in which exogenously determined litigation costs can enhance the welfare of market participants. However, they assume that the auditor can, in a perfectly competitive setting, incorporate the risk of loss from litigation into the audit fee. Further, their model does not allow for litigation loss when no audit failure has occurred.

The *foreseeability* standard does not provide a reasonable basis for determining the future risks to be priced because of its indeterminate class of potential plaintiffs and the indeterminate amount of loss that such plaintiffs might incur. The fact that many accounting firms are excluding audit services or certain sectors of audit clients from their practices supports the contention that firms are unable to adequately price indeterminate risk. Further, there is evidence that many insurers have either abandoned or sharply reduced the coverage they offer (Goldwasser 1988), which suggests that increased insurance coverage is not a viable option for the auditor.[11] The *foreseeability* standard suffers from the inability to adequately specify to whom the auditor's liability extends. For this reason, the *foreseeability* standard has not gained popularity among courts or commentators (Bilek 1985; Gormley 1984; Siliciano 1988).

The *intended beneficiary* standard, as stated in Section 552 of the Restatement (Second) of Torts, limits liability to those for whose benefit and guidance the information was intended or to whom the supplier of the information knows the information will be provided.[12] This standard creates no auditor liability to parties to whom the auditor had no reason to believe the information would be made available. Further, if the client's transaction materially changes from that represented to the auditor so as to increase the risk of exposure, there is no auditor liability for losses arising from the altered transaction. Thus, if the auditor's work product either is used in a manner not intended or is provided to a party whom the auditor did not intend to benefit, auditor liability for negligence does not apply. Although it is a more expansive standard than strict *privity*, limiting liability to intended beneficiaries is similar to *privity* in that the auditor has prior knowledge of the parties to whom liability can extend. Extending liability beyond strict *privity* is necessary given that the specific identity of parties for whom financial information is intended may be unknown. This standard holds the auditor liable for negligence to a known class of intended recipients and permits the auditor to more accurately assess the degree of risk assumed than does the *foreseeability* standard. The auditor can then price the audit product to reflect the risk assumed or, if more cost efficient, shift the risk through purchase of an insurance contract.

BILY V. ARTHUR YOUNG & CO.: DEFINING THE SCOPE OF AUDITOR LIABILITY

Bily[13] adopts a standard of auditor liability that is neither as broad as the potentially unlimited liability of the *foreseeability* standard nor as narrow as strict *privity*. The *Bily* case arose from the failure of Osborne Computer. In 1983, individual investors as well as pension funds and venture capitalists made certain "bridge" loans or provided secured letters of credit to support third party loans to Osborne that were intended to provide operating funds until the time of an initial public offering (IPO) planned for later that same year. In exchange for assistance in obtaining the loans, certain plaintiffs received warrants that were intended to provide sizable profits when the IPO was consummated. Other plaintiffs purchased Osborne stock through private placements. Robert Bily, who was a director of the company, purchased shares in 1983 from Adam Osborne, the founder of the company.

Arthur Young and Co. issued unqualified audit opinions on the financial statements for 1981 and 1982. In 1983, Osborne filed for bankruptcy, and the plaintiffs eventually lost their entire investment. With the exception of one plaintiff who had not read the 1982 audit opinion, the plaintiffs claimed reliance on the 1982 unqualified audit report in making their investments. At trial, an expert witness testified to more than 40 deficiencies in the audit, including understatement of liabilities by approximately $3 million, failure to detect weaknesses in internal control procedures, and failure to disclose discovered deviations. The expert asserted gross professional negligence on the part of Arthur Young. The jury returned a verdict against Arthur Young for professional negligence, which was upheld by the California Court of Appeals. The California Supreme Court reversed and remanded the decision, declining to permit all foreseeable third parties to recover from an auditor for professional negligence.

The majority opinion in *Bily* distinguished three parties to whom the auditor may be liable, with a different standard of liability applying to each. A general duty of care applies only to the client for whom the audit is prepared. The auditor can then be held liable for general negligence only to the client. General negligence applies when, in fulfilling a contract for professional services, an accountant fails to exercise that degree of skill and competency reasonably expected of persons in the profession. However, intended beneficiaries of the audit report can recover for negligent misrepresentation. Negligent misrepresentation arises when a defendant makes false representations, honestly believing that they are true but without reasonable ground for such belief.[14] Finally, reasonably foreseeable third parties can recover only for intentional fraud. A finding of fraud requires that the auditor make a false representation of a material fact with the intent to induce the plaintiff to act. The false representation must be made with knowledge that it is false, although the knowledge requirement is satisfied if the statement is made with reckless disregard for the truth.[15]

The majority opinion noted that the risk assumed by an auditor is necessarily a function of the number and character of persons affected and the nature and extent of the proposed transaction. The court provided an example where an auditor is engaged by an individual considering a $10 million investment. The auditor is able to identify the specific risk assumed and to "encounter, limit, or avoid the risk," which is not possible when a "generic" audit is performed.[16] Because it is difficult to ascribe a causal relationship between the audit report and an economic loss suffered by an investor, and because plaintiffs in auditor liability cases tend to be relatively sophisticated, the majority found that contract liability would be a more effective means of adjusting risk between the respective parties.[17] The court stated that increasing the liability exposure of auditors would not necessarily lead to more careful audits. Rather, "the economic result of unlimited negligence liability could just as easily be an increase in the cost and decrease in the availability of audits and audit reports with no compensating improvement in audit quality."[18] If audit quality cannot be significantly improved to deal with expansive liability, the deterrent effect of liability actions could actually be reduced.[19]

AUDITOR RESPONSIBILITIES

Uniform adoption of the *Bily* standard would clearly define the scope of responsibility that the auditor assumes to third parties. By limiting auditor exposure to parties who have contracted for the auditor's services (general negligence exposure) and parties who are intended beneficiaries of the auditor's work product (negligent misrepresentation), the auditor can better price the risk of the audit. This may result in accepting audit work at a fee that compensates for the risk of loss, rejecting audit work because the risks cannot be adequately compensated, or shifting the risk through the purchase of insurance, which is then priced into the audit fee. Of course, "risk" of loss implies that there will be some variance associated with an expected loss function. Nevertheless, a clear and uniform standard for when the auditor may be liable will reduce that variance. In the extreme, if the expected loss were known with certainty, the auditor could accurately price the risk and all market participants would be expected to experience welfare gains because the parties at fault would ultimately bear the cost of the negligence.[20]

Although we believe that *Bily* appropriately restricts accountants' liability for damages arising from general negligence to clients, we concur with the dissenting opinion of Justice Kennard that, "If audit reports were not a substantial factor in the decisions of investors and lenders, businesses would have little need for independent auditing services. Thus, accountants can hardly argue that third party reliance is anything other than a routine and predictable response."[21] In fact, the American Institute of CPAs (AICPA) specifically recognizes the responsibilities of the profession to the public at large (AICPA 1988, Article II). Rather than limit the accountant's liability to intended beneficiaries, the *Bily* dissent argues that a jury should be permitted to separate the "wheat from the chaff" and fix liability on the parties at fault. The accounting profession has long recognized the benefits of emphasizing the independence and objectivity of the professional auditor and has profited from the public view of the auditor as a "public watchdog." However, it has been demonstrated that the public view of the assurances provided by an audit report, and the profession's view of such assurances, are quite different (Epstein and Geiger 1994). This "expectations gap" raises questions with respect to the ability of a jury to separate the wheat from the chaff in assessing damages for an economic loss suffered by users of financial statements.[22]

Nevertheless, the views expressed in the dissenting opinion in the *Bily* case cannot, and should not, be ignored. Prior to the stock market crash of 1929, the auditor's primary responsibility was to management. The market crash, and the subsequent enactment of the 1933 and 1934 Securities Acts, shifted the emphasis of the profession to parties outside management (Weiss 1992). The profession itself must take more responsibility in defining and satisfying its responsibilities to the public (Tarantino 1993). A uniform standard of to whom an auditor is liable for negligence is a necessary, but not sufficient, condition to reaching a solution to the litigation crisis. Given the importance of the independent audit in the financial markets, regulation of the audit function is a reality that cannot be ignored. Ultimately, if the public is not satisfied with the accounting profession's service, work, product, or behavior, the public will exercise its power through regulatory or judicial means (Ponemon 1992).

In analyzing how the profession could improve its self-regulation, we believe the profession must address the perception that it wants to "have it both ways." That is, the profession benefits from the public perception that an audit provides assurances that financial statements accurately present the financial position of a firm and are free of fraud. Reducing the liability exposure of the auditor cannot occur without also reducing the public perception of the nature of the audit process and the audit product. Changes in perception would also affect the value of the monitoring role of the independent auditor. Self-regulation efforts must be meaningful and the profession must be willing to accept the potential for adverse consequences resulting from a reduction in the public perception of the degree of assurance provided by a standard audit report. However, meaningful self-regulation can also counter the adverse publicity that the profession has received during the current litigation explosion. The litigation "crisis" can be viewed as an opportunity to enhance the practices and reputation of the profession. The *Bily* standard cannot completely resolve the litigation crisis because there will still be legitimate debate with respect to the identity of intended beneficiaries of the auditor's work product. Self-preservation has induced the profession to adapt its practices in the past (Weiss 1992), and the opportunity should not be lost on the present generation of accounting professionals.

REFORM MEASURES: AUDIT PRACTICE AND RECOGNIZING THE INHERENT LIMITATIONS OF AUDITS

In March of 1993, the Public Oversight Board (POB) of the AICPA SEC Practice Section issued a report that proposed changes in the liability system, revisions to audit practice, and additional disclosures in accountants' reports (Public Oversight Board 1993).[23] Issuance of the report was met by a critical commentary in the *New*

York Times, in which the POB was characterized as an "undemanding" self-regulatory group that recommends legislation to shield auditors from liability while also suggesting higher audit fees to justify a more thorough audit (Cowan 1993). We believe this characterization of the POB and its recommendations is catchy but unfair. The POB proposals were thorough; however, some of the recommendations are not necessary under the *Bily* standard for auditor liability and could damage the value of the audit product. Other recommendations for self-regulation are well-founded and may be needed to avoid unwanted regulatory intervention by parties unfamiliar with the audit process.

The POB recommendation likely to receive the most attention by the public is to replace joint-and-several liability with separate-and-proportionate liability. Replacing joint-and-several liability is inappropriate under the *Bily* standard because *Bily* enables the auditor to better ascertain the risk assumed by a particular audit engagement. Joint-and-several liability is based on the belief that an innocent plaintiff should not suffer a loss when one or more defendants who cause an indivisible harm are able to pay the damages. In practice, joint-and-several liability differs from proportionate liability only when one or more defendants is unable to pay his share of the damages. Allegations of audit failures arise when a financial loss has been suffered, and the company that is the subject of the audit report is often unable to pay any damages. The accountant, as the "deep pockets" defendant, is then subjected to the risk of bearing the entire cost of the loss although the accountant's actions may be only a small part of the cause of the loss. This perceived problem with joint-and-several liability is not unique to the accounting profession. However, joint-and-several liability is defended on the grounds that the innocent plaintiff would otherwise bear the loss associated with the financial inability of a defendant to pay. When the issue is framed as one of a guilty codefendant bearing a cost out of proportion to the codefendant's individual blame because of the insolvency of the other guilty codefendants, joint-and-several liability seems inequitable. If the issue is instead framed as one of a blameless plaintiff bearing a loss for which codefendants, some of whom are solvent and others insolvent, have been found liable, joint-and-several liability can be readily defended.

Replacing joint-and-several liability with proportionate liability reduces the value the auditor's deep pockets bring to the audit product. The significant potential for loss if the auditor delivers a lower than contracted product can signal a high quality product (Bar-Yosef and Livnat 1984; Klein and Leffler 1981). The public's perception of the quality of an audit is not accidental and is based, in part, on the potentially unlimited liability of the CPA for his harmful actions. This factor should not be ignored in developing solutions to the liability crisis. Finally, because of the contracting relationship among codefendants (i.e., the auditor, management, and the board of directors), proportionate sharing of liability may not apply to losses arising from negligence in an audit (Hill, Metzger, and Schatzberg 1993).[24] If the courts hold that proportionate liability does not apply to audits, reforms of joint-and-several liability may have little effect on the auditor's liability for loss. However, efforts to achieve such reforms create the perception that the auditor is unwilling to stand behind the audit report.

With the exception of the POB's support for the elimination of joint-and-several liability for damages, the POB report contains several excellent recommendations for action by the SEC Practice Section Committee. More rigorous self-regulation, including the imposition of sanctions, would improve both the quality of audits and public perception of the profession. Under AICPA bylaws, any member firm that audits SEC clients must be a member of the SEC Practice Section of the Division for CPA Firms. SEC Practice Section firms must undergo a peer review at least once every three years.[25] The POB report indicates that 25% of the firms that had an initial peer review in 1991 were found to have significantly flawed quality control systems but that 93% of the firms that had repeat reviews were found to have satisfactory quality control systems. Unfortunately, firms that do not belong to the SEC Practice Section but that nonetheless audit SEC clients cannot be regulated by the AICPA system. The POB report recommends that the SEC act to require SEC registrants to disclose whether their auditors have had a peer review and, if so, the date of the most recent review and the results.[26]

A second important self-regulation mechanism under the direction of the AICPA Division of CPA firms is the Quality Control Inquiry Committee (QCIC) Program. Members of the SEC Practice Section are required to report allegations of deficient audits to the QCIC, which then investigates whether the firm needs to take corrective measures and also whether the deficiencies point to a need to revise generally accepted auditing standards. The POB report recommends that firms be required to report to the QCIC the audit guidance that the firm believes might have avoided the allegations brought against the firm. The QCIC could then analyze such information, together with any gathered by the peer review teams, as a basis for developing audit guidelines for accounting professionals. A former chief accountant of the SEC Enforcement Division (Sack 1990) and a well-known member of the plaintiff's bar (Weiss 1992) both note that training and education is needed to reduce the liability exposure of the profession. QCIC disclosures could be of value in alerting accounting professionals to the types of situations and transactions that can lead to audit failures. Such disclosures can be of value in improving the standards of the profession. The profession must be willing to learn from its mistakes and QCIC disclosures represent an essential part of the learning process.

The POB's strongest call for change is in the area of accountants' responsibilities for detecting fraud. Epstein and Geiger (1994) report survey evidence that 71% of investors believe that audited financial statements should contain absolute assurances that the financial statements are free from material misstatements. Although recognizing that it is unreasonable to expect the auditor to guarantee the honesty and integrity of information contained in audited financial statements, the POB report suggests that the primary responsibility for narrowing the "expectations gap" rests with the profession. To this end, the report recommends that the profession improve its standards and practices, particularly in the area of detecting management fraud. The report also calls for disclosure of the inherent limitations of an audit of financial statement information as a means of detecting management fraud.

While it is clear that the profession cannot detect all cases of management fraud, the POB believes that additional steps should be taken to *enhance* the ability of the auditor to detect such fraud. Information obtained from QCIC reports of the SEC Practice section could be used to alert member firms to factors leading to audit failures and factors suggesting the presence of management fraud. The POB suggests that auditors are not consistently complying with SAS 53, the auditing standard that requires auditors to assess the risk that management fraud may cause the financial statements to be materially misstated. Self-regulation by the profession could be of assistance in developing comprehensive audit guidelines to assess the risk of fraud and in specifying additional audit procedures to be followed when fraud is suspected.

Reducing the expectations gap through improved communication of the inherent limitations of the audit process should also include two other recommendations of the POB. Auditor evaluations of the adequacy of company internal control procedures could be misinterpreted to mean that the company is well managed such that there will be no future surprises for investors and lenders. Auditing standards should be revised to more clearly communicate inherent limitations of internal control assurances provided by an audit report. Also, when a client's historical financial statements include estimates of value, such as the carrying value of a real estate project under development, the audit report should clearly communicate the nature of the estimate to avoid the implication that the value is determined with the same degree of accuracy that would be used for a recently purchased asset. Financial projections of projects under development should be clearly identified as prospective financial information subject to a lower standard of auditor assurance. The audit report should permit sufficient flexibility to distinguish valuation estimates from historical financial information. Once again, this is expected to reduce the public's perception of the assurances provided by the audit report and may then reduce the value of the report to the client. However, the profession must be willing to accept any reduced value that may result from narrowing the expectations gap.

Reducing the expectations gap should also involve efforts on the part of the profession to educate the investing public to the inherent limitations in financial statements and assurances provided by an audit report. If for no other reason than because an informed jury pool will be less likely to award damages against an auditor, this recommendation may appear to be of obvious benefit to the profession. However, reducing the expectations gap may also be expected to reduce the value of the audit report. The lower the public's perception of the role of the audit in providing assurances of the accuracy of financial statements, the lower will be the demand for audit services. Of course, this expectations gap has had negative consequences for auditors, but it is important to recognize that it has also benefitted auditors by increasing their role in providing assurances regarding clients' financial reports and other assertions.

The POB recommends that the Financial Accounting Standards Board (FASB) add to its agenda a project to design a brief statement explaining the limitations of financial statements. For example, it could be noted that financial statements contain estimates of amounts that depend on future, uncertain events; their relevancy may decline rapidly when conditions within the reporting entity or the external environment change; and the statements are only one of the sources of information that should be consulted before making an investment or extending credit to a company. Such an explanation, made part of every set of financial statements described as being in accordance with generally accepted accounting principles, could assist in reducing the expectations gap. However, the profession must also be willing to accept any reduction in the value of the audit report caused by reducing the public's perception of the assurances provided by audited financial statements.

In addition to reducing the public's expectations of the ability of the auditor to provide assurances that financial statements are free from material misstatements, it is also important to reduce clients' expectations that the auditor will assume an advocacy role. Professional accountants who testify in support of positions favored by clients impair the appearance of independence. The competitive environment facing the accounting profession creates short-term financial incentives to accept clients that may lack integrity and to agree to report positions taken by the client that may reduce the quality of the financial statements. The POB recommends that firms avoid partner performance measures that make it necessary to play an advocacy role for fear of jeopardizing a continued relationship with the client. The profession has always been concerned with professional independence, both in fact as well as in appearance, and self-regulation to avoid the appearance of an advocacy role by auditors would help to reduce the perception that auditors are inextricably linked to management actions that result in material misstatements (Weiss 1993).

Walter Schuetze, chief accountant for the SEC, noted in a speech to an AICPA session (Doyle 1994) that he was "vexed and bewildered" by auditors "not standing up to their clients" when the clients demand acquiescence to reporting positions that "lack any reasonable foundation." Schuetze also criticized major firms that, in the 1970s and 1980s, favored revisions to the accounting treatment of executive stock options but that now publicly criticize the 1993 FASB proposal *Accounting for Stock-Based Compensation*, which requires a charge to earnings for stock option grants. He does not accuse the profession of bending to client pressures[27] but notes that such a change in position without a full explanation could lead to the perception "that the switch was in response to the fear of losing clients or other forms of retaliation." The public perception of the independence of the auditor is clearly important in fulfilling the responsibilities of the profession to the public, and it is important for the profession to embrace any recommendations that would improve the public's perception. Similarly, Sack (1990) cautions firms to be aware of subtle cultural aspects of the organization that may imply that firm policies are more for show than for actual practice. For example, penalizing employees for standing up to a client sends a message that is more powerful than any written firm policy of independence.

CONCLUSION

Increased audit risk exposure has resulted in many professional CPA firms either not accepting audit engagements or limiting the type of work that they will perform (Cook et al. 1992). The reduction in the availability of audit services should be of concern to both the public and the profession. A significant concern to the profession is the risk of liability to an indeterminate number of parties under the common law standard that accountants owe a general duty of care to *foreseeable* third parties. A more reasonable rule is that developed by the California Supreme Court in *Bily v. Arthur Young & Co.*, in which the court considered the minor role of the auditor in the success or failure of a business venture and rejected the *foreseeability* standard as out of proportion to the accountant's degree of fault. The imposition of the *foreseeability* rule, when applied to accountants' reports, the distribution of which is beyond the control of the accountant, encourages third parties to use the legal system to recover their losses rather than relying on their own prudence in evaluating business prospects. Replacing joint-and-several liability with proportionate liability does not cure this problem, because the accountant is still liable to an indeterminate class of investors and may not be entitled to proportionate protection because of the contracting relationship between the accountant and management.

Additionally, joint-and-several liability also reduces the risk that a blameless investor or creditor will bear the loss arising from the negligent or fraudulent performance of those who benefitted from the financial transaction, only some of whom are insolvent. Accountants should direct their efforts toward influencing other jurisdictions to follow *Bily* and the long-standing *privity* or the equivalent of *privity* standard promulgated by the New York courts. Adoption of the *Bily* standard will enhance accountants' ability to ascertain the risk assumed from audit engagements and then better price the risk or shift the risk through the purchase of insurance.

However, the profession must also improve its own procedures to meet its professional obligations to those parties with contractual privity and to the intended beneficiaries recognized by the *Bily* court. Many of the suggestions made in this paper will assist in reducing the expectations gap, but reducing the perception of the assurances provided is also likely to reduce the public perception of the value of the audit report. To the extent that it induces greater demand for the audit report, the profession benefits from the expectations gap. Reducing litigation against professional accountants below the "crisis" level requires that the profession be willing to improve its audit standards and practices, enhance the ability to detect management fraud, and improve public disclosure of the inherent limitations of the accountants' report on financial statements. Overall, by improving the ability of the profession to perform the independent auditor's function and to fulfill its legal duties, these changes, combined with judicial limitations on the degree of risk assumed by the auditor, will benefit both the profession and the public.

NOTES

1. *Bily v. Arthur Young & Co.*, 834 P.2d 745 (Cal. 1992).
2. *Ernst & Ernst v. Hochfelder et al.*, 425 U.S. 185 (1976).
3. The discussion in this paper is limited to the typical case alleging auditor negligence liability to third parties. In such a case, it is alleged that the audited financial statements or other financial information contained material misstatements or omissions that would have been detected by the auditor had the auditor not been negligent in the conduct of the audit. It is typically the auditor's negligence, rather than the auditor's knowledge of the misstatement contained in the client's financial information, that is alleged.

4. Decisions following the *privity* standard include *Robertson v. White*, 633 F. Supp. (W.D. Ark. 1986); *Gordon v. Etue, Wandlaw & Co.*, 511 So.2d 384 (Fla. 1987); *Toro v. Krouse, Kern & Co.*, 644 F. Supp. 986 (N.D. Ind. 1986); and, *Pennine Resources, Inc. v. Dorwart Andrew & Co.*, 639 F. Supp. 1071 (E.D. Pa. 1986). Four states have enacted statutes following the *privity* standard: Illinois, Utah, Arkansas, and Kansas. In the Kansas statute, Kan. Stat. Ann. Sec. 1-402 (Supp. 1987), a third party can recover if the auditor is aware of its reliance and the party has been identified in writing to the auditor and the specific transaction described. The Illinois statute, Ill. Ann. Stat. ch. 111, 5535.1 (Smith-Hurd Supp. 1987), the Utah statute, Utah Code Ann. Sec. 58-26-12 (1990), and the Arkansas statute, Ark. Code Ann., Sec. 16-114-302 (Michie Supp. 1987), all provide that the auditor can limit its negligence liability to those third parties the auditor identifies in writing.

5. In addition to *Bily v. Arthur Young & Co.*, 834 p. 2d 745 (Cal. 1992), the *intended beneficiary* standard has been adopted by courts in Alaska (*Selden v. Burnett*, 754 P.2d 256 [Alaska, 1988]); Florida (*First Florida Bank v. Max Mitchell & Co.*, 558 So.2d 9, 12-15 [Fla. 1990]); Georgia (*Badische Corp. v. Caylor*, 356 S.E. 2d 198 [Ga. 1987]); North Carolina (*Raritan River Steel Co. v. Cherry*, 407 S.E. 2d 178 [N.C. 1991]); Ohio (*Ohio National Bank v. Schiesswehl*, 33 Ohio App. 329 [Ohio 1986]); Tennessee (*Bethlehem Steel Corporation v. Ernst & Whinney*, 822 S.W. 2d 592 [Tenn. 1991]); Texas (*Bluebell, Inc. v. Peat Marwick Mitchell*, 715 S.W. 2d 408 [Tex. App. 1986]); Washington (*Haberman v. Pub. Power Supply Sys.*, 744 P. 2d 1032, 1067-1068 [Wash. 1988]); and West Virginia (*First Nat'l Bank v. Crawford*, 386 S.E. 2d 310, 311-312 [W.Va., 1989]).

6. *Glanzer v. Shephard*, 135 N.E. 275 (N.Y. 1922).

7. *Ultramares v. Touche*, 174 N.E. 441 (N.Y. 1931); *Credit Alliance v. Arthur Andersen & Co.*, 483 N.E. 2d 110 (N.Y. 1985), reaffirming *Ultramares*.

8. *Ultramares v. Touche*, at 444. A dissenting opinion in *Bily v. Arthur Young & Co.* argues that the auditor's liability may be indeterminate, like any tort liability, but is not limitless. The auditor's liability would be finite because the financial statements would become obsolete within a few years, and is not limitless because only parties who relied on the financial statements could sue the auditor.

9. See, for example, *Citizens State Bank v. Timm, Schmidt & Co.*, 335 N.W.2d 361 (Wis. 1983), and *International Mortgage Co. v. John P. Butler Accountancy Corp.*, 223 Cal. Rptr. 218 (Cal. App. 1986).

10. 461 A.2d. 138 (N.J. Super. App. Div. 1987).

11. Underwriting practice and insurance regulations typically require that the amount of insurance premiums accepted be limited to a multiple of the insurer's capital. The ratio is between two-and-a-half and five, to one, with the higher ratios allowed for lower risk lines (fire and marine) and the lower ratios required for the higher risk categories (professional liability). From 1985 to 1987, when confronted with market losses on investments and high insurance claims, premiums collected were at the limit for capital reserves. Insurers were forced to reduce the number and value of policies issued in high risk categories.

12. Restatement (Second) of Torts §552(2) (1977).

13. 834 P. 2d 745 (Cal. 1992).

14. 5 Witkin, *Summary of Cal.Law Torts*, §720 at 819 (9th ed. 1988).

15. *State Str. Trust Co. v. Ernst*, 15 N.E. 2d 416 (N.Y. 1938).

16. *Bily v. Arthur Young & Co.*, 834 P.2D 745,757.
17. 834 P.2D 745, 761.
18. 834 P.2D 745, 766, quoting from Siliciano, "Negligent Accounting and the Limits of Instrumental Tort Reform," 86 Mich.L.Rev. 1929 (1988).
19. 834 P.2D 745,766, quoting from Fischel (1987, p. 1055): "The deterrent effect of liability rules is the difference between incurring liability when performance meets the required standard and the probability of incurring liability when performance is below the required standard. Thus, the stronger the probability that liability will be incurred when performance is adequate, the weaker is the deterrent effect of liability rules. Why offer a higher quality audit product if you will be sued regardless whenever there is a precipitous decline in stock prices?"
20. Joint-and-several liability imposes a disproportionate share of the loss experienced by financial investors on auditors because the company in which the investment was made is often insolvent by the time the loss is realized. If the auditor could perfectly price the risk associated with each client into the audit fee, the audit client would bear the cost of economic losses through payments when the firm was solvent. "Good" firms would pay lower fees and "bad" firms, higher fees. If the audit fee were sufficiently high, the firm might choose not to be audited or to engage a low-reputation auditor with little capital at stake, which itself would signal the financial markets of the status of the firm. The firm would then pay a price in the form of higher costs of capital. Under such a system, joint-and-several liability need not be an impediment to the practice of auditing. In fact, joint-and-several liability would ensure that the damaged party would be able to recover from someone at fault.
21. *Bily v. Arthur Young & Co.* 834 P.2D 745,778.
22. Two investigations conducted by Congress in the late 1970s and one in 1985 dealt with the public responsibilities of CPAs and questioned whether self-regulation was promoting the public interest, giving rise to the term expectation gap.
23. The SEC Practice section is one of two sections of the AICPA Division for CPA Firms (the other is the Private Companies Practice section). AICPA bylaws provide that no member of the AICPA can be associated with a firm that audits SEC clients unless the firm is a member of the SEC Practice Section. The section administers a peer review process and a quality control inquiry for allegations of audit failures.
24. In *National Surety v. Lybrand*, 9 N.Y.S.2d 554 (N.Y. 1939), the court ruled that management negligence is a defense only when management negligence contributed to the auditor's failure to perform his contracted duties. In *Lincoln Grain, Inc. v. Coopers & Lybrand*, 345 N.W.2d 300 (Neb. 1984), the court applied the *National Surety* test on the grounds that to do otherwise would "render illusory the notion that an accountant is liable for the negligent performance of his duties.
25. The peer review evaluates the firm's quality control system in general and also whether the quality control system is adequately communicated to employees and whether the system is being followed. The peer review also determines whether the member firm is complying with SEC Practice Section membership requirements. The POB report states that the SEC Practice Section requirements affect more than 105,000 professionals at 1,214 member firms, which audit more than 14,750 SEC clients.

26. The SEC previously considered such a requirement but was uncertain with respect to its authority to mandate such a disclosure provision.

27. Favoring changes to the treatment of accounting for stock-based compensation obviously does not imply that any proposed change would be favored.

REFERENCES

American Institute of CPAs (AICPA). 1988. *Principles of Professional Conduct.* New York: AICPA.

Bar-Yosef, S., and J. Livnat. 1984. Auditor selection: An incentive-signalling approach. *Accounting and Business Research* (Autumn): 301-309.

Bilek, T.E. 1985. Accountants' liability to the third party and public policy: A Calabresi approach. *Southwestern Law Journal* 39: 689-708.

Cook, J.M., E.M. Freedman, R.J. Groves, J.C. Madonna, S.F. O'Malley, and L.A. Weinbach. 1992. The liability crisis in the United States: Impact on the accounting profession, a statement of position. *Journal of Accountancy* (November): 19-23.

Cowan, A. 1993. The messy business of audits. *The New York Times* (March 5): C3.

Doyle, J.M. 1994. Outside auditors must hang tough, SEC official says. *Albuquerque Journal* (January 17): 11 (Business Outlook section).

Epstein, M.C., and M.A. Geiger. 1994. Investor views of audit assurance: Recent evidence of the expectations gap. *Journal of Accountancy* (January): 60-66.

Fischel, D.R. 1987. The regulation of accounting: Some economic issues. *Brooklyn Law Review* 52: 1057-1056.

Goldwasser, D. 1988. Policy considerations in accountants' liability to third parties for negligence. *Journal of Accounting, Auditing & Finance* (Summer): 217-231.

Gormley, R.J. 1984. The foreseen, the foreseeable, and beyond—accountants' liability to nonclients. *Seton Hall Law Review* 14: 528-573.

Hard-hit accountants hope to limit liability. 1992. *National Law Journal* (December 7): 35.

Hill, J.W., M.B. Metzger, and J.W. Schatzberg. 1993. Auditing's emerging legal peril under the *National Surety* doctrine: A program for research. *Accounting Horizons* (March): 12-28.

Klein, B., and K.B. Leffler. 1981. The role of market forces in assuring contractual performance. *Journal of Political Economy* (August): 615-641.

Kothari, S.P., T. Lys, C.W. Smith, and R.L. Watts. 1988. Auditor liability and information disclosure. *Journal of Accounting, Auditing & Finance* (Fall): 307-339.

Liebman, J.H., and A.S. Kelly. 1992. Accountants' liability to third parties for negligent misrepresentation: The search for a new limiting principle. *American Business Law Journal* 30(November): 347-439.

Melumad, N.D., and L. Thoman. 1990. On auditors and the courts in an adverse selection setting. *Journal of Accounting Research* (Spring): 77-120.

Ponemon, L.A. 1992. Discussant's response to "Litigation risk broadly considered." In *Proceedings of the 1992 Deloitte and Touche University of*

Kansas Symposium on Auditing Problems, 60-72. Lawrence, KS: University of Kansas.

Public Oversight Board. 1993. *A Special Report by the Public Oversight Board of the SEC Practice Section* (March 5). Stamford, CT: Public Oversight Board.

Roddy, K. 1993. Professionals' liability for violations of the federal securities law, RICO, and state claims. *Practicing Law Institute, Corporate Law and Practice Course Handbook* 803 (January): 593.

Sack, R.J. 1990. The expectations gap: What dare we expect of ourselves? In *The Abraham J. Briloff Lecture Series on Accounting and Society*, 5-16. Binghamton, NY: School of Management, Binghamton University, State University of New York.

________. 1996. Securities litigation bill is now law. *Journal of Accountancy* (February): 13-14.

Siliciano, J.A. 1988. Negligent accounting and the limits of tort reform. *Michigan Law Review* 86: 1929-1980.

Tarantino, D.A. 1993. Financial reporting: Meeting the demands of a new age. *Accounting Today* (November 15): 4, 43.

Weiss, M.I. 1992. Why auditors have failed to fulfill their necessary professional responsibilities-and what to do about it. In *The Abraham J. Briloff Lecture Series on Accounting and Society*, 23-36. Binghamton, NY: School of Management, Binghamton University, State University of New York.

________. 1993. Auditors: Be watchdogs, not just bean counters. *Accounting Today* 7(November 15): 40-42.

Wiener, H.B. 1983. Common law liability of the certified public accountant for negligent misrepresentation. *San Diego Law Review* 20: 233-263.

VALUE JUDGMENTS USING BELIEF FUNCTIONS

Rajendra P. Srivastava

ABSTRACT

The main purpose of this paper is to show how the belief-function framework can be used to model human behavior when making decisions that involve value judgments. A rule of decision making is presented in the form of a proposition. This proposition is simple and intuitive. It predicts correctly the observed behavior, even the behavior that is considered to be irrational under the expected utility theory. I use the empirical data of Tversky and Kahneman (1981, 1986) to show how well the proposed rule predicts the observed behavior. Also, I discuss the relevance of this study to moral reasoning and to making ethical judgments using the empirical results of Arnold and Ponemon (1991).

Research on Accounting Ethics, Volume 2, pages 109-130.

ISBN: 1-55938-997-4

INTRODUCTION

The main purpose of this paper is to show how the belief-function framework can be used to model human behavior when making decisions that involve value judgments. A rule of decision making is presented in the form of a proposition. This proposition is simple and intuitive. It predicts correctly the observed behavior, even the behavior that is considered to be irrational under the expected utility theory (EUT).

The empirical work over several decades has shown that neither probability theory nor expected utility theory fully explains human decision-making behavior. There are numerous situations where we run into problems if we use probability theory to model uncertainties encountered in the real world (see, e.g., Buchanan and Shortliffe 1984; Davis, Buchanan, and Shortliffe 1977; Einhorn and Hogarth 1986; Kahneman and Tversky 1979; Shafer and Srivastava 1990; Srivastava 1993). In fact, the straightforward use of probability theory to model uncertainties in certain situations has often led to paradoxes. For example, the Ellsberg (1961; see also Einhorn and Hogarth 1986) paradox stems from the fact that we are not able to model correctly the uncertainties involved in his situations using probabilities. Consider the following situation. Suppose you have two urns. Each urn contains 100 balls of red and black colors. However, you are told that one urn has unknown proportions of red and black balls (a situation of complete ignorance), and you are told that the other urn contains 50 red and 50 black balls (a situation of complete knowledge). If we use probabilities to represent uncertainties involved in the above example, then we are not able to distinguish between the two situations since we are forced to assign the same value 0.5 to the probability of picking a red ball and to the probability of picking a black ball from either urn. This inability of probability theory to distinguish between the two situations led to the Ellsberg paradox as elaborated by Einhorn and Hogarth (1986). A belief-function treatment of the problem resolves the paradox (see, e.g., Srivastava 1994).

Schoemaker (1982) presents a good summary of the problems we have had in justifying some of the basic axioms of the expected utility theory (see also Kahneman and Tversky 1979; Tversky 1969; Tversky and Kahneman 1986). Simon (1986) points out several situations where decisions are made based not on the utility maximization rule but on the context, taking into consideration all the factors of the environment in the decision process. Simon emphatically states under several situations that "utility maximization is neither a necessary nor a sufficient condition for the conclusion that was reached (p. S215)." He makes further comments on how decisions are procedurally made and how a neoclassical economist thinks that such a decision should be made:

> The rational person of neoclassical economics always reaches the decision that is objectively, or substantively, best in terms of the given utility function. The rational person of cognitive psychology goes about making his or her decisions in a way that is procedurally reasonable in the light of the available knowledge and means of computation (p. S211).

Simon's last sentence above is the essence of the decision-making process using the belief-function framework. It aggregates all the information available in the context and then makes the decision. The present paper deals with value judgments [1]. This domain of decision making is beyond the domain of utility theory. However, for the last several decades, we have been using EUT to rationalize behavior and have failed in our efforts. As Simon (1986) puts it:

> Embracing a substantive theory of rationality has had significant consequences for neoclassical economics and especially for its methodology. Until very recently, neoclassical economics has developed no strong empirical methodology for investigating the processes whereby values are formed, *for the content of the utility function lies outside its self-defined scope* (p. S211, emphasis added).

We do not plan to repeat all the problems with EUT that are already discussed in the literature. Rather, we show how one can use the belief-function framework to make value judgments. We use extensively the empirical data of Tversky and Kahneman (1981, 1986) to demonstrate the usefulness of the belief-function framework for decision making. One situation is of special interest. When the same information is presented in two versions, positive and negative, the decision maker has two different responses which are inconsistent according to EUT. They violate the invariance axiom and, thus, have puzzled both the theorists and the empiricists. However, as stated by Tversky and Kahneman (1986), this behavior has been observed repeatedly and even with the same group:

> On several occasions we presented both versions to the same respondents and discussed with them the inconsistent preferences evoked by the two frames. Many respondents expressed a wish to remain risk averse in the "lives saved" version and risk seeking in the "lives lost" version, although they also expressed a wish for their answers to be consistent (p. S260).

Prospect theory was developed by Kahneman and Tversky (1979) to account for preferences that are anomalous in the normative theory. It is interesting to see that the rule proposed in this paper for making decisions that involve value judgments predicts all the observed anomalous behaviors.

The remaining part of the paper is divided into five sections and an Appendix. In the second section, we discuss the belief-function approach to decision making. In the third section, we discuss a proposition for value judgments. In the fourth section, we discuss more examples of value judgments. In the fifth section, we discuss the relevance of this study to moral reasoning and ethical decisions. In the sixth section, we provide a summary. Finally, in the Appendix, we present an introduction to belief functions.

THE BELIEF-FUNCTION APPROACH TO DECISION MAKING

Recently, several approaches to making decisions under the belief-function framework have been proposed (for details, see Jaffray 1989, 1994; Nguyen and Walker 1994; Smets 1990a, 1990b; Strat 1990, 1994; Yager 1990). However, since the value judgments are outside the domain of utility theory, we do not want to use the expected utility theory approach of decision making here. Rather, we want to explore how the belief-function framework can help us understand human behavior in value judgments.

In general, the theory of belief functions provides a framework for aggregating evidence—the evidence that is available at the time of decision making. Thus, the belief-function framework not only provides a way to model uncertainties encountered by decision makers but also provides a framework to integrate all that we know about the contextual situation in a specific decision problem. The contextual situation has been emphasized by Simon (1986) and many others, especially by researchers in AI (Artificial Intelligence).

There are three basic functions in the belief-function framework that are important in our context (see Appendix for an introduction). The *basic probability assignment function,*[2] $m(A)$, represents the uncertainty mass assigned to an assertion A. This assignment may be a single assessment of the decision maker for the level of support on A or a combination of such assessments based on several items of evidence that are relevant to A. The belief function, $Bel(A)$, represents the *total belief or support* for A considering all the evidence that directly relate to the assertion. The plausibility function, $Pl(A)$, represents the *maximum possible support that could be assigned to the assertion* given the current knowledge of the situation. For example, $Bel(A) = 0.3$, and $Pl(A) = 0.9$, imply that we have direct evidence that A is true with a level of support of 0.3 but the maximum possible support that could be assigned to A is 0.9. It simply means that we have 0.6 ($= 0.9 - 0.3$) level of support unassigned that could be assigned to A if further evidence in its favor were collected.

A PROPOSITION FOR VALUE JUDGMENTS USING BELIEF FUNCTIONS

The proposition listed below determines the rule for decision making under uncertainty involving value judgments.

Proposition 1. When making a choice of an alternative from a group of alternatives based on the value judgment, the decision maker will select the alternative that has the highest belief in favor of the alternative being good/fair. If this rule results in the decision maker being indifferent among the alternatives, then he or she will choose the alternative that has the lowest belief of it being bad/unfair (i.e., the highest plausibility of it being good/fair).

This proposition is intuitive. We collect all that we know from the contextual situation about all the alternatives. Next, we determine the beliefs in favor of them being good/fair and select the one that has the highest belief in favor of it being good/fair. This process may involve combining both positive and negative items of evidence. The formal way to combine this information is to use Dempster's rule of combination (see, e.g., Shafer 1976; Shafer and Srivastava 1990;

Srivastava and Shafer 1992). However, the decision maker uses his or her intuitive judgment to aggregate all the evidence in favor of and against the alternative to determine the total belief. In the case where we have the same belief for each alternative of being good/fair, then we should use the beliefs for the alternatives being bad/unfair and select the one that has the least belief for it being bad/unfair—that is, select the alternative that has the highest plausibility of it being good/fair. We demonstrate below how well this decision-making rule fits with the empirical data.

We consider Problems 5 and 6 in Tversky and Kahneman (1986; see also Tversky and Kahneman 1981, p. 453) to illustrate the process. The description of the situation is as follows:

> Problem 5 ($N = 152$):
>
> Imagine that the U.S. is preparing for the outbreak of an unusual Asian disease, which is expected to kill 600 people. Two alternative programs to combat the disease have been proposed. Assume that the exact scientific estimates of the consequences of the programs are as follows:
>
> If Program A is adopted, 200 people will be saved [72%].
>
> If Program B is adopted, there is 1/3 probability that 600 people will be saved, and 2/3 probability that no people will be saved [28%].

The symbol N above represents the total number of subjects used in the study. The figures in parentheses next to program descriptions represent the percent of subjects that prefer that particular program.

The information about the two programs above has been presented in a positive way, because it describes how many people will be saved. Death incidences are implied in the statement but are not made explicit. As a dccision maker, when you receive this information and need to respond quickly, you start processing this information as a positive piece of evidence in favor of the program being described. Before we can make the decision about our choice of program, we need the belief for each program being good. The historical information that we have on each program does not directly provide these beliefs. We need to estimate them from the evidence. This situation is quite different from the situation of decision making with monetary payoffs under a game of chance. There, the decision maker knows all the probabilities and, thus, all the beliefs and plausibilities or can compute the beliefs and plausibilities given the information about the game (Srivastava 1994). In the present problem, we need to estimate them from the data as described below.

Based on the statistics, 200 people will be saved for sure in Program A. This is a positive item of evidence in support of the program being good. How strong is this support? We cannot exactly quantify it but let us say it supports the hypothesis that Program A is good with a level of belief a, that is, $Bel(G_A) = a$ $(1 > a > 0)$. Similarly, for Program B, we have information that if implemented, it will save 600 people with 1/3 probability and none with 2/3 probability. This information is again interpreted as a positive item of evidence in favor of B but the level of support is not known precisely. Let us say, the support is some amount b, that is, $Bel(G_B) = b$ $(1 > b > 0)$. Now, the question is which is higher of the two; is $a > b$ or $b > a$? Let us reason it out and see which inequality is true. Based on what we know about the two programs, we see that in A we are sure to save 200 people and in B we have only 1/3 probability to save on average 200 people. This analysis suggests that Program A is better than B, that is, $Bel(G_A) = a > Bel(G_B) = b$. This means that we will select Program A based on Proposition 1. This is what the empirical data show. Note that 72% chose Program A and 22% chose Program B (see Problem 5 above).

Let us consider Problem 6 of Tversky and Kahneman (1986):

> Problem 6 ($N = 155$):
>
> If Program C is adopted, 400 people will die [22%].
>
> If Program D is adopted, there is 1/3 probability that nobody will die, and 2/3 probability that 600 will die [78%].

This information is presented in a negative way because it only talks about how many people will die if a particular program is adopted. Also, as in the previous case, it does not directly give us the beliefs for the programs being good or bad. However, we can estimate these beliefs based on what we know about the programs. For Program C, 400 people will die for sure. This immediately implies that it is related to the program being bad (not good). Let us say the belief assigned to the hypothesis that Program C is not good is c, that is, $Bel(\sim G_C) = c$. Also, since there is no direct evidence in support of Program C being good, the corresponding belief is zero: $Bel(G_C) = 0$.

With a similar argument as above, we can assign a zero value to the belief that Program D is good and a value of d to the belief that it is not good: $Bel(G_D) = 0$, and $Bel(\sim G_D) = d$. The only question is whether $c > d$ or $d > c$? Once we establish this, we can select the program. Let us again reason it out. Based on what we know about the two programs, we see that in C, we are sure that 400 people will die but in B we have only 2/3 probability that on average 400 people will die. This information makes us feel that Program C is worse than program D, that is, $Bel(\sim G_C) = c > Bel(\sim G_D) = d$. Here, although we do not know how good are the two programs [$Bel(G_C) = 0$, and $Bel(G_D) = 0$], we do know, in relative terms, how bad are the two programs. Thus, if we want to select a program to be adopted, we will of course choose the one that is not as bad as the other. Which means we will choose Program D. Proposition 1 suggests the same choice and the empirical data support it too: 22% selected C and 78% selected D (see Problem 6 above).

However, if we had a well-informed individual, he or she would immediately recognize, even if he or she received only one version of the story, that if 200 people will be saved in Program A for sure, then 400 will die, too. Similarly, for Program B, if 600 people will be saved with the probability 1/3, then 600 will die too with probability 2/3. If we analyze the above information altogether in the belief-function framework, then we will have the following beliefs: $Bel(G_A) = a$, $Bel(\sim G_A) = c$, $Bel(G_B) = b$, and $Bel(\sim G_B) = d$. Let us assume that the same inequalities hold as we discussed earlier—that is, $a > b$, and $c > d$. *In probability theory, the above inequalities will not make sense.* We cannot express such feelings about the evidence in probability terms. This is one of the reasons why Einhorn and Hogarth (1986) proposed their ambiguity model.

How can we determine which alternative is better in the above situation? Let us use Proposition 1. It tells us to pick an alternative with the highest belief that it is good/fair. In the present case, we have $Bel(G_A) = a > Bel(G_B) = b$. Thus, we should select Program A based on the proposition. Let us further investigate and see if A is the right choice. Consider now the worst scenario case and look at the plausibility (see Appendix for the definition) for each program to be bad. The plausibility value for each program to be bad represents the maximum possible belief that could be assigned to it being bad. The plausibilities that the two programs are bad are: $Pl(\sim G_A) = (1 - a)$, and $Pl(\sim G_B) = (1 - b)$. We find that in the worst scenario case, Program A is not as bad as Program B because the plausibility of A being bad is less than the plausibility of B being bad: $Pl(\sim G_A) = (1 - a) < Pl(\sim G_B) = (1 - b)$. This inequality is true because $a > b$. Thus, based on the above argument, we find Program A to be overall better than Program B. This is what Proposition 1 suggests.

MORE EXAMPLES OF VALUE JUDGMENTS

In this section, we consider the rest of problems discussed by Tversky and Kahneman (1986) related to value judgment and show how Proposition 1 predicts all of the observed behaviors.

Problem 1

Problem 1 of Tversky and Kahneman (1996) comes from McNeil et al. (1982).

Problem 1

Survival frame: ($N = 247$)

Surgery: Of 100 people having surgery, 90 live through the postoperative period; 68 are alive at the end of the first year, and 34 are alive at the end of five years [82%].

Radiation Therapy: Of 100 people having radiation therapy, all live through the treatment; 77 are alive at the end of one year, and 22 are alive at the end of five years [18%].

Mortality frame: ($N = 336$)

Surgery: Of 100 people having surgery, 10 die during surgery or the postoperative period; 32 die by the end of the first year, and 66 die by the end of five years [56%].

Radiation Therapy: Of 100 people having radiation therapy, none die during treatment; 23 die by the end of one year, and 78 die by the end of five years [44%].

In order to explain the results, let us first consider the evidence based on the survival frame. Looking at the Surgery statistics, we feel that all the evidence points toward the treatment being good. This can be expressed as a positive belief that the Surgery is good: $Bel_s(G_S) = a$ $(1 > a > 0)$. There is no negative evidence; therefore, the belief that Surgery is bad (not good) is zero: $Bel_s(\sim G_S) = 0$. (G stands for good; the subscript S of G stands for Surgery, and the subscript *s* of *Bel* stands for survival frame). Similarly, for Radiation Therapy, all the evidence again points toward the treatment being good and none to it being bad. These beliefs can be written as: $Bel_s(G_R) = b$ $(1 > b > 0)$, and $Bel_s(\sim G_R) = 0$.

Now, how do we find which treatment is better unless we know the relative values of the two beliefs that the programs are good? Let us look at the factors involved in the above judgment: 90 versus all live during the treatment; 68 versus 77 are alive at the end of first year, and 34 versus 22 are alive at the end of five years. We see that 34 people in Surgery will be alive at the end of five years compared to only 22 in Radiation Therapy. However, the other two items of evidence are not as favorable for Surgery. Assuming that a treatment is better than another if more people who are treated by it live longer than those treated by the other, then the belief that Surgery is good is higher than the belief that Radiation Therapy is good: $Bel_s(G_S) = a > Bel_s(G_R) = b$. Therefore, the choice should be Surgery according to Proposition 1. This is what the data show: 82% chose Surgery and only 18% chose Radiation Therapy (see Problem 1 above).

On the other hand, when we consider the evidence produced in mortality frame, we find that all the evidence in the case of Surgery points to it being bad (not good). Therefore, we have a nonzero belief that Surgery is not good and a zero belief that Surgery is good: $Bel_m(G_S) = 0$, and $Bel_m(\sim G_S) = c$ $(1 > c > 0)$, where the subscript *m* stands for mortality. For Radiation Therapy, we have both kinds of evidence; that none die during the treatment is a good sign; however, there are two other items of evidence that tell us that Radiation Therapy is not good. Thus, we have a mixed situation. We can express this feeling by nonzero beliefs for both the treatment being good and the treatment being bad, that is, $Bel_m(G_R) = b''$, $(1 > b'' > 0)$ and $Bel_m(\sim G_R) = d$ $(1 > d > 0)$. The value of b'' may be very small but it is not zero.

Proposition 1 suggests that Radiation Therapy is better because the belief that Radiation Therapy is good is higher than the belief that Surgery is good, that is, $Bel_m(G_R) = b'' > Bel_m(G_S) = 0$. The preferred choice based on this argument is Radiation Therapy. However, there would be many individuals who might evaluate the situation by considering both aspects of the evidence. In that case, Surgery has a higher support for it being good because 34 instead of 22 people live more than five years. Thus, they will prefer Surgery over Radiation Therapy. We will have a mixed response in this case.

This is evident from the empirical data. While there is a significant increase in response to Radiation Therapy from 18% in the survival frame to 44% in the mortality frame, still 56% preferred Surgery in the mortality frame. Thus, the data support our reasoning.

Problem 12

Problem 12 comes from Tversky and Kahnemann (1986).

Problem 12 ($N = 72$)

In the treatment of tumors, there is sometimes a choice between two types of therapies: (i) a radical treatment such as extensive surgery, which involves some risk of imminent death, (ii) a moderate treatment, such as limited surgery or radiation therapy. Each of the following problems describes the possible outcome of two alternative treatments, for three different cases. In considering each case, suppose the patient is a 40-year-old male. Assume that without treatment, death is imminent (within a month) and that only one of the treatments can be applied. Please indicate the treatment you would prefer in each case.

Case 1

Treatment A: 20% chance of imminent death and 80% chance of normal life, with an expected longevity of 30 years [35%].

Treatment B: certainty of a normal life, with an expected longevity of 18 years [65%].

Case 2

Treatment C: 80% chance of imminent death and 20% chance of normal life, with an expected longevity of 30 years [68%].

Treatment D: 75% chance of imminent death and 25% chance of normal life, with an expected longevity of 18 years [32%].

Case 3

Consider a new case where there is a 25% chance that the tumor is treatable and a 75% chance that it is not. If the tumor is not treatable, death is imminent. If the tumor is treatable, the outcomes of the treatment are as follows:

Treatment E: 20% chance of imminent death and 80% chance of normal life, with an expected longevity of 30 years [32%].

Treatment F: certainty of normal life, with an expected longevity of 18 years [68%].

In all the above cases, again, we do not have the beliefs on whether a treatment is good or bad. We need to assess them. For Treatment A in Case 1, the evidence that 20% will die supports that the treatment is not good ($\sim G$), but the evidence that 80% will live a normal life for 30 years supports that the treatment is good (G). Thus, we have the following beliefs: $Bel(G_A) = a$, $Bel(\sim G_A) = a''$. Both a and a'' are nonzero and, of course, less than 1. For treatment B in Case 1, the evidence that everyone lives a normal life of 18 years is a strong support for the treatment to be good. There is no direct evidence that the treatment is bad. For this case, we have the following beliefs: $Bel(G_B) = b$, $Bel(\sim G_B) = 0$. Since the decision is to be based on the belief of the treatment being good, we need to determine which belief is higher. Is $a > b$, or $b > a$? This is a difficult question. In one case, we have 80% people live a normal life for 30 years, and in the other case, we have everyone living a normal life for 18 years. However, if we give equal importance to everyone's life then everyone living 18 years of normal life is better than only 80% living a normal life for 30 years. This argument, we believe, is pretty strong because we are talking about people's lives and everyone should have equal opportunity to live. However, the situation may be reversed if we had everyone living only for few years—say, five years—of normal life. Thus, in light of our discussion, $Bel(G_B) = b > Bel(G_A) = a$ and the choice will be Treatment B. The empirical data agree with our result: 65% chose Treatment B and 35% chose Treatment A.

We will not discuss Cases 2 and 3 in detail. However, if we follow a similar logic as above, we can predict the results. The only important point to note is that whether 20% people living a normal life for 30 years is better than 30% living only 18 years. This is again a difficult question. Many may believe that it is better for fewer people to live a longer life than for more people to live a shorter life, especially when there is no guarantee of who lives and who dies. With this argument, we can explain the findings of Case 2. For Case 3, the empirical data can be explained using the same logic as used in Case 1. The decision maker has no control over whether the tumor is treatable or not treatable. However, when it is treatable, he should prefer to choose alternative F based on the arguments presented earlier.

Discounts and Surcharges

There is ample empirical evidence that when it comes to preferences, people prefer things that are positive—good news, discounts, and so forth—over things that are negative—bad news, surcharges, and so forth—even if the information may have the same economic consequence for the well-being of the decision maker (Bazerman 1983; Kahneman, Knetsch, and Thaler 1986; Schelling 1981; Thaler 1980). However, this behavior has been considered as irrational behavior because economic theories do not predict such a behavior. Based on the decision rule proposed in this paper, such a behavior is normal; the decision maker makes the decision based what he or she knows about the situation, bringing in all cognitive capabilities to process the information. If the information appears to be negative, then that is how he or she is going to process it. The decision maker may not be a sophisticated economist who looks at all the consequences even though they are not given in the information and then makes the decision.

Let us consider a simple example of a judgment about being fair or unfair. This example and the empirical data have been taken from Kahneman, Knetsch, and Thaler (1986). The subjects are answering the question of whether the company is being unfair to employees:

> *Positive information:* A company is making a small profit. It is located in a community experiencing a recession with substantial unemployment and inflation of 12%. The company decides to increase salaries only 5% this year [22%].
>
> *Negative information:* A company is making a small profit. It is located in a community experiencing a recession with substantial unemployment but no inflation. The company decides to decrease wages and salaries 7% this year [62%].

In the case of positive information, we get the impression that the company is doing a favor to the employees by giving a 5% raise to the employees rather than laying off anyone. However, some may interpret the information that they are giving only a 5% raise when inflation is 12% as an item of evidence supporting unfairness of the company. In this situation, we may have a nonzero value for both the beliefs: the belief that the company is being fair (F), and the belief that the company is not being fair ($\sim F$): $Bel_P(\mathrm{F}) = a$, and $Bel_P(\sim F) = b$, where $1 > a > 0$, and $1 > b > 0$ and the subscript of *Bel* stands for positive evidence. Some may argue for $b = 0$, which is acceptable.

Let us analyze the negative evidence. It tells us that the company is being unfair to the employees by decreasing wages and salaries by 7%. This evidence has a direct support for the company being unfair and no support for the company being fair, which yields the following beliefs: $Bel_N(F) = 0$, and $Bel_N(\sim F) = c$. Based on Proposition 1, if we had to choose whether the company was being fair, we see that in the positive case we have support in favor of the company being fair, that is, $Bel_P(F) = a > 0$, whereas we have no evidence to support that the company is being fair in the negative case [$Bel_N(F) = 0$]. Thus, in the positive case the company is being fair, but in the negative case the company is being unfair. The empirical data support our argument (see the problem description above).

MORAL REASONING AND ETHICAL DECISIONS

Moral reasoning and ethical decisions are similar to value judgments; the decision maker takes into consideration all the information relevant to the context based on the individual values and beliefs (e.g., see the discussion in Arnold and Ponemon 1991). Kohlberg (1969) has developed a theory of cognitive moral reasoning and development. Arnold and Ponemon (1991) use Kohlberg's model to examine the internal auditor's perceptions of whistleblowing behavior within the context of his or her level of moral reasoning. It is interesting to note that their experimental situation fits very well within the domain of this study. Their experiment involves judgments related to whether an individual discovering a management fraud will report the findings to higher authorities—that is, blow the whistle. The subjects were 106 internal auditors from the public and private sectors. Since the subjects acted as third persons in making their judgments, the experimental design is beyond the domain of the traditional expected utility theory. Rather, the situation is similar to value judgments as discussed in the third and fourth sections above. Before providing a belief-function treatment of their problem, we briefly describe one version of their case presented to the subjects with two levels of treatment (Arnold and Ponemon 1991, 7):

> Tim is an internal auditor with an organization that is a primary contractor for the U.S. government. Tim recently completed an audit of a subsidiary business unit (ABC plant) which is completing significant (large dollar) contracts for various government agencies. The billings of the subsidiary have been audited previously and no major problems were detected. During the present audit, Tim discovered, within the subsidiary's billing system, a series of bogus (inflated or falsified) invoices to customers that had already been paid. Tim reported this finding to the director of internal audit. The director said that he would report it to authorities within the company. After a few days, the director told Tim, "Forget about it!"

Tim demands further action. The director says:

Treatment level–affiliation. "If your findings are reported, the company will be forced to close the ABC plant." Two of Tim's very close friends are employees in the plant.

Treatment level–penalty. "If you pursue this, you will be fired!"

The subjects were asked to make a prediction as to whether Tim *did* or *did not* blow the whistle. This question is similar to value judgment; the subjects were asked to make a value judgment on whether the individual in the case acted ethically (E) or not ($\sim E$). We do not discuss all their cases in the present paper. However, in order to illustrate the belief-function treatment of such a problem, we consider the scenario where the individual discovering the fraud is an internal auditor and faces two situations if he or she blows the whistle: (1) two friends lose their jobs, or (2) Tim gets fired.

The decision maker (*DM*, the subject) has to make the judgment whether Tim will act ethically (E)—that is, blow the whistle under situation 1 or situation 2. A belief-function treatment of the problem follows. Let us assume that *DM* does not know anything else about Tim in terms of his moral and ethical values except the information given above about the two situations. In situation 1, the knowledge that Tim's two friends will lose their jobs if he reports the fraud provides direct evidence that Tim will not report the fraud—that is, he will act unethically ($\sim E$). Thus, this evidence provides a positive nonzero belief, say a, that Tim will act unethically, that is, $Bel_1(\sim E) = a$ ($1 > a > 0$) where the subscript on *Bel* represents the first situation. Since there is no evidence in support of E, the belief that Tim will act ethically (E) is zero, that is, $Bel_1(E) = 0$.

In situation 2, the evidence that Tim will be fired provides direct evidence that he will not report the fraud—that is, he will not act ethically. Thus, the belief that Tim will act unethically is again nonzero—say, an amount b—that is, $Bel_2(\sim E) = b$, and again, since there is no evidence in favor of E, $Bel_2(E) = 0$. The question is, which alternative will the *DM* pick? The answer depends on the relative values of a and b. Let us analyze the situation. It seems reasonable to assume that without any other information about Tim's background regarding his moral and ethical values, he will be more willing to act unethically when it comes to losing his own job in comparison to having his friends lose their jobs. This reasoning suggests that $a < b$. Thus, using Proposition 1, we find that *DM* will pick situation 1. This is because the belief that Tim will act ethically is zero in both situations [$Bel_1(E) = Bel_2(E) = 0$] and the belief that he will act unethically in situation 1 is lower than the belief that he will act unethically in situation 2 [$Bel_1(\sim E) = a < Bel_2(\sim E) = b$]. This implies that it is more plausible that Tim will act ethically in situation 1 than in situation 2. In other words, *DM* will suggest that it is more plausible that Tim will report the fraud in situation 1 than in situation 2. This is what Arnold and Ponemon found: the subjects perceived whistleblowing to be less likely under conditions of job termination than under plant closure and employee layoffs (1991, p. 10). One can analyze the other cases of Arnold and Ponemon in a similar fashion.

SUMMARY

In summary, we have described a rule for making decisions that involve value judgments using belief functions. The rule is presented in the form of a proposition which is simple and intuitive. We have shown how well the rule predicts the observed behavior by using the empirical data of Tversky and Kahneman (1981, 1986). It is interesting to see that the proposed rule predicts correctly even those behaviors that are considered irrational under EUT. Also, we have discussed, using the empirical results of Arnold and Ponemon (1991), how the present work can be used to model behaviors when making ethical judgments.

ACKNOWLEDGMENT

This research was partially supported by Deloitte & Touche through their Faculty Fellowship at the School of Business. The author would like to thank the accounting and finance workshop participants at The University of Kansas—in particular, Peter Gillett, Keith Harrison, Mark Hirschey, Maurice Joy, and George Pinches—for their invaluable comments and suggestions.

APPENDIX

The Belief-Function Framework

Belief functions[3] are not new; they have antecedents in the seventeenth-century work of George Hooper and James Bernoulli (Shafer 1976). The works by Dempster in the 1960s and by Shafer in the 1970s comprise the current form of the belief-function formalism known as Dempster-Shafer theory of belief functions. We give only the basics of belief functions. Since the present paper does not deal with combination of evidence, we do not give Dempster's rule of combination. Interested readers are advised to see Shafer (1976) for details.

The basic difference between probability theory and the belief-function framework is in the assignment of uncertainties to a set of mutually exclusive and exhaustive states or assertions under consideration (we will call this set a *frame* and represent it by the symbol Θ). In probability theory, we assign uncertainty to each individual element of the frame and call it the probability of occurrence of the element. The sum of all these probabilities equals one.

Let us consider an auditing example. The accounts receivable balance is not materially misstated (*ar*) and it is materially misstated (~*ar*) are the two assertions representing a mutually exclusive and exhaustive set. Here, the frame consists of the two elements:[4] $\Theta = \{ar, \sim ar\}$. In probability theory, we will assign probability to each element of the frame, that is, $P(ar) \geq 0$, and $P(\sim ar) \geq 0$. Also, we know that $P(ar) + P(\sim ar) = 1$. In the belief-function formalism, uncertainty is assigned not only to the single elements of the frame but also to all other proper subsets of the frame and to the entire frame. We call these uncertainties *m*-values, or the *basic probability assignment function.*

m-values (The Basic Probability Assignment Function)

Similar to probabilities, all these *m*-values add to one. For the example considered above,[5] we will have $m(ar) \geq 0$, $m(\sim ar) \geq 0$, and $m(\{ar, \sim ar\}) \geq 0$, and $m(ar) + m(\sim ar) + m(\{ar, \sim ar\}) = 1$. Let us assume that the auditor has performed analytical procedures relevant to the accounts receivable balance and found no significant difference between the recorded value and the predicted value. Based on this finding, he feels that the recorded value appears reasonable and is not materially misstated. However, he does not want to put too much weight on this evidence. He feels he can assign a small level of assurance—say, 0.3 on a scale of 0-1—that the account is not materially misstated. We can express this feeling in terms of *m*-values as: $m(ar) = 0.3$, $m(\sim ar) = 0$, and $m(\{ar, \sim ar\}) = 0.7$. The belief function interpretation of these *m*-values is that the auditor has 0.3 level of support to *ar*, no support to ~*ar*, and 0.7 level of support remains uncommitted, which represents ignorance.

However, if we had to express the above feelings in terms of probabilities, then we get into problems because we will assign $P(ar) = 0.3$ and $P(\sim ar) = 0.7$, which implies that there is a 70% chance that the account is materially misstated, but we know that this is not what the auditor is trying to say. The auditor has no reason to believe that the account is materially misstated. Thus, we can use *m*-values to express the basic judgment about the level of support or assurance the auditor obtains from an item of evidence for an assertion. An example of a negative item of evidence which will have a direct support for ~*ar* would be the following set of inherent factors: (1) in the prior years, the account has had major problems; and (2) there are economic reasons for management to misstate the account. In such a case, we can express the auditor's feelings as $m(ar) = 0$, $m(\sim ar) = 0.2$, and $m(\{ar, \sim ar\}) = 0.8$, assuming that the auditor feels a low, say 0.2, level of support for ~*ar*.

The auditor can express a mixed type of evidence in terms of *m*-values without any problems. For example, consider that the auditor has accumulated several environmental factors, some in support of and some against the assertion that the accounts receivable balance is not materially misstated. He assesses that there is a moderate—say, 0.4—level of support in favor of the assertion and a low level of support—say, 0.1—for its negation and feels that he cannot assign the remaining 0.5 level of support to any particular state. We can express this feeling as: $m(ar) = 0.4$, $m(\sim ar) = 0.1$, and $m(\{ar, \sim ar\}) = 0.5$. In probability theory, we cannot express such a feeling.

Belief Functions

So far, we have talked about probabilities and *m*-values. Let us now define the belief function, $Bel(A)$ for a subset A of elements of the frame. $Bel(A)$ represents the total belief in A. This belief will be more than $m(A)$. Actually, $Bel(A)$ is equal to $m(A)$ plus the sum of all the m-values for the set of elements that are contained in A. In terms of symbols:

$$Bel\,(A) = \sum_{B \subseteq A} m(B).$$

By definition, belief in the empty set is zero.

Consider an example to illustrate the definition of belief functions. Suppose you have a friend who lives on the East Coast in the New Jersey area. The only contact you have with him is through greeting cards that he sends you periodically with no return address. You want to find the belief that your friend lives in New Jersey. After looking through all the cards you have received over the years, you can identify the following post-office seals marked on the cards: 10% of the cards are marked North Brunswick; 20%, East Brunswick; 10%, Philadelphia; and 15%, Newark. Twenty-five percent of the cards have only the Brunswick part legible, which means you cannot determine from what part of Brunswick these cards were mailed. For the remaining 20%, nothing is legible on the seals. These numbers can be interpreted as nonzero m-values for different subsets of the frame that your friend lives somewhere on the East Coast near New Jersey. Based on just this evidence, you wish to form your total belief that the friend lives in New Jersey. This belief will be the sum of the m-values that he lives in North Brunswick, East Brunswick, Brunswick, and Newark. For this example, the belief is 0.70. Similarly, the belief that the friend lives in Brunswick—which includes North Brunswick and East Brunswick—will be 0.55 (10% North Brunswick, 20% East Brunswick, 25% Brunswick).

Going back to our auditing example of analytical procedures, the auditor's assessment of the level of support in terms of m-values was: $m(ar) = 0.3$, $m(\sim ar) = 0$, and $m(\{ar, \sim ar\}) = 0.7$. Based on analytical procedures alone, the belief that the account is not materially misstated is 0.3 [i.e., $Bel(ar) = 0.3$] and no support that the account is materially misstated [$Bel(\sim ar) = 0$]. In general, a zero belief in the belief-function formalism means that there is no evidence to support the proposition. In other words, a zero belief in a proposition represents lack of evidence. In contrast, a zero probability in probability theory means that the proposition cannot be true, which represents an impossibility. Also, one finds that beliefs for *ar* and $\sim ar$ do not necessarily add to one, that is, $Bel(ar) + Bel(\sim ar) \leq 1$, whereas in probability, it is always true that $P(ar) + P(\sim ar) = 1$.

Belief functions differ from probabilities in representing ignorance. In probability theory, we represent ignorance by assigning equal probability to all the outcomes or elements of the frame. In the belief-function framework, we represent ignorance by assigning an m-value of one to the entire frame and an *m*-value of zero to all its proper subsets. The belief-function formalism becomes the Bayesian formalism when nonzero *m*-values exist only for single elements of the frame. In such a case, *m*-values become probabilities, that is, $m(a_i = P(a_i)$, and Dempster's rule in the belief-function formalism becomes Bayes' rule in the probability theory (Shafer 1976).

Plausibility Functions

By definition, the plausibility of A is equal to one minus the belief in $\sim A$, that is, $Pl(A) = 1 - Bel(\sim A)$ where $\sim A$ represents the set of elements that are not in *A*. Intuitively, the plausibility of *A* is the degree to which *A* is plausible given the evidence. In other words, $Pl(A)$ is the degree to which we do not assign belief to its negation $\sim A$.

In our example of analytical procedures, we have $Bel(ar) = 0.3$, $Bel(\sim ar) = 0$. These values yield the following plausibility values. $Pl(ar) = 1$, and $Pl(\sim ar) = 0.7$. $Pl(\sim ar) = 1$ indicates that *ar* is maximally plausible since we have no evidence against it. However, $Pl(\sim ar) = 0.7$ indicates that if we had no other items of evidence to consider then the maximum possible risk that the account is materially misstated would be 0.7, even though we have no evidence that the account is materially misstated ($Bel(\sim ar) = 0$).

NOTES

1. Moral reasoning and making ethical judgments are similar to value judgments; they all depend on the contextual information available to the decision maker.

2. The *basic probability assignment function* (*m*-values) in the belief-function framework is similar to probability function with the one difference that *m*-values are defined, in general, on all possible subsets of the frame of interest whereas probabilities are defined only on singletons (see Appendix for details). In the case where nonzero *m*-values exist only for the singletons, the belief-function framework reduces to the Bayesian framework (Srivastava and Shafer 1992).

3. This Appendix is taken from Srivastava (1993).

4. In the case of n elements in the frame, we will have $P(a_i) \geq 0$ and $\sum_{i=1}^{n} P(a_i) = 1$, where a_i represents the ith element of the frame.

5. For a frame of n elements, we will have, in general, m-values for each individual elements, each set of two elements, each set of three elements, and so on, to the m-value for the entire frame. All such m-values add to one, that is, $\sum m(A) = 1^{A \subseteq \Theta}$ where A represents all the proper subsets of the frame Θ. The m-value for the empty set is zero.

REFERENCES

Arnold, D.F., Sr., and L.A. Ponemon. 1991. Internal auditors' perceptions of whistle-blowing and the influence of moral reasoning: An experiment. *Auditing: A Journal of Practice and Theory* 10(2, Fall): 1-15.

Bazerman, M.H. 1983. Negotiator judgment. *American Behavioral Scientist* 27: 211-228.

Buchanan, B.G., and E.H. Shortliffe. 1984. *Rule-Based Expert Systems: The MYCIN Experiments of the Stanford Heuristic Programming Project.* Reading, MA: Addison-Wesley.

Davis, R., B. Buchanan, and E.H. Shortliffe. 1977. Production rules as a representation for a knowledge-based consultation system. *Artificial Intelligence* 8: 15-45.

Dempster, A.P. 1967. Upper and lower probabilities induced by a multivalued mapping. *Annals of Mathematical Statistics* 38: 205-339.

________. 1968. A generalization of Bayesian inference. *Journal of the Royal Statistical Society, Series B* 30: 205-247.

Einhorn, H.J., and R.M. Hogarth. 1986. Decision making under ambiguity. *The Journal of Business* 59(4, Pt. 2, October): S225-S250.

Ellsberg, D. 1961. Risk, ambiguity, and the savage axioms. *Quarterly Journal of Economics* 75: 643-669.

Jaffray, J-Y. 1989. Utility theory for belief functions. *Operations Research Letters* 8: 107-112.

________. 1994. Dynamic decision making with belief functions. In *Advances in the Dempster-Shafer Theory of Evidence,* eds. R.R. Yager, M. Fedrizzi, and J. Kacprzyk, 331-352. New York: John Wiley and Sons.

Kahneman, D., J.L. Knetsch, and R.H. Thaler. 1986. Fairness and the assumptions of economics. *The Journal of Business* 59(4, Pt. 2, October): S85-S300.

Kahneman, D., and A. Tversky. 1979. Prospect theory: An analysis of decision under risk. *Econometrica* 47(2): 263-291.

Kohlberg, L. 1969. Stages and sequences: The cognitive developmental approach to socialization. In *Handbook of Socialization Theory and Research*, ed. D. Goslin. Chicago: Rand McNally.

McNeil, B.J., S.G. Pauker, H.C. Sox, Jr., and A. Tversky. 1982. On the elicitation of preferences for alternative therapies. *New England Journal of Medicine* 306: 1259-1262.

Nguyen, H.T., and E.A. Walker. 1994. On decision making using belief functions. In *Advances in the Dempster-Shafer Theory of Evidence,* eds. R.R. Yager, M. Fedrizzi, and J. Kacprzyk, 311-330. New York: John Wiley and Sons.

Schelling, T.C. 1981. Economic reasoning and the ethics of policy. *Policy Interest* 63: 37-61.

Schoemaker, P.J.H. 1982. The expected utility model: Its variants, purposes, evidence and limitations. *Journal of Economic Literature* XX(June): 529-563.

Shafer, G. 1976. *A Mathematical Theory of Evidence.* Princeton, NJ: Princeton University Press.

Shafer, G., and R.P. Srivastava. 1990. The Bayesian and belief-function formalisms: A general perspective for auditing. *Auditing: A Journal of Practice and Theory* (Supplement): 110-148.

Simon, H.A. 1986. Rationality in psychology and economics. *The Journal of Business* 59(4, Pt. 2, October): S209-S224.

Smets, P. 1990a. The combination of evidence in the transferable belief model. *IEEE Transactions on Pattern Analysis and Machine Intelligence* 12(5, May): 447-458.

________. 1990b. Constructing the pignistic probability function in a context of uncertainty. *Uncertainty in Artificial Intelligence,* vol. 5, ed. M. Henrion, R.D. Shachter, L.N. Kanal, and J.F. Lemmer. North-Holland: Elsevier.

Srivastava, R.P. 1993. Belief functions and audit decisions. *Auditors Report* 17(1, Fall): 8-12.

________. 1994. Decision making under ambiguity: A belief-function perspective. Working Paper No. 262, School of Business, The University of Kansas, Lawrence (June).

Srivastava, R.P., and G. Shafer. 1992. Belief-function formulas for audit risk. *The Accounting Review* (April): 249-283.

Strat, T.M. 1990. Decision analysis using belief functions. *International Journal of Approximate Reasoning* 4(5): 6.

________. 1994. Decision analysis using belief functions. In *Advances in the Dempster-Shafer Theory of Evidence,* eds. R.R. Yager, M. Fedrizzi, and J. Kacprzyk, 275-309. New York: John Wiley and Sons.

Thaler, R.H. 1980. Towards a positive theory of consumer choice. *Journal Economic Behavior and Organization* 1: 39-60.

Tversky, A. 1969. Intransitivity of preferences. *Psychological Review* 76: 105-110.

Tversky, A, and D. Kahneman. 1981. The framing of decisions and the psychology of choice. *Science* 211: 453-458.

________. 1986. Rational choice and the framing of decisions. *The Journal of Business* 59(4, Pt. 2, October): S251-S278.

Yager, R.R. 1990. Decision making under Dempster-Shafer uncertainties. Technical Report MII-915, Iona College, New Rochelle, NY.

ETHICAL OBLIGATIONS OF CPAs IN ADVERTISING AND SOLICITATION:

PUBLIC INTEREST CONSIDERATIONS

Kathy S. Moffeit, Steven M. Mintz, and
Ruth Lesher Taylor

ABSTRACT

This paper analyzes the ethical, professional, and legal issues related to CPA advertising and solicitation practices in light of the 1993 U.S. Supreme Court ruling in *Edenfield v. Fane* that Florida's ban on direct uninvited solicitation is unconstitutional. A review of the rules of professional conduct in the 54 jurisdictions indicated that very few state boards of accountancy provide any guidance for CPAs as to what are acceptable and professional practices. Supreme Court rulings in lawyer cases clearly establish that a state can prohibit false and deceptive practices and that states can establish other guidelines that serve their asserted interests. However, rules that go beyond

Research on Accounting Ethics, Volume 2, pages 131-157.

ISBN: 1-55938-997-4

prohibiting these practices have been consistently judged to be unconstitutional because they prohibit the free flow of commercial information that is essential to our free market economy. A stricter set of prohibitions on soliciting audit and other clients for whom attest services will be performed may be defensible if it could be demonstrated that the public's interest in independent CPA services justified such restrictions. In today's competitive environment for professional services, the possibility exists that unethical CPAs may be tempted to solicit clients by promising to overlook financial misstatements or by promising to give a favorable opinion on the client's financial statements. Independence is impaired if it appears that a CPA might compromise his or her ethical standards when engaged in direct uninvited solicitation. The American Institute of Certified Public Accountants (AICPA) should conduct a study of the public's perception of the objectivity and independence of CPAs when engaged in an uninvited solicitation of potential clients. Additional recommendations are made for state boards of accountancy, state CPA societies, and practitioners. Future research should be undertaken to determine whether there is a relationship between a CPA who commits an ethics violation and how that CPA advertises to obtain clients.

INTRODUCTION

For many years the accounting profession considered advertising and direct uninvited solicitation practices to be unprofessional conduct for CPAs because such forms of communication could mislead or intimidate a potential client, thereby disserving the client's interest. During 1977-1978, the Antitrust Division of the Department of Justice challenged the American Institute of Certified Public Accountant's (AICPA) blanket prohibition of these practices as being against the public interest because it prevented the client from making comparisons of price, quality, and the scope of a CPA's services. Following a U.S. Supreme Court decision that a total ban on lawyer advertising was unconstitutional, the AICPA in 1978 lifted its 61-year ban on advertising and solicitation and amended Rule 502 in its *Code of Professional Conduct* (Code) to permit both advertising and solicitation so long as they are not false, misleading, or deceptive.

According to the *Report of the Special Committee on Solicitation* (1981, 4-5) that was formed by the AICPA subsequent to the lifting of these prohibitions, members were concerned that direct uninvited solicitation practices might undermine the professionalism of CPAs and create the potential to negatively affect the public image of CPAs. Consequently, the committee recommended that Rule 502 should be amended to prohibit certain forms of "unscrupulous solicitation practices ... that are detrimental to the public and the profession." Specifically, it recommended that solicitation by the use of coercion, duress, compulsion, intimidation, threats, overreaching, or vexatious or harassing conduct should be prohibited. Ultimately, a new rule was adopted at the time of restructuring the Code on January 12, 1988. A prohibition of solicitation by the use of coercion, overreaching, or harassing conduct was added to the proscription of false, misleading, or deceptive advertising and solicitation practices (AICPA 1988, 16).

An important finding of the Committee was that no empirical data existed to support a complete ban on direct uninvited solicitation. That is, no instances were uncovered of a lack of independence of audit clients who were obtained by direct uninvited solicitation or the failure of an auditor to maintain independence in mental attitude toward a client who might be subjected to direct uninvited solicitation by another CPA. However, the Committee's investigation of this issue was made in 1980, only eight years after the AICPA lifted its ban on competitive bidding (Rule 3.03) and just one year after the encroachment rule (Rule 401) was repealed. Both of these rules addressed concerns related to the solicitation of clients of another CPA. Since 1980, a significant increase in competition for professional services has occurred; therefore, the results of the AICPA's investigation may not be valid in today's competitive environment.

On July 26, 1990, the Federal Trade Commission (FTC) issued a final order pursuant to a consent agreement between the FTC and the AICPA prohibiting the AICPA from "Restricting, regulating, impeding, declaring unethical, advising members against, or interfering with" a list of practices. Two of these practices are direct solicitation of a potential client and advertising that (1) is "self-laudatory or comparative," (2) contains "any testimonial or endorsement," or (3) is "not considered by the AICPA to be professionally dignified or in good taste" (FTC 1990, 3-4). It was made clear in the FTC order, however, that the AICPA can make and enforce guidelines against false or deceptive practices in solicitation and advertising.

On April 26, 1993, the U.S. Supreme Court affirmed in *Edenfield v. Fane* the Eleventh Circuit Court of Appeals' ruling striking down Florida's ban on "direct, in-person, uninvited solicitation." The decision raises important questions about the ethical and professional responsibilities of CPAs in advertising and solicitation and the enforceability of state bans on uninvited solicitation of a potential client.

The purpose of this paper is to analyze the ethical, professional, and legal issues related to CPA advertising and solicitation and to make recommendations to improve the profession's ethical standards in light of the FTC consent order, the Supreme Court decision in *Edenfield*, and other Supreme Court cases related to advertising and solicitation by lawyers. The recommendations should be of interest to both the business and accounting communities because of the need to market professional services in an ethical and professional manner and the importance of a free flow of commercial information to our free enterprise system. State boards of accountancy also should be interested in the results of the study because of their regulatory role.

In the remainder of this paper, we first identify the ethical issues to be explored. This is followed by a discussion of the role of the accounting profession in society, including the purpose of the AICPA Code, the growth in CPA nonattest services, the public interest aspect of a CPA's services, and state regulation of advertising and solicitation practices. The next section contains a description of the research method used to obtain and analyze information related to advertising and solicitation in light of the FTC consent order and the Supreme Court decision in *Edenfield*. The next section explores some of the legal considerations, including the effect of the *Edenfield* ruling and other Supreme Court opinions in lawyer advertising and solicitation cases on what might be acceptable practices for CPAs. Then, future issues are explored and recommendations are made to enhance CPA advertising and solicitation practices. Finally, concluding comments are made about the importance of protecting the public's interest when CPAs engage in advertising and solicitation practices.

ETHICAL ISSUES

This paper addresses the two sides of the advertising and solicitation controversy. One side is that advertising and solicitation practices provide useful information to potential purchasers about the cost and availability of professional accounting services that enhances the ability of consumers to make informed comparisons. This is the type of argument that was used by the FTC in challenging the AICPA's restrictions on advertising and solicitation as being anticompetitive. The other side of the issue centers on the need for objectivity and independence—in fact and appearance—in the performance of auditing and other services. The accounting profession is concerned that advertising and solicitation practices may impair the ability of CPAs to be objective in the performance of professional services.

An interesting contrast can be made between CPAs and lawyers and the potential for advertising and solicitation practices to inhibit service to a client. It is a well-accepted belief that lawyer advertising has negatively affected the public's image of attorneys. However, this does not mean that lawyers who advertise or solicit clients cannot fulfill their professional obligations. They can still satisfy those obligations if they defend their clients well. Lawyers serve as advocates for their clients. There is no expectation that lawyers will be independent of their clients or objective in presenting their clients' cases.

In contrast to lawyers, CPAs are expected to be independent of their audit clients. Even the appearance of a lack of independence can impair the public's perception of the reliability of audited financial statements. The appearance of independence refers to the impression of others with regard to whether the auditor can act with integrity and objectivity. Thus, the auditor should avoid any relationships with the client that may even appear to impair objectivity in rendering audit or other attest services. This is a much stricter standard than exists for lawyers. The stricter standard exists because CPAs must be concerned about the perceptions of stockholders, creditors, and others who may rely on the audited financial statements. The lawyer, on the other hand, is primarily concerned with the client's interests.

Questionable advertising and solicitation practices potentially affect the credibility of CPAs to a much larger extent than that of lawyers. Whereas the lawyer primarily serves the client, the CPA has an ethical responsibility to the public interest that is of paramount importance. If the public perceives that the credibility of a CPA is diminished as a result of advertising and solicitation, then its reliance on the audited financial statements also may be reduced. The end result may be a loss of confidence in the audit function and, perhaps, the accounting profession.

THE ACCOUNTING PROFESSION

Society grants professions such as medicine, law, and accounting monopolies to practice because of the required level of expertise and specialized knowledge that professionals need to carry out their responsibilities. In exchange for their monopoly rights, professionals promise to use their expertise to benefit society. A profession is allowed to self-regulate the behavior of its members and, typically, a code of ethics is the mechanism used to monitor the activities of the members of a profession.

In addition to expressing the profession's public-service ideal, the AICPA Code serves two functions. One is to emphasize the importance of high standards of ethical conduct in relationships between accounting professionals and their clients or the general public. In this regard, the Code's rules require: strict independence from clients for whom attest services are performed; integrity, objectivity, and due care in the performance of all professional services; the maintenance of client confidentiality; and compliance with the profession's technical standards in rendering services, including expressing an opinion on the fairness of the presentations in the client's financial statements. The Code's other function is to promote harmony within the profession by addressing relationships among the professionals themselves. The questionable link between this function and the public interest is at the heart of the prohibition of an uninvited solicitation. As pointed out earlier, the federal government challenged the prohibition of this and other advertising practices as being against the public interest in that it impeded the free flow of commercial information to the public.

Scope of Services

The AICPA's rules of professional conduct have evolved over a long period of time, dating back to 1917. Most of the rules were developed at a time when the scope of a CPA's professional services was limited to auditing and income tax preparation and tax planning. During the 1960s and 1970s, the scope of services was broadened to include sophisticated tax planning, both on an individual and a corporate level, and a variety of management advisory services. During the 1980s and 1990s, the scope of services was further expanded to include other forms of advisory services, such as personal financial planning and litigation support. Currently, advisory services come under the umbrella of six consulting functions and include a broad range of services. Also, since 1978 the AICPA has issued standards for the performance of attest services other than auditing, including reviews of financial statements, which provide limited assurance about the conformity of the financial statements with generally accepted accounting principles, and such services as a compilation of financial statements and examination of prospective financial information.

Growth in the magnitude of nonattest services during the 1970s and 1980s is apparent in the results of two studies. Previts (1985) determined that the average percentage of fees earned through audit services performed by the then Big Eight CPA firms was 70%. By 1984, the percentage had declined to 62%. Read and Tomczyk (1992) surveyed the fee distribution of each of the Big Eight firms during the 1982-1988 period and found that one firm's average fees were higher for tax and MAS services combined than for attest-type services. The range of distribution was from a low of 32% to a high of 53% for tax and MAS services. Moreover, the 13 "second and third tier" firms had similar distributions, with two firms earning a larger percentage of their fees from nonattest services. The range for these firms was 35%-57%.

The services performed by CPAs can be categorized as either public services or client services. Auditing and other attest-related services are public services because investors and creditors rely on the financial statements for their decision-making needs. It is the independence of the auditor from the client—both in fact and appearance—that adds value to the auditor's opinion on the financial statements. Unlike audited financial statements that typically result from a Securities and Exchange Commission requirement or are submitted as part of a loan request, tax and consulting services are performed because of the client's need for these services. Thus, it is the client that primarily relies on the objectivity of the CPA when performing nonattest services and independence is not required.

The Public Interest

According to the AICPA Code as amended on January 14, 1992 (AICPA 1994, 5), CPAs are expected to discharge their professional responsibilities in a way that will serve the public interest. The public interest is defined as the collective well-being of the community of people and institutions the profession serves, including clients, credit grantors, governments, employees, investors, the business and financial community, and others who rely on the objectivity and integrity of CPAs to maintain the orderly functioning of commerce.

The accounting profession has always recognized its responsibility to the public. The cornerstone of this responsibility is the attest function. The auditor's expert opinion is relied on by the users of the financial statements to make the investment and credit decisions that help provide for the efficient allocation of economic resources in our free market economy. Society grants monopoly rights to the accounting profession because of the public interest component of the attest function. Typically, only CPAs can perform the attest function, although some states have grandfathered "registered" accountants and permit them to attest to the fairness of financial statements. A few states even permit non-CPAs to perform the attest function as long as they do not hold themselves out to be CPAs. As a practical matter, a public corporation would engage only a CPA to attest to the fairness of its financial statements. On the other hand, non-CPAs can and do perform accounting services in industry and government, prepare tax returns, provide advice on personal financial planning, and engage in a variety of consulting services.

The primacy of the attest function was recognized by the Supreme Court in *U.S. v. Arthur Young & Co.* Commenting on the difference between the attorney's role as the client's confidential adviser and advocate and the role of the independent CPA, the Court stated that (1984, 1503):

> By certifying the public reports that collectively depict a corporation's financial status, the independent auditor assumes a *public* responsibility transcending any employment relationship with the client. The independent public accountant performing this special function owes ultimate allegiance to the corporation's creditors and stockholders, as well as to the investing public. This "public watchdog" function demands that the accountant maintain total independence from the client at all times and requires complete fidelity to the public trust.

State Regulation of CPAs

CPAs are licensed to practice in a particular state by that state's Board of Accountancy. Each state board has its own rules, which may conflict with AICPA rules. The result could be confusion on the part of a CPA who is uncertain as to what is or is not an acceptable practice under one or the other set of rules. Even though the ethical responsibility of a CPA in this situation is to follow the more restrictive rule, confusion is likely to exist because of the liberalization of AICPA rules following its agreement with the FTC. The potential for confusion increases when a CPA has different clients in different states, in which case the CPA may be permitted to engage in an advertising or solicitation practice in one state but not in another.

Following the FTC consent order, some states revised their rules and dropped their bans on testimonials or endorsements in advertising and direct uninvited solicitation, while other states did not. Some of the restrictive language in state codes is inconsistent with the consent order and, as a result, state board rules may be subject to legal challenge as violating a CPA's freedom of commercial speech, as occurred in *Edenfield.* Also, CPAs in states with restrictive language in their code may be subject to disciplinary proceedings if they advertise and solicit in a way that is consistent with the consent order but violates the state's rules on advertising and solicitation. This raises the following questions: (1) how are advertising and direct solicitation practices currently addressed by the state codes of professional ethics? and (2) what, if any, guidance is provided in the rules to ensure that advertising and solicitation practices are carried out in an ethical and professional manner?

RESEARCH METHOD

This research was begun in 1992 when the state boards of accountancy in all 50 states were asked to provide their codes of ethics. Six states indicated that they followed the AICPA's *Code of Professional Conduct*, of which five did not have separate state codes. The codes of professional ethics of the other 44 states were reviewed and it was determined that the largest number of differences between state rules and the requirements of the FTC consent order were the rules related to direct uninvited solicitation and testimonials and endorsements. Table 1 outlines the provisions of all 50 states. If advertising/solicitation is not addressed or if the language prohibits false or deceptive advertising and solicitation or coercive solicitation practices, then the state is considered "in agreement with FTC order."

Table 1. Analysis of State Rules (as of June 1992)

	Solicitation		*Advertising*	
	Agrees with FTC	*Prohibits Uninvited Solicitation*	*Agrees with FTC*	*Prohibits Testimonials/ Endorsements*
Alabama	X		X	
Alaska	X		X	
Arizona	X		X	
Arkansas	X			X
California	X		X	
Colorado	X		X	
Connecticut	X		X	
Delaware (AICPA)	X		X	
Florida		X	X	
Georgia	X			X_1
Hawaii	X			X
Idaho		X		X
Illinois	X		X	
Indiana (AICPA)	X		X	
Iowa (AICPA)	X		X	
Kansas	X		X	
Kentucky	X		X	
Louisiana		X		X
Maine (AICPA)	X		X	
Maryland	X		X	
Massachusetts		X	X	
Michigan		X	X	
Minnesota		X		X_1
Mississippi		X		X
Missouri	X		X	
Montana	X			X_1
Nebraska	X		X	
Nevada	X		X	
New Hampshire	X			X
New Jersey	X			X
New Mexico		X		X
New York	X			X
N. Carolina	X		X	
N. Dakota	X		X	
Ohio		X	X	
Oklahoma	X		X	
Oregon	X			X_1
Pennsylvania	X		X	
Rhode Island (AICPA)	X		X	
S. Carolina	X			X_1
S. Dakota	X		X	
Tennessee	X		X	

(continued)

Table 1. *(Continued)*

Texas		X	X	
Utah	X			X
Vermont	X		X	
Virginia	X		X	
Washington	X		X	
W. Virginia	X		X	
Wisconsin	X		X	
Wyoming	X			X[1]
Totals	40	10	34	16

Note: [1]These six states have qualifying language that would appear to make the prohibition consistent with the FTC order.

State Rules Analyzed

The results indicate that the solicitation rules in 40 states were in accord with the FTC order in 1992, while 10 states had rules violating the order by prohibiting direct, uninvited, or in-person solicitation of nonclients. Additionally, rules in 16 states were in violation of the order in that they prohibited testimonials or laudatory statements in advertising, although six of these states had qualifying language in their codes that appeared to make their rules consistent with the FTC order which allows the AICPA to establish guidelines for false and deceptive practices. Of the 10 states that had advertising rules in violation of the order, four also prohibited uninvited solicitation. Therefore, six states prohibited only testimonials and endorsements, and they did not have the aforementioned qualifying language. Overall, 16 states[1] were in violation of the consent order in 1992 in that they prohibited either uninvited solicitation (ten states) or testimonials or other laudatory statements (six states).

The rules in several states that prohibited uninvited solicitation indicated that a distinction was made between three types of solicitation: (1) face-to-face solicitation, (2) telephone solicitation, and (3) solicitation through written communication. Most of these states prohibited face-to-face solicitation (in-person) and telephone communication (direct) but permitted solicitation through the mail so long as it was not false, fraudulent, misleading, or deceptive. The reason for prohibiting in-person solicitation is the possibility of coercive or overreaching conduct on the part of the CPA when soliciting a potential client face-to-face, while telephonic communication was prohibited because it invades the privacy of a client who does not invite the solicitation. On the other hand, a mail solicitation can be discarded by the potential client, so it does not pose the same threat of overreaching behavior.

Guidance in the Rules

Laudatory statements can deceive the potential client if claims are made that are not supportable by the facts. For example, a CPA who advertises that he or she is the best CPA in town should bear the burden of proof in substantiating such a claim. The public interest is served by creating limits on the ability of CPAs to make, or allow others to make, laudatory statements. As mentioned above, only six of the 16 states that prohibited testimonials or endorsements tied the prohibition to false or deceptive practices. Thus, the rules in these six states were consistent with the consent order because truthful and nondeceptive testimonials or endorsements should not be prohibited. In each of the six states, a qualifying statement was added to the rules to the effect that only testimonials, endorsements, or other laudatory statements that were not supported by verifiable facts were prohibited. This qualification seems to make the rules consistent with certain Supreme Court rulings discussed below. For the other 10 states that had a blanket ban on testimonials or endorsements, the question is: how does such a prohibition serve the public interest, or is this another example of trying to "promote harmony within the profession"?

Three of the six states (Georgia, Minnesota, and Wyoming) with qualifying language also gave detailed examples of what constitutes a false, fraudulent, misleading, deceptive, or unfair statement or claim in violation of the advertising and solicitation rule. Georgia's Rule 20-12-.15 in its *Code of Professional Conduct* (pp. 50-51) is a good example of the kind of guidance that is helpful in determining the ethical obligations of a CPA who undertakes to advertise or solicit potential clients. Item (f) notwithstanding, the eight examples appear to be consistent with the FTC order and Supreme Court rulings. The Rule in its entirety is as follows:

20-12-.15 Advertising and Solicitation

(1) A licensee shall not use or participate in the use of any form of public communication having reference to his professional services which contains a false, fraudulent, misleading, deceptive or unfair statement

or claim. A false, fraudulent, misleading, deceptive or unfair statement or claim includes but is not limited to a statement or claim which:

(a) Contains a misrepresentation of fact; or
(b) Is likely to mislead or deceive because it fails to make full disclosure of relevant facts; or
(c) Contains any testimonial or laudatory statement, or other statement or implication that the licensee's professional services are of exceptional quality if not supported by verifiable facts; or
(d) Is intended or likely to create false or unjustified expectations of favorable results; or
(e) Implies educational or professional attainments or licensing recognition not supported in fact; or
(f) States or implies that the licensee has received formal recognition as a specialist in any aspect of the practice of public accounting, except in accordance with rules adopted by the Board; or
(g) Represents that professional services can or will be competently performed for a stated fee when this is not the case, or makes representations with respect to fees for professional services that do not disclose all variables affecting the fees that will in fact be charged; or
(h) Contains other representations or implications that in reasonable probability will cause an ordinarily prudent person to misunderstand or be deceived.

(2) A licensee shall not by any communication use coercion, duress, compulsion, intimidation, threats, overreaching, or vexatious or harassing conduct in the course of offering, soliciting, or advertising to perform an engagement.

New York and Utah provide the most specific solicitation guidelines in their state codes. The New York State Education Department rules (pp. 47-48) first detail the advertising and direct solicitation techniques not in the public interest, including false, fraudulent, deceptive, or misleading practices and those that intimidate or pressure the client. Second, the rules define what is deemed an appropriate means of informing the public of the availability of professional services, focusing primarily on the prices established for such services. Third, requirements are given for the maintenance of copies of advertisements. Last, prohibited activities are described including media "push" money and advertised portrayals of professional practice.

The Utah Committee for Public Accountancy rules (pp. 4-5) provide descriptive examples of information and objective advertising that is permitted under the rules. For example, advertising of services offered, fees charged, educational and professional attainments, and statements of policy or position that address a subject of public interest are all considered to be appropriate information to be included in an advertisement. The rules also describe false, misleading, or deceptive advertising or other forms of solicitation including testimonials or endorsements and self-laudatory statements that are not based on verifiable facts.

AICPA Update

Subsequent to the Supreme Court decision in *Edenfield*, the AICPA State Legislation Department conducted a survey of state laws and regulations on the use of advertisements and solicitation by CPAs. We requested a copy of the July 20, 1993, summary in order to update our 1992 analysis of state rules. According to the report, four states (Idaho, Minnesota, Mississippi, and Ohio) that had prohibited direct uninvited solicitation now permit it. The AICPA also provided information on the rules in four additional jurisdictions—the District of Columbia and Guam, both of which have rules consistent with the consent order; Puerto Rico, which prohibits advertising or promotion of services in any publication and prohibits solicitation; and the Virgin Islands, which has no provisions on either advertising or solicitation, which, therefore, does not prohibit such practices.

Changes Since AICPA Update

We decided to communicate directly with the other seven jurisdictions (including Puerto Rico) that prohibit uninvited solicitation to determine whether any of them anticipated eliminating their state's prohibition in light of the *Edenfield* ruling. A letter was sent to the executive director of each of the jurisdictions requesting a copy of any position statement that described the Board's intent. State boards that did not respond to the request were telephoned and information was sought directly from the executive director. As a result of this procedure, it was determined that three additional states—New Mexico, Massachusetts, and Texas—deleted the prohibition of uninvited solicitation from their rules. One state, Louisiana, sent a position statement announcing that the Board will cease enforcement of its rule "categorically banning direct, uninvited telephone or personal solicitation of client engagements." The Louisiana Board plans to amend its rules to delete the prohibition. Another state, Michigan, indicated that it had decided to cease enforcement and would amend its rules. Florida amended its solicitation rule on September 23, 1993, to conform with the Supreme Court ruling. Therefore, only Puerto Rico still prohibits direct uninvited solicitation.[2]

As part of the update, it was determined that one state that had prohibited testimonials or endorsements—New Mexico—now permits it. Therefore, only nine states still prohibit such practices without having the qualifying language previously referred to in the paper.[3]

All of the 10 states that prohibited direct uninvited solicitation, as determined in the 1992 survey by the authors, now permit it or have proposed rule changes that would permit solicitation. However, only the new rule in Texas provides any guidance to CPAs about what is or is not an acceptable solicitation practice. The rule in Texas prohibits the solicitation of an engagement or any other form of communication about professional services which is accompanied by coercion, duress, compulsion, intimidation, threats, or overreaching, or vexatious or harassing conduct.

The new rule in Texas also establishes a mechanism whereby the Texas State Board of Public Accountancy can determine whether a relationship exists between substandard services performed by a CPA who was investigated for an ethics violation and unprofessional advertising practices of that CPA. Specifically, the rule requires certificate or registration holders to retain a copy of the actual mailing used in a direct mail communication, along with a list of the persons who received the communication, for at least 36 months from the date of the last transmission or use. A similar requirement exists for radio and television broadcast communication. This is an important and forward-looking provision because it enables the Board to review a particular CPA's advertising practices after a complaint has been filed against the CPA. Obviously, it would not be practical for the State Board to review the advertising practices of all licensed CPAs. However, it is feasible for the Board to review the practices of those CPAs who have allegedly violated the rules. Thus, the Board can better protect the public's interest in having truthful and nondeceptive advertising.

LEGAL CONSIDERATIONS

The state action doctrine provides immunity from state court challenge of actions by a state regulatory board if it can be shown that the board acted according to a clearly articulated policy to displace competition. For example, if state board rules prohibiting direct uninvited solicitation were also incorporated into the state's statutes, then challenges to the rules could only be made on constitutional grounds. This was the situation in Florida when, in 1991, the U.S. Eleventh Circuit Court of Appeals ruled in *Fane v. Edenfield* that a Florida statute prohibiting CPAs from engaging in in-person solicitation was an impermissible restriction of commercial speech in violation of the First Amendment; the ruling stated that the statute was not tailored narrowly enough to directly advance the state's asserted interest in protecting a CPA's integrity, independence, and objectivity while performing the attest function. Thus, the Court reasoned that (1993, 1518):

> Even if there were evidence before us to indicate that allowing CPAs who perform audit and review [attest] engagements to solicit in-person would undermine the integrity of financial statements, that still would not justify the total prohibition of in-person solicitation by all CPAs.

Edenfield v. Fane

The Supreme Court opinion in *Edenfield v. Fane* (1993, 1594) provides some insight into the legal defensibility of prohibitions of direct uninvited solicitation and what guidance can be provided to state boards of accountancy in their regulatory role. The opinion recognizes the potential value of solicitation because it enables the buyer to meet and evaluate the person offering the product or service, and it allows both the buyer and the seller to discuss and negotiate the desired form for the transaction or professional relationship. Ironically, these benefits also provide the opportunity for overreaching conduct, a practice that can be restricted according to the Court.

The Court's ruling clearly states that targeted prohibitions of fraudulent or deceptive practices or solicitation that intimidates or harasses the recipient are constitutionally supportable. Beyond that, little guidance is provided about which practices might be appropriately banned by a state.

Fane's challenge to the Florida Department of Professional Regulation statute prohibiting direct uninvited solicitation by necessity also encompassed the State Board of Accountancy's rule because, while prohibiting personal solicitation, the statute does make an exception for "constitutionally protected speech as determined by the rules of the

Board" (Florida 1993, 21). As previously mentioned, the Florida Board did drop its ban on uninvited solicitation in light of the Supreme Court ruling in *Edenfield.*

One aspect of the challenge to the Florida statute was Fane's contention that it violated the equal protection provision of the constitution in that the state's prohibition of in-person solicitation by CPAs does not apply to non-CPA financial professionals who are not prohibited from utilizing personal contacts to solicit new clients. The Supreme Court did not rule directly on this issue, yet it has important implications for the scope of a CPAs services with regard to whether the AICPA should consider a separate solicitation rule when soliciting attest services for a potential client and a more liberal rule when soliciting nonattest services, similar to current rules on contingent fees and commissions.

The Supreme Court in *Edenfield* was not as generous as the Florida Court of Appeals in its interpretation of whether a ban on direct uninvited solicitation of attest clients might withstand a constitutional challenge. The Florida Board of Accountancy argued that "solicitation compromises the independence necessary to perform the audit and attest functions, because a CPA who needs business enough to solicit clients will be prone to ethical lapses." The Board claimed that "the public perception of CPA independence will be undermined if CPAs behave like ordinary commercial actors," even if actual misconduct does not occur. The Supreme Court acknowledged the state's substantial interest in maintaining CPA independence and ensuring against conflicts of interest. However, it stated that the Board failed to demonstrate that the blanket "ban on CPA solicitation advances its asserted interests in any direct and material way." In reaching this conclusion, the Court emphasized that the Board failed to provide any evidence to support its contention.

The Board attempted to use the aforementioned AICPA report on CPA solicitation as support for its position. However, as the Supreme Court correctly noted the findings of the Special Committee on Solicitation contradict the Board's position. Moreover, the statement that a CPA who solicits clients is more prone to ethical lapses totally ignores the fact that today most CPAs solicit potential clients in some form or another. The critical issue is one of perception. The requirement of independence precludes relationships that may appear to impair a member's objectivity in rendering attest services.

The AICPA report on solicitation that was issued in 1981 failed to identify any specific instances of actual impairment of independence. However, the report did not attempt to determine whether the *public perception* might be that, when a CPA engages in direct uninvited solicitation of potential clients for whom attest services will be performed, the appearance of objectivity is lacking and, therefore, there exists a lack of independence.

The only relevant questions in the solicitation report were asked of CPAs and not the public. CPAs were asked (AICPA 1981, 4) whether they agreed or disagreed with the proposition that there would be an impairment of independence because CPAs do not maintain their independence in mental attitude toward those clients subjected to direct uninvited solicitation by another CPA. The survey disclosed that 11% were in "total agreement" with the proposition that impairment occurred, whereas 34% were in "total disagreement." Not only were the wrong people asked to respond, but the question does not even address the perception issue or why there might be an impairment of independence. That is, given the competitive environment for professional services, the CPA might be soliciting a client who desperately wants to find a CPA who will provide a favorable opinion on the client's financial statements. Thus, there is an incentive for dishonest CPAs to solicit clients by promising to overlook financial misstatements or by promising to render a favorable opinion. The lack of evidence in 1981 that such practices had occurred is as much a reflection of the fact that there is no practical way to verify such an assertion as it is a reflection of the fact that the survey did not cover a long enough period of time after the AICPA lifted its bans on competitive bidding and encroachment.

Other Rulings

Supreme Court opinions in cases involving lawyers provide additional insight into the Court's point of view about various solicitation practices. The Court ruled in *Ohralik v. Ohio Bar Association* (1978, 1912) that a State Bar rule preventing lawyer solicitation of clients was justified only in situations "inherently conducive to overreaching and other forms of misconduct," which were found to exist in this case. Ohralik solicited business from two young accident victims, approaching one while she lay in traction in a hospital bed. He employed a concealed tape recorder to assist him in his solicitation efforts and emphasized the contingent nature of his fee to make his offer appear cost-free and irresistible. In addition, he refused to withdraw even when requested to do so by his client and he misrepresented himself to the insurance company. The Supreme Court opinion in *Edenfield* references the *Ohralik* ruling, stating, "Unlike a lawyer, a CPA is not a 'professional trained in the art of persuasion.' A CPA's training emphasizes independence and objectivity, not advocacy." The Court noted that Fane's prospective clients are sophisticated and experienced business executives with knowledge and understanding of a CPA's services.

The Court's statement that a CPA is not trained to be persuasive ignores the fact that, if a client's accounting procedures are not consistent with acceptable standards, the accountant is then obligated to try to persuade the client to follow generally accepted accounting principles and should not allow his or her judgment to be subordinated to the client's will. One can only wonder whether, based on the Court's opinion in *Ohralik*, a state board of accountancy could successfully defend a prohibition of direct uninvited solicitation of clients if it could demonstrate that the CPA's solicitation reflected a degree of persuasion inconsistent with "rational and considered decision making by the prospective client," somewhat like the "uninformed acquiescence" to which the accident victims in *Ohralik* were prone.

Contrary to the Court's support of the solicitation practice in *Edenfield*, its ruling in *Ohralik* emphasizes the potential dangers of face-to-face solicitation. Comparing this practice to general advertising, the Court stated that (1919), "Unlike a public advertisement, which simply provides information and leaves the recipient free to act upon it or not, in-person solicitation may exert pressure and often demands an immediate response, without providing an opportunity for comparison or reflection." Perhaps the Supreme Court was not particularly concerned about this possibility in *Edenfield* because of its belief that CPAs are fair-minded and will act more professionally than a lawyer when engaged in an uninvited solicitation.

Two additional Supreme Court rulings further differentiate acceptable lawyer solicitation practices. The Court's opinion in *Zauderer v. Office of Disciplinary Counsel of the Supreme Court of Ohio* (1985, 2265) clearly indicates its position that printed advertisements generally pose less of a risk of overreaching conduct and undue influence. According to the opinion, a printed advertisement "may convey information and ideas more or less effectively, but in most cases it will lack the coercive force of the personal presence of a trained advocate" (2277). The Court's opinion in *Shapero v. Kentucky Bar Association* (1988, 1916) is consistent with its ruling in *Zauderer*. The Court ruled in *Shapero* that the potential for undue influence is significantly less in a targeted direct-mail solicitation when compared with in-person solicitation. The Court reasoned that, "the recipient of such advertising is not faced with the coercive presence of a trained advocate or the pressure for an immediate yes-or-no answer to the representation offer but can simply put the letter aside to be considered later, ignored, or discarded" (1918).

An important aspect of the Court's opinion in *Zauderer* is its recognition that disclosure requirements may be added to rules of conduct that prohibit false, fraudulent, or misleading advertising and solicitation or coercive solicitation practices, so long as the "disclosure requirements are reasonably related to the State's interest in preventing deception of consumers" (2282). The Court emphasized that because disclosure requirements more narrowly affect an advertiser's interests than do flat prohibitions on speech, its prior decisions in commercial speech cases recognize that, "warning[s] or disclaimer[s] might be appropriately required ... in order to dissipate the possibility of consumer confusion or deception" (2282).

Supreme Court Guidance

The following generalizations can be made in light of the Supreme Court rulings in *Edenfield, Ohralik, Zauderer*, and *Shapero*.

1. State boards of accountancy must tailor their prohibition of advertising and direct solicitation narrowly enough to serve their asserted interests. Prohibitions of fraudulent and deceptive practices and coercive solicitation consistently have been held to be constitutionally supportable.
2. In-person solicitation is fraught with the opportunity for undue influence, pressure, and intimidation of potential clients. However, it is difficult to justify a blanket ban on this practice because, unlike a targeted mail solicitation, there is no documentation of the details of the face-to-face encounter.

3. Absent any documentary evidence or survey results to support a ban on direct uninvited solicitation of clients for whom audit or other attest-related services are to be performed, the Supreme Court is not likely to uphold a targeted ban based on the type of services performed by a CPA.
4. State board rules can encompass disclosure requirements that serve a state's asserted interests in regulating advertising and solicitation practices. However, such requirements should be specific and should not be broader than is required to serve the state's asserted interests.

FUTURE ISSUES AND RECOMMENDATIONS

Increasing competition for professional accounting and auditing services has created an environment in which CPAs now think of themselves as both business people and trained professionals. Although the use of marketing techniques by CPAs is increasing and many CPAs serve clients in two or more states, a lack of uniformity exists as to what CPAs in various states may or may not do with regard to advertising practices such as testimonials and other laudatory statements. While all states now permit CPAs to solicit potential clients so long as their practices are not false, fraudulent, misleading, deceptive, or conducted with coercion or overreaching conduct, very few states provide any guidelines for the ethical obligations of CPAs when soliciting new business from potential clients. The rules of conduct in nine states currently contain unqualified prohibitions of testimonials or endorsements. That is, the rules do not tie the prohibition to statements that are made that lack objectivity and verifiability and, therefore, may potentially mislead the solicited client. More states need to provide the kind of guidance that Georgia does in its rules. The public interest is best served when CPAs are given clear guidance as to what is and is not an acceptable advertising or solicitation practice.

Even though no states currently prohibit direct uninvited solicitation, an important issue that has not been addressed by the profession is whether a ban on solicitation of potential clients for whom audit or other attest-related services are to be performed might withstand a constitutional challenge. Such a limited ban would be consistent with the AICPA's current rules that prohibit a CPA from accepting contingent fees or commissions from attest clients but permit CPAs to accept contingent fees and disclosed commissions from nonattest clients. Such a limited ban would serve the public interest if it can be demonstrated that the perception of the public is that there is an impairment of independence when a CPA engages in a direct uninvited solicitation of clients for whom attest services will be performed.

Survey the Public

The Supreme Court relied heavily on the AICPA's solicitation report in its opinion in *Edenfield*, stating that no evidence existed of a lack of independence when a CPA performs attest services for a client who was directly solicited on an uninvited basis. Therefore, short of an actual situation occurring in the future where an impairment of independence can be demonstrated, the Court is not likely to support a state board prohibition of direct uninvited solicitation unless evidence can be provided to counteract the findings of the 1981 report.

The profession itself is at fault on this matter because it has not attempted to determine whether the public perception is that objectivity may be lacking when a CPA performs attest services for a solicited client and, therefore, independence is impaired.[4] Future research is needed to assess the opinions of the various publics served by the CPA on this matter. In particular, the investing public, institutional investors, and creditors should be surveyed because these are the groups that rely on the independence of the auditor in rendering an opinion on the fairness of the client's financial statements.

Emphasize Professionalism

Virtually all state rules on advertising and solicitation are written from the perspective of "thou shalt not," rather than providing helpful information to the public. What is needed now is to concentrate more on what we want to accomplish through advertising and solicitation and less on what we must prevent. A positive ethics approach accomplishes that by incorporating both compliance with formal standards and the promotion of individual ethical responsibility.

The first recommendation is that the accounting profession, through the AICPA and in cooperation with individual states, take a united stand and make a positive statement of how a CPA can maintain professionalism while obtaining new clients and promoting new services. Unlike the approach of a rule to be enforced, this position would reflect the spirit of the 1988 revision of the AICPA Code toward a set of principles that are goal-oriented and aspirational. One idea would be a revision of the current AICPA Code in the form of an addendum to Article II—The Public Interest. Language could be incorporated that emphasized a CPA's responsibility to market professional services in a form and content that reflects a level of professionalism consistent with the Principles of the Code. An extension of such a statement is that advertising and solicitation activities should be conducted with the highest sense of integrity. Rules that prohibit false, misleading, deceptive, coercive, or harassing conduct and rules that prohibit statements that are not supported by verifiable facts are clearly consistent with the intent of these principles. Separate rules prohibiting practices such as testimonials or endorsements are not needed because it would be a violation of the existing rule to advertise or solicit in a manner that is false, misleading, or deceptive or if the communication is not supported by verifiable facts.

Another recommendation is that educational seminars should be offered on the use of marketing techniques that not only enhance business opportunities but also encourage adherence to ethical responsibilities. These seminars should help dissipate some of the feelings that "marketing has harmed the accounting industry" which seem to be present in the current literature. Advertising and solicitation practices are here to stay. State CPA societies in particular should educate their members as to what constitutes acceptable, professional practice.

Future Research

As previously mentioned, the Texas State Board of Public Accountancy recently adopted a new advertising and solicitation rule that requires licensed CPAs in Texas to retain records of direct mail communication and copies of broadcast communication for 36 months from the date of the last transmission or use. It is recommended that other state boards should adopt similar requirements. The purpose would be to enable a state board to determine whether a particular CPA who has been found to have violated a rule of conduct such as independence, integrity, and objectivity or due care in the performance of professional services, also advertises in a unprofessional manner. Realistically, a state board probably would not review the retained information unless a complaint was filed against a particular CPA for improper advertising or solicitation practices. However, the existence of such information provides an opportunity for accounting educators to do research on the correlation between a particular CPA violating the aforementioned rules and questionable advertising practices. Accounting educators could approach their state board of accountancy and propose such a cooperative effort between the academic and professional communities.

Suggestions for the Practicing CPA

Since it is difficult to determine when and even if there will be an organized effort at the national level to unify AICPA and State Board rules on advertising and provide better guidance to CPAs when soliciting potential clients, the following advice is offered to the practicing CPA. First, be familiar with the state rules and any differences that might exist between them and the AICPA's rules. Violating a state's rules subjects the practitioner to disciplinary action including reprimand, censure, probation, scope of practice limitations, and the imposition of fines and administrative costs. For the most serious violations, the CPA's license to practice may be suspended or revoked. Second, seek advice before advertising or making a solicitation that might be in violation of the rules. An individual CPA's ethical responsibility includes the consideration of the possible consequences of an action prior to taking it. State boards typically will respond to inquiries about the acceptability of specific practices. Staff members sometimes take issues to committees or to the full board for discussion and resolution before providing a response. Finally, state CPA societies should consider developing continuing education courses that focus on the ethical responsibilities of CPAs. Such courses could be used as a mechanism to discuss with practicing CPAs the rules of the state board of accountancy, as well as those of the AICPA and state CPA societies. This could help to sensitize CPAs to the differences that exist in advertising and solicitation rules as well as in other areas of practice, such as commissions, and what are the ethical expectations for CPAs when the rules differ.

Suggestions for the AICPA

The AICPA should form a committee to study the public's perception of the objectivity and independence of CPAs who solicit attest clients and clients for whom nonattest services are to be performed. Almost 15 years have gone by since the 1981 solicitation study was completed by the Institute. During that time, the scope of a CPA's services has dramatically expanded and the environment has become increasingly more competitive. Over the years, allegations have been made that some CPAs underbid to obtain audit clients and use attest services as a "loss leader" to obtain more lucrative consulting services. Opinion shopping is alleged to be an all-too-common practice. In this kind of environment, the likelihood exists that a CPA might be tempted to "give in" to the client's demand for a favorable opinion. The public's perception might be that independence is impaired when a CPA solicits a client on an uninvited basis in much the same way that a CPA who bids at or below cost to obtain an audit client could have an "appearance" problem. In both instances, the public perception may be that audit quality is lessened.

CONCLUSION

Both the FTC consent order and the Supreme Court's rulings reflect a belief that the public has a right to a free flow of commercial information. An analysis of the Court's opinions indicates that only narrowly tailored prohibitions of advertising and solicitation can withstand a constitutional challenge. In the past, rules that prohibit fraudulent and deceptive practices and those that proscribe coercive or intimidating behavior have been upheld by the Court because they further the state's interest in protecting the public.

Questions persist about the professionalism of CPAs who engage in advertising and solicitation practices. Guidance should be provided by the accounting profession to emphasize the positive aspects of a CPA's ethical responsibility when advertising and soliciting potential clients. In order to protect the public interest, research is needed to determine the public's perception of a CPA's objectivity and independence in performing the attest function for solicited clients and whether that perception is any different for those CPAs who solicit clients to perform nonattest services.

NOTES

1. The 16 states include: Arkansas, Florida, Hawaii, Idaho, Louisiana, Massachusetts, Michigan, Minnesota, Mississippi, New Hampshire, New Jersey, New Mexico, New York, Ohio, Texas, and Utah.
2. Repeated efforts to get the Puerto Rico State Board of Public Accountancy to send information have been unsuccessful. We assume that Puerto Rico eventually will drop its ban on uninvited solicitation, as did the 10 states that prohibited the practice as of June 1992.
3. The nine states include: Arkansas, Hawaii, Idaho, Louisiana, Mississippi, New Hamphsire, New Jersey, New York, and Utah.
4. In 1986, Louis Harris and Associates, Inc., conducted a comprehensive survey of the public's perception of the ethical standards of CPAs. The survey covered 1,200 members of the general public, which included 681 members of the public who claimed to be knowledgeable about accountants and accounting and 550 people who owned common stock and equities. The survey covered 104 different probe areas, including the background and qualifications of CPAs, the role of the government in regulating the profession, the public perception of CPA independence and objectivity in performing professional services, and the role of CPAs in performing non-audit services. Several questions addressed the issue of whether CPAs should be allowed to receive commissions and contingent fees from audit clients and non-audit clients. However, not one question asked whether CPAs should be allowed to solicit audit and non-audit clients on an uninvited basis or what was the public perception of a CPA's objectivity and independence when soliciting clients for whom attest and nonattest services are to be performed.

REFERENCES

American Institute of Certified Public Accountants (AICPA). 1981. *Report of the Special Committee on Solicitation.* New York: AICPA.

________. 1988. *Code of Professional Conduct, as amended January 12, 1988.* New York: AICPA.

________, State Legislation Department. 1993. *Summary of U.S. Supreme Court Opinion: Edenfield et al v. Fane.* New York: AICPA.

________. 1994. *Code of Professional Conduct as amended January 14, 1992.* New York: AICPA.

Florida, Department of Professional Regulation. 1993 (May). *Law and Rules of Florida Board of Accountancy.*
The University of the State of New York State Education Department. 1989 (May). *Public Accountancy Handbook.*
Division of Occupational and Professional Licensing, Department of Business Regulation. 1988 (January). *Utah Rules of the Committee for Public Accountancy.*
Edenfield v. *Fane,* Supreme Court of the United States, No. 91-1594, April 26, 1993.
Fane v. *Edenfield,* 945 F. 2d 1514, 1516 (11th Cir. 1991).
Federal Trade Commission, Docket No. C. 3297, July 26, 1990.
Georgia State Board of Accountancy. 1992 (July). *Rules and Regulations.*
Ohralik v. *Ohio State Bar Association,* 98 S. Ct.1912 (1978).
Previts, G.J. 1985. *The Scope of CPA Services.* New York: Wiley.
Read, W.R., and S. Tomczyk. 1992. An examination of changes in scope of services performed by CPA firms. *Accounting Horizons* (September): 42-51.
Shapero v. *Kentucky Bar Association,* 104 S. Ct. 1916 (1988).
United States v. *Arthur Young & Company et. al.,* 104 S. Ct. 1495 (1988).
Zauderer v. *Office of Disciplinary of the Supreme Court of Ohio,* 105 S. Ct. 2265 (1985).

INTEGRATING ETHICS INTO INTERMEDIATE ACCOUNTING:

AN EXPERIMENTAL INVESTIGATION INCORPORATING ATTRIBUTION THEORY

Sara York Kenny and Martha M. Eining

ABSTRACT

Integrating ethical awareness and reasoning components into undergraduate accounting education curricula has been advocated by various groups, individuals, and organizations for decades (Accounting Education Change Commission 1990; American Accounting Association 1986; Loeb 1988; Ponemon 1993; National Commission 1987). Despite the fact that ethics is an appropriate topic for financial accounting (Scribner and Dillaway 1989; Mintz 1990), many accounting curriculums tend to relegate discussions of ethics and ethical dilemmas to a separate ethics course or within the specific segments of the auditing course (Cohen and Pant 1989).

Research on Accounting Ethics, Volume 2, pages 159-186.

ISBN: 1-55938-997-4

The purpose of this study is to investigate the effectiveness of different methods of integrating ethics into intermediate financial accounting. The characteristics of the tasks performed by the financial accountant differ from those performed by the auditor and can be explained and studied using the perspective of attribution theory. Attribution theory suggests that individuals behave differently when they are the actors as opposed to the observers in ethical situations. Based on the characteristics of the tasks, the financial accountant can be considered an actor, while the auditor performs the role of an observer. This actor-observer effect may well limit the effectiveness of auditing-based ethics pedagogies when used in intermediate financial accounting courses.

In the current study, we conduct two separate experiments. In the first experiment, we document the actor-observer effect for intermediate accounting students. In the second experiment, we document the relative ineffectiveness of several traditional auditing pedagogies for integrating ethics when used in financial accounting.

The results of the two experiments have important ramifications for the successful integration of ethical awareness exercises into intermediate accounting classes. Recognizing the existence of the actor-observer effect suggests that pedagogies for integrating ethical awareness exercises must take into account the students' tendencies to apply differential standards in different situations. Accordingly, we suggest that successful pedagogies will focus on analysis of long-term consequences to a wide range of participants in financial accounting and reporting situations. Suggested pedagogies are discussed in the paper.

INTRODUCTION

Integrating ethical awareness and reasoning components into undergraduate accounting education curriculums has been advocated by various groups, individuals, and organizations for decades. Most recently, the Accounting Education Change Commission (1990, Appendix B-2) suggested that accounting students should be taught to "identify ethical issues and apply a value-based reasoning system to ethical questions." Further, both the Treadway Commission (National Commission 1987) and the Bedford Committee (AAA 1986) recommended integration of ethics into most accounting courses. Although Mintz (1990) and Scribner and Dillaway (1989) suggest that ethics is an appropriate topic in financial accounting, studies indicate a paucity of coverage in these classes (Cohen and Pant 1989). McNair and Milam (1993) report an increased coverage of ethics but indicate that many accounting curriculums still tend to relegate discussions of ethics and ethical dilemmas to a separate ethics course or to the module in the auditing course which discusses the AICPA Code of Ethics.

The approach of teaching ethics in isolation appears to have limited affect on the moral development of accounting students as measured by the Defining Issues Test (DIT) (Shaub 1991; St. Pierre et al. 1990). Weber (1990), reviewing prior research, reports that, while ethical awareness and reasoning skills tend to improve after taking an ethics course, the effects appear to be short term. Within a time as short as one semester, students' ethical awareness and reasoning skills seem to revert back to their pre-ethics course level.[1] In addition, the limited study of the integration of ethics into accounting has typically concentrated on the auditing course (Poneman 1992; Hiltebeitel and Jones 1991). Poneman (1993) suggests that the integration of ethics into accounting may require specific kinds of programs or instructions. Loeb (1991) has also argued for the need to assess the outcomes from teaching ethics in accounting courses. The current study seeks to explore some specific programs for introducing ethics into financial accounting courses.

For the current research, we conducted two different experiments to (1) assess attribution models as they relate to teaching financial accounting, and (2) assess the relative effectiveness of two traditional pedagogies commonly used to integrate ethics into accounting courses. We document the presence of the actor-observer effect noted in attribution theory for students in intermediate financial accounting. The pedagogies that have been used effectively in auditing courses were not effective in the intermediate financial accounting course. We argue that the presence of the actor-observer effect explains the ineffectiveness of these traditional pedagogies.

The results of the two experiments have important ramifications for the successful integration of ethical awareness exercises into intermediate accounting classes. Recognizing the existence of the actor-observer effect suggests that pedagogies for integrating ethical awareness exercises must take into account the students' tendencies to apply differential standards in different situations. Accordingly, we suggest that successful pedagogies will focus on analysis of long-term consequences to a wide range of participants in financial accounting and reporting situations.

ATTRIBUTION THEORY AND HYPOTHESIS DEVELOPMENT

Attribution Theory

Attribution theory posits that individuals employ logical models to assess, analyze, and interpret their relationships within a social context (Heider 1958; Kelley 1967). Within the context of these various models, individuals also make judgments regarding their behavior and the behavior of others (Heider 1958; Kelley 1967; O'Connor 1988; Weiner 1990). Although the models tend to be logical and fairly consistent, they are also biased (Jones and Nisbett 1972). A common bias is the actor-observer effect, which describes the divergent tendencies between the actor (the protagonist) and the observer (the person observing the behavior of the actor) (Jones and Nisbett 1972). Although the research involving actor-observer effects indicates that the effect may be context-specific, the basic finding is that actors tend to be more lenient in judgment of their own actions than in the evaluation of the actions of others (Jones and Nisbett 1972; Watson 1982). The closer the circle of influence (such as self or in-group), the more likely the individual is to employ a situational attribution model (Jones and Nisbett 1972; O'Connor 1988). Further, the closer the circle of influence, the more likely individuals are to seek information which confirms their original judgment or opinion concerning the behavior of the actor (Snyder and White 1981).

The actor-observer effect has been well documented in a variety of contexts, including clinical psychology (Wilkins et al. 1990; Bernard et al. 1987; Bernard and Jara 1986), altruistic situations (Schlenker et al. 1983), and general conversational behavior (O'Connor 1988). In accounting research, attribution models have been applied in cost accounting situations (Shields et al. 1981; Harrison et al. 1988) and auditing contexts (Arrington et al. 1985). Consistent with extant research in other areas of social science, accountants tend to apply different attributional models to themselves than to people outside themselves (i.e., the actor-observer effect has been noted).

Attribution Theory Applied in Financial Accounting and Auditing Tasks

Although actor-observer effects have been noted in a variety of disciplines, the strength of the effect and the magnitude of its occurrence seems to be, at least in part, a function of the context (O'Connor 1988). Actors, when attributing their own behavior, are naturally more aware of the complexities of the schema surrounding them and their actions at the time, and, thus, their evaluations and attributions are more situational-based than the evaluations and attributions of a distant observer.

Applying this reasoning in ethical dilemma scenarios, research finds that individuals tend to hold themselves to a lower standard than they apply to others in the same scenario (Wilkins et al. 1990; Bernard and Jara 1986). While they may understand what they *should* do in a particular situation, individuals often respond that they *would* do something else (Wilkins et al. 1990).

Consistent with the basic assumptions of attribution theory, we believe that the very nature of financial accounting and auditing tasks are fundamentally different and lead students to relate to them differentially. In addition, the reasoning process employed in financial accounting tasks is different than that in auditing. The major differences are summarized in Table 1. In auditing, the auditor is viewing transactions after the fact and is evaluating someone else's work. The auditor has the advantage of hindsight and the critical advantage of reviewing, rather than recording, the transaction. Contrast the audit process to the financial accounting process. The financial accountant is recording the transaction as it occurs and in conjunction with many other transactions. He or she does not have the advantage of hindsight, nor is he or she reviewing what someone else has already done. Rather, the accountant is directly involved at the start of the process. In addition, the auditor's main focus is on the aggregated balance of an account, which allows him or her to consider the overall impact. The financial accountant concentrates on each individual transaction and may not focus on the combined impact of a number of transactions.

Stated in terms of attribution theory and actor-observer effects, auditing tasks require actors to observe and judge the actions of someone else. Usually the relationship is not close, which in an

Table 1. Comparison of Auditing and Financial Accounting

	Auditing	*Financial Accounting*
Description of task	Review work of others	Record transactions
Involvement in task	Review work of different company	Record transactions from own company
Timing of task	Examine past transactions	Record current transactions
Level of aggregation	Focus on account balances	Focus on individual transactions

actor-observer context implies that the auditor is likely to hold the person being audited to a higher (ethical) standard that he or she would hold him or herself. Accordingly, the approaches to introducing ethics in an auditing class, which require the student to critically evaluate the recording of the transaction well after the fact and with a global perspective, are entirely consistent with promulgating the natural distance documented in actor-observe attribution theory research.

Financial accounting, on the other hand, requires students to make a quick decision based upon limited transaction-specific information. Financial accounting transactions are recorded by the actor and, in the case of financial accounting courses, are also evaluated by the actor. Further, the financial accountant makes a number of transactions while the auditor reviews the account balance arising from many entries. The financial accountant in this situation may view each transaction as less important than the auditor will view the account balance. In addition, the financial accountant performs a task for his or her own company while the auditor reviews the financial records of another company. Thus, consistent with attribution theory, one would expect students to be more generous with their evaluations of their own behavior. Accordingly, approaches to integrating ethics into financial accounting classes, which require students to critically evaluate their own behavior, are unlikely to solicit radical behavior changes because students *cannot* hold themselves to as high a standard as they would an unknown or distant person. Thus, we hypothesize:

Hypothesis 1. Students will apply higher standards of ethical behavior to others than they apply to themselves.

Strategies for Integrating Ethics into Curricula

Arlow and Ulrich (1983, 1985, 1988) noted that accounting students began the term with higher ethical awareness and reasoning skills than students in other majors. Their explanation was that accounting students were exposed to ethics in several other courses in their curriculum. However, Arlow and Ulrich (1983, 1985, 1988) also noted that accounting students' ethical awareness and reasoning skills did not significantly improve during the ethics course, suggesting that accounting students gained little in the ethics course which was not already well addressed in other accounting courses. Furthermore, since the post-test four years later revealed that the subjects tended to revert to their pre-ethics course level of ethical awareness and reasoning, this means the accounting students tended to retain whatever ethical awareness and reasoning skills they had gained in their accounting curriculum. Thus, we hypothesize:

Hypothesis 2. Ethical awareness and reasoning skills taught in the course of accounting curriculums tend to be retained.

To assess the degree to which ethics was introduced and covered in accounting curricula during the time frame of the Arlow and Ulrich studies (the 1980s), we reviewed a broad range of accounting textbooks from the era. Ethics was discussed in several auditing texts, in terms of the AICPA Code of Ethics and the ethics portion of the CPA exam. We found virtually no mention of ethics in elementary, financial, managerial, tax, or information systems texts. Our review leads us to believe that the integration of ethics touted by Arlow and Ulrich occurred primarily in the auditing course. Given the placement of the ethics course in typical undergraduate curriculums, the students entering the ethics courses in Arlow and Ulrich's studies may have also been taking or have just completed their auditing course. Accordingly, students may have perceived an emphasis on ethics by virtue of the fact that they experienced ethics topics in two courses over a relatively short time. That being the case, we hypothesize that if students are inundated with ethics throughout their accounting curriculum, they will perceive its importance and will develop stronger ethical awareness and reasoning skills:

Hypothesis 3. The more exposure students receive to ethical awareness and reasoning exercises, the more likely students are to retain over longer periods of time the knowledge and skills gained in those areas.

While the Arlow and Ulrich studies indicate that integration of ethics into the accounting curriculum seems to be "successful," we find little discussion of the method of integration and/or the relative success of various methods of integrating ethics. In addition, the AECC, the Treadway Commission, and the Bedford Committee all discuss the importance of the integration of ethics into the curriculum. However, no specific means of doing so is specified. Thus, the operationalization of "integration of ethics" has not been well described. Burton et al. (1991) describe two basic methods of introducing ethics into other disciplines: (1) a business scenario open discussion system in which students discuss the ethical implications inherent in several business scenarios or (2) a philosophical lecture regarding ethical philosophies and moral reasoning. Their study indicates that how ethics is introduced in other disciplines does have an effect on students' perceptions, but they draw few conclusions about the relative effectiveness of either approach.

The research design employed in this study allowed us to test the relative effectiveness of at least two different approaches to integrating ethics. First, we considered the operationalization of the term "integration" with respect to ethics in financial accounting curriculum and the ethics content or coverage a course needed to include in order to be considered "integrated." Second, our experience with ethical dilemmas led us to believe that most of the ethical dilemmas that get accountants into trouble are subtle and fall into the "gray" areas where GAAP is not descriptive. This reasoning led us to question how well students could identify ethical dilemmas and if their recognition skills would increase if we gently introduced them to ethics situations. Thus, our goal was to assess the means by which we could teach students how to recognize subtle ethics questions as opposed to the philosophies inherent in either of Burton's et al. (1991) work. Given this prior research, we hypothesize:

Hypothesis 4. The more subtle the introduction of ethics into the curriculum, the less likely students will be to improve their ethical awareness and reasoning skills.

RESEARCH DESIGN AND RESULTS

We conducted two different experiments to test our hypotheses. We tested Hypothesis 1 in experiment one , and Hypotheses 2, 3, and 4 in experiment two. Undergraduate accounting students enrolled at a major state university served as subjects in both experiments. However, the two experiments were conducted on different students to avoid any bias. Table 2 reports demographic information and descriptive statistics regarding the subjects in both experiments. As Table 2 indicates, there were no significant demographic differences between the two experimental groups. The students take the intermediate series upon admission to the School of Business. Admittance to the School of Business requires completion of all prerequisite background courses and also a grade point of at least 3 on a 4-point scale.

Actor-Observer Experiment

One hundred and twenty-five (125) undergraduate accounting students enrolled in the first upper division (junior level) accounting class were surveyed in this experiment (see Appendix for survey instrument). To provide a valid measure of the actor-observer effect, the scenarios were varied so that half the subjects received accounting scenarios in which they were the actor and the other half received accounting scenarios in which they observed someone else's behavior.

Table 2. Selected Demographic Data

	Attribution $n = 125$	*Spring* $n = 56$	*Summer* $n = 36$	*Final Group* $n = 44$
Age	25.2	24.9	24.0	25.0
GPA	3.39	3.42	3.46	3.39
Years in school	3.76	3.66	4.00	3.75
Marital status				
Married	62	30	21	24
Not Married	59	26	14	20
Religious Preference (yes)	109	41	26	36
Gender				
Male	71	35	22	27
Female	46	20	11	17

Note: Not all items add up to the total due to nonresponses.

The subjects who received accounting scenarios in which they were the actor were presented with a nonaccounting problem in which they observed behavior, and the opposite was true for those who observed behavior for the accounting scenario. This resulted in two treatments: treatment one included subjects who were actors in an accounting scenario and observers in a nonaccounting scenario, and treatment two included subjects who were observers in an accounting scenario and actors in a nonaccounting scenario. The presentation of the scenarios was randomized within subject groups. Analysis indicated that there were no differences in demographics between the two treatment groups.

Actor-Observer Experiment Results

The results of the actor-observer experiment are presented in Table 3. In the nonaccounting scenario, we observe that the students were quite likely to "do nothing" if they were cast in the role of the actor in the case. Conversely, if the students were cast as observers, they were far more likely to prescribe definitive action. As Table 3 indicates, the differences between actors and observers is significant, with a chi-square of 17.562 ($df = 2$) and a p-value of $<.0001$. In other words, the actor-observer effect is clearly and significantly documented in this experiment.

Table 3. Results of Actor Observer Experiment

	Do Nothing	*Make the Change*
	Panel A. Accounting Scenario	
Actor	0	61
Observer	5	58
Chi-square = 5.045		
P-value = 0.025		

	Contact Principal	*Contact Parents*	*Do Nothing*
	Panel B. Nonaccounting Scenario		
Actor	7	13	40
Observer	10	33	18
Chi-square = 17.562			
P-value = < .0001			

The accounting case, though statistically significant, is not quite as clear as the nonaccounting scenario. In the accounting case, both actors and observers were likely to recommend immediate correction of the error, but five observers recommended no action. This result, though statistically significant, is seemingly contradictory to the actor-observer effect. Since one of the cells in this aspect of the experiment contains no observations, the statistical significance of the analysis may be invalid; that is, the five observations are likely to be spurious (or, in this case, the subjects may have been unclear about the accounting treatment in the case). The strength of the results from the nonaccounting (ethics) tends to counteract the unusual results in the accounting scenario.

Ethics Awareness Strategy Experiment

The second experiment was conducted over a 10-month period at the same major university with undergraduate accounting students enrolled in Intermediate Accounting I and II. Since Intermediate Accounting I was offered in both the spring and summer sessions, we had two separate test groups during part of the 10-month time frame and one test group at the end. Students in all groups were surveyed at least four times: at the beginning and end of Intermediate I and at the beginning and end of Intermediate II. Figure 1 graphically depicts the survey procedure.

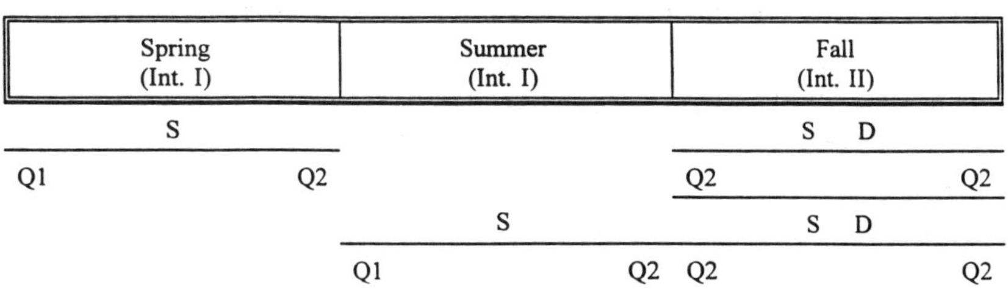

Key: Q1: Pretest survey, including demographic and work experience information.
Q2: Posttest survey.
S: "Subtle" treatment.
D: "Direct" treatment.

Figure 1. Experimental Procedure

In total, 92 students participated in the study, 56 from the spring term and 36 from the summer term. We attempted to anonymously identify the surveys so we could trace the progress of individual students. The students were asked to use a number known only to them which they entered on all of the surveys they completed. At the conclusion of the study, 44 subjects could be matched through all phases of data collection. These 44 are referred to as the summary group for the remainder of the paper. Responses were tabulated separately for the spring and summer terms and analyzed for any possible differences, but no significant differences were noted.

Demographic data was collected on all subjects at the beginning of the survey period. Table 1 presents demographics for the two starting groups and the 44 subjects in the summary group. The only significant difference between the groups was noted in number of years in school, with the summer group (Group 2) having more years in school than the spring group; however, the summary group was not statistically different than either the spring or summer group. A check of these students' transcripts revealed that the Group 2 students had no more accounting classes than Group 1 students and actually had virtually no more business classes than did the Group 1 students. Rather, the Group 2 students seemed to just be taking longer to get through their undergraduate programs than the Group 1 students. We find no theoretical linkage indicating that this difference should contribute to an ethical attitude or reasoning differential.

The initial survey given at the start of Intermediate I consisted of six parts. In the pretest—that is, at the beginning of the spring and summer quarters—we gathered information about accounting work experience, educational background, and demographics. These parts of the survey were not repeated in any of the posttests.

The remainder of the survey consisted of three parts: accounting scenarios, accounting attitudes, and ethical attitudes (see Appendix for survey instrument). The accounting scenarios were developed from real world examples and presented a financial accounting and an ethical dilemma. In each scenario, the actor made a choice between several alternatives, and the students were asked to agree or not agree (using a Likert-type scale) with the actor's decision. Then the students were given a series of factors which may have influenced their decision and were asked to rank the factors in terms of importance in their decision-making process. The accounting attitude questions were developed to glean the students' attitudes toward both the role and the responsibilities of accounting and accountants in society. Responses were tracked on a Likert-type scale. Finally, the Survey of Ethical Theoretic Aptitudes (Brady 1990) was included. This survey measures an individual's approaches to ethical situations from formalist or utilitarian philosophies. The survey is valuable in ascertaining how people reason through ethical situations because it displays their underlying philosophy with respect to ethical decision making.[2]

The survey was pilot tested using a group of Intermediate Accounting I students enrolled in the winter quarter. These students were surveyed at the beginning of the quarter only to provide feedback on the instrument. Relatively minor wording and phraseology changes were made to the instrument as a result of the pilot testing.

Administration of the survey was handled by the researchers. The researchers entered the classroom, read a prepared statement regarding participation in the survey, and distributed the surveys. Students generally needed about 20 minutes to complete the pretest surveys and 15 minutes for each survey thereafter. The researcher waited in the classroom while the students completed the survey and collected the survey instruments prior to leaving the room.

The study employed, in essence, two treatments. During Stage 1, we used a "subtle" approach in integrating ethics into the classroom. Specific ethical awareness cases, which dealt with actual business occurrences, were assigned in class. No formal discussion of the ethical implications of the cases or the ethical philosophies inherent in the companies' behaviors occurred in class. Rather, students were asked to analyze the cases out of class and arrive at a financial reporting solution. The students brought their responses to class and discussed their solutions. During the course of those discussions, occasionally the "social good" of the transaction or the accounting treatment arose, but the instructor did not try to guide the students into such a discussion. Rather, the instructor asked students to consider the economic ramifications of the transaction in question and then asked the students to consider which group (i.e., shareholders, creditors, general public, employees, and so on) was most affected by the transaction. Thus, words such as "ethics," "morality," "right," and so on were not introduced by the instructor. These words did, however, occasionally come up in the students' discussions.

Stage 2 employed a more direct method of integrating ethics into the classroom. The treatment was a combination of the two approaches discussed in Burton et al. (1991) and consistent with Cooper (1985) and involved two steps: (1) in-class lecture/discussion of ethics in general and ethics in financial accounting, and (2) out-of-class written assignment. The in-class portion, which included a handout, focused on concepts of ethical decision making. The lecture was followed by an in-class discussion of the concepts applied to various accounting topics studied during the course such as revenue recognition, valuation of receivables and long-term assets. A class period later, the students were assigned an out-of-class written case, which was an ethics scenario with financial accounting implications. Ethics was specifically mentioned in each step.

We used the subtle method of integrating ethics first to provide for a clear test of this method. During the Intermediate II class, the students received the direct method. We chose this sequence since it appeared that if any differences were noted they should be stronger for the direct method than for the subtle method.

Ethics Awareness Strategy Experiment Results

Our initial analyses of the data revealed no significant changes for any of our measures. We noted no changes in either group from the beginning of the quarter to the end and no change at the beginning of the last quarter of testing. Thus, Hypotheses 2, 3, and 4 were not supported. Not only did the students' ethical attitudes and attitudes about accounting remain virtually constant over this period of time, their solutions to the scenarios also remained constant. This was somewhat of a surprise since the topics addressed in the scenarios were studied in Intermediate I. The study of the topics should lead to renewed thinking about those areas but obviously did not change the perspective of the ethical implications.

To provide further insight, we analyzed the data further. Brady (1990) describes formalists as persons who look for rules to guide them as they make ethical choices. This behavior pattern might be expected of accounting students, especially in the intermediate accounting classes where knowledge of the rules generally is so important. Brady (1990) describes utilitarians as those who evaluate ethical situations based upon perceived costs and benefits to the people involved. This behavior might also be expected of accounting students, who are taught cost/benefit analysis in several classes and who are introduced to the FASB's conceptual framework which discusses the relative costs and benefits of certain accounting treatments.

This analysis of the ethical theoretic survey revealed that the students in all groups were neither strong formalists nor utilitarians as defined by Brady (1990). Rather, the students appear to be firmly entrenched in the middle ground, which Brady describes as "mugwump." Students enter Intermediate Accounting I with the "mugwump" attitude and retain it throughout both Intermediate Accounting I and II. Further, the variance is small, indicating that most of the students tend to fall in the "mugwump" category. Even the intrusive and direct treatment in Stage 2 did not dislodge the students' ethical theoretical attitudes. Table 4 provides the analysis for the summary group.

We also examined the data to determine if gender or religious preference may have led to any differences. The results of this analysis are presented in panels B and C of Table 4. Gender did not have a significant effect on the students' theoretical attitudes. There is a difference between those who declare a religious preference and those who do not, but given the very small number of students who expressed no religious preference, we question the usefulness of the result.

Table 4. Ethical Theoretic Aptitudes
$n = 44$

	Mean	*Standard Deviation*	*Minimum*	*Maximum*	*P-value*
		Panel A: Summary Group—Longitudinal			
Beginning (Q1)	.2045	2.646	-6	5	.7770
Ending (Q2)	.3636	2.606	-6	5	
		Panel B: Summary Group by Gender			
Male ($n = 27$)	.2222	2.6794	-6	4	.6523
Female ($n = 17$)	.5882	2.8509	-5	5	
		Panel C: Summary Group by Religious Preference			
Preference ($n = 36$)	-.0555	2.6180	-6	5	.0047
No Preference ($n = 8$)	2.250	1.5811	1	5	

Key: + 7 > score > + 5: "flaming utilitarian."
+ 4 > score > + 2: "moderate utilitarian."
+ 1 > score > - 1: "mugwump."
- 2 > score > - 4: "moderate formalist."
- 5 > score > - 8: "ice-cold formalist."

Source: Adapted from Brady (1990).

DISCUSSION

The results of both experiments lead us to question the effectiveness of the two major pedagogical tools presently suggested for integration of ethics into accounting courses. We have documented the actor-observer effect, and we have found that the students are not strong formalists, so we question whether a rule-based approach is effective in financial accounting. In addition, since we found that the students are not strong utilitarians, the cost/benefit analysis may also not be effective. We found that the subtle approach of integrating ethics into the class was also not effective, which may be indicative of students' "mugwump" tendencies. Even the intrusive, direct approach introduced near the end of the last quarter (when any effect should have been magnified) was not effective. We interpret all of these results in light of the actor-observer effect. We find that students apply a different standard of ethical behavior to others than they hold for themselves. Accordingly, when the traditional ethics pedagogies are used in financial accounting classes, the student (who is the actor in this case) is applying a different standard of ethical behavior to his/her actions than has been documented in auditing classes.

Our results appear to conflict with other research which provides some evidence of the effectiveness of teaching ethics in a separate ethics course or integrating ethics into the auditing class. However, there is very little empirical research focused on the effectiveness of integrating ethics into financial accounting classes. We interpret our results to suggest that the presence of the actor-observer effect mitigates the effectiveness of the traditional pedagogies in financial accounting classes.

We suggest that pedagogies which do not take into account the actor-observer effect will be ineffective in enhancing ethical awareness in financial accounting courses. We suggest that the pedagogies that will be effective are those that specifically force the student to examine the complete ramifications, both short term and long term, of possible accounting alternatives.

CONCLUSIONS AND FURTHER RESEARCH

Our purpose in undertaking this research was to assess various operationalizations of "integration of ethics into the accounting curriculum," with emphasis in financial accounting. We tested the relative effectiveness of two approaches which have been suggested in the literature: a "subtle" approach, which did not directly discuss ethics or ethical reasoning and a more "direct" approach, in which an ethical theory discussion and ethics case were introduced simultaneously. We administered the "subtle" treatment over a longer period of time because we thought it might take a longer period of time for the students to focus on ethics under this method. We thought this method might prove effective, however, if for no other reason than its continued exposure. We introduced the direct approach near the end of the testing period to magnify its effect, if any.

Our initial results indicate that neither approach significantly increases students' ethical awareness or reasoning skills, at least over a six-or seven-month period. In another experiment, we document the presence of the actor-observer effect, which we interpret as a potential explanation for the ineffectiveness of traditional auditing-type ethical awareness exercises in financial accounting classes.

The two experiments described in this paper contribute to the literature by examining ethics specifically in a financial accounting context. We found that the methods which have worked in ethics and auditing classes do not appear to be effective in financial accounting. Our results led us to conclude that the process of reasoning underlying financial accounting activities is fundamentally different than that underlying auditing, where ethics has been traditionally introduced in accounting. While we do not question the need for integration of ethics in financial accounting classes, our results lead us to question the effectiveness of the methods presently used in auditing for integration in financial accounting. Rather, we see the need for innovative pedagogical tools to introduce ethics in financial accounting which are consistent with the financial accounting reasoning process.

APPENDIX: SURVEY INSTRUMENT

Portions Included in Experiment 1 and in Pretest of Experiment 2

Attitudes

Please indicate your response by circling the number that most closely corresponds to your opinion.

	Strongly Disagree						*Strongly Agree*
1. Accountants are ethical if they adhere to generally accepted accounting principles.	1	2	3	4	5	6	7
2. The primary purpose of financial accounting is bookkeeping.	1	2	3	4	5	6	7
3. Public accounting encourages accountants to behave ethically.	1	2	3	4	5	6	7
4. If an accountant uncovers something wrong at his/her workplace, he/she will "blow the whistle."	1	2	3	4	5	6	7
5. Accountants will not behave ethically without specific codes of conduct.	1	2	3	4	5	6	7
6. Corporate America expects accountants to behave ethically.	1	2	3	4	5	6	7
7. Accountants should always "tell it like it is."	1	2	3	4	5	6	7
8. Corporations will not knowingly sell a dangerous product.	1	2	3	4	5	6	7
9. Bluffing in business negotiations is unethical.	1	2	3	4	5	6	7
10. The social responsibility of a business is to increase its profits.	1	2	3	4	5	6	7
11. The culture of a corporation determines its ethical values.	1	2	3	4	5	6	7
12. Laws are necessary to insure that corporations behave ethically.	1	2	3	4	5	6	7
13. Accountants are more ethical than other professionals.	1	2	3	4	5	6	7
14. An accountant's primary responsibility is to safequard the interests of his/her client.	1	2	3	4	5	6	7

Attitudes

Think about the alternative presented after each statement. Mark the statement that you think best represents your feelings.

1. Persons' actions should be described in terms of being
   ______ good or bad. ______ right or wrong.
2. When making an ethical decision, one should pay attention to
   ______ one's conscience. ______ others' needs, wants, and desires.
3. Solutions to ethical problems are usually
   ______ some shade of gray. ______ black and white.
4. It is of more value to societies to
   ______ follow stable traditions and maintain a distinctive identity.
   ______ be responsive and adapt to new conditions as the world changes.
5. When thinking through ethical problems, I prefer to
   ______ develop practical, workable alternatives.
   ______ make reasonable distinctions and clarifications.
6. When people disagree over ethical matters, I strive for
   ______ some point(s) of agreement. ______ workable compromises.
7. Uttering a falsehood is wrong because
   ______ depending on the results, it can lead to further problems.
   ______ it wouldn't be right for anyone to lie.
8. Thinking of occupations, I would rather be a
   ______ wise judge, applying the law with fairness and impartiality.
   ______ benevolent legislator, seeking an improved life for all.
9. I would rather be known as a person who
   ______ has accomplished a lot and achieved much.
   ______ has integrity and is a person of principle.
10. The aim of science should be
    ______ to discover the truth. ______ to solve existing problems.
11. Whether a person is a liar is
    ______ a matter of degree. ______ a question of kind.

12. A nation should pay more attention to its
    ______ heritage, its roots. ______ its future, its potential.
13. It is more important to be
    ______ happy. ______ worthy.
14. Unethical behavior is best described as
    ______ violation of a principle of law. ______ ausing some degree of harm.
15. The purpose of government should be
    ______ to promote the best possible life for its citizens.
    ______ to secure justice and fair treatment.

Source: Adapted from Brady (1990).

Accounting/Work Experience

1. I am currently employed, or I have been employed sometime during the last two years: ______Yes ______ No

If no, go to Part V. If yes, please answer the following questions.

a. Information about the company.

   The size of the company is (check only one):
   ______ Local ______ Service
   ______ Regional ______ Retailing
   ______ National ______ Manufacturing
   ______ Multinational ______ Banking/Financial Services
   Other, Please identify__________
   I work(ed) at the (check only one):
   ______ Only Office / Department ______ Home Office/ Department

b. Information about the job

   My job title is: ______________________

   During the course of my job(s), I have performed the following tasks: (check all that apply)

   ______ Reconciled Bank Statements
   ______ Balanced Accounts Receivable
   ______ Written Journal Entries

______ Prepared SEC Reports
______ Operated a Cash Register
______ Prepared Financial Statements
______ Balanced Accounts Payable
______ Prepared Bank Deposits
______ Billed Customers
______ Kept the Books
______ None of the above

Educational Background

1. Year in School: __ Freshman. __ Sophomore. __ Junior. __ Senior. __Graduate School.
2. Major: ____________________ Overall GPA: ______
3. For each of the courses listed below, indicate the quarter that the class was taken or this quarter if currently enrolled. Leave the space blank if you have not taken the course.

   ______ LIBED 110 Problems in Human Values
   ______ SOC 160 Current Social Problems in America
   ______ PHIL 243 Ethics
   ______ ACCT 509 Tax
   ______ MGMT 640 Business Ethics
   ______ PHIL 344 Bioethics
   ______ PHIL 250 Philosophy of Religion

Demographics

1. Age: ______
2. Gender: ______ M ______ F
3. Marital Status: ______ Married ______ Single
4. Number of children ______
5. Do you have a religious preference? ______ Yes ______ No
   If yes, would you please indicate preference: ____________
6. Place of Birth: ______________________________
7. Number of years you have lived in Utah: ______________
8. Parents' occupations: Mother ____________________
   Father ____________________

Portion Included in All Iterations of Experiment 2

Accounting Scenarios

Please read the following scenarios and respond to the questions that follow each by circling the letter that most closely corresponds to your opinion.

Scenario 1: ComData is a computer software development company. ComData ships software packages to its distributors, who in turn sell the product to retailers throughout the country. ComData unconditionally guarantees its product to the distributors. ComData recognizes revenue at the time the product is shipped to the distributors. Several years ago, the company developed an enormously successful statistics program, Crunch. Versions 1 and 2 of Crunch were highly reliable, statistically accurate and well received in the marketplace. Version 3, however, was inherently flawed. The company was unaware of the flaws in the software until after several hundred thousand copies had been delivered to distributors. Eventually, ComData recalled all of Version 3. ComData's auditors required ComData to restate the financial statements, in essence "unrecognizing" the revenue associated with Version 3. ComData immediately began research and development efforts to introduce Version 4. Version 4 has been extensively tested and is ready to ship to distributors. ComData plans to recognize revenue on Version 4 when the product is shipped to distributors.

	Strongly Disagree						Strongly Agree	No Opinion
1. Do you agree with ComData's accounting treatment for Version 4?	1	2	3	4	5	6	7	0

Please indicate the *importance* of the following factors in making your decision:

	None						Great	No Opinion
2. Accounting treatment for Version 4 is consistent with that for Versions 1 and 2.	1	2	3	4	5	6	7	0
3. Version 3's problems were irrelevant to Version 4.	1	2	3	4	5	6	7	0

4. The amount of money involved 1 2 3 4 5 6 7 0
5. The shareholders want ComData to report the greatest amount of revenue possible. 1 2 3 4 5 6 7 0
6. Accounting treatment for Version 4 should be consistent with the most recent experience, i.e., Version 3. ....1 2 3 4 5 6 7 0
7. The extensive testing of Version 4 justifies the accounting treatment. ...1 2 3 4 5 6 7 0
8. ComData should follow GAAP. 1 2 3 4 5 6 7 0
9. The effect of the accounting treatment on earnings per share. 1 2 3 4 5 6 7 0
10. The shareholders need correct information..........................1 2 3 4 5 6 7 0

Scenario 2: Chris is the chief accountant for a medium size manufacturing firm. Chris completed preparation of the company's annual financial statements and delivered them to the company controller. He congratulated Chris on a job well done and said that he was very excited because the company's net income is higher than he thought it would be. "This is great news," he said, "because my bonus is based upon net income, and now I know my bonus this year will be huge!" After returning to the office, Chris begins checking the financial statements more carefully and realizes that ending inventory has been misstated. Because of the misstatement, net income is significantly overstated. If the error is corrected, net income will be less than the company originally forecast and much less than the number the controller has just received. If the error is not corrected this year, next year's net income will be understated, but by next year-end, retained earnings will be O.K. (i.e., the inventory errors counterbalance).

1. What should Chris do? (Check the appropriate line):
   _____ Let the error "correct" itself over the next year.
   _____ Correct the error this year.

Please indicate the **importance** of the following factors in making your decision:

	None Great	No Opinion
2. If someone else finds Chris' error, he may be fired.	1 2 3 4 5 6 7	0

3. Correcting the error will require a lot of work.	1 2 3 4 5 6 7	0
4. The controller is counting on the bonus.	1 2 3 4 5 6 7	0
5. Since the error will "correct" by next year-end, there's no reason to cause trouble now.	1 2 3 4 5 6 7	0
6. Accountants should always "tell it like it is."	1 2 3 4 5 6 7	0
7. Chris will be embarrassed if the error is dislcosed.	1 2 3 4 5 6 7	0
8. The error is a timing difference.	1 2 3 4 5 6 7	0
9. People may make decisions based upon the reported financial results.	1 2 3 4 5 6 7	0
10. Financial statements must be reliable.	1 2 3 4 5 6 7	0

Portion Included Only in Experiment 1

Scenarios

Case 1. John (You)[1] works in the Data Processing Unit of the City Police Department. The Police Department's computer system is linked to a centralized data bank that contains criminal information for the entire country. One day, while working on the computer, John (you) accidentally entered the highly classified "sex crime suspect profiles" which John is not authorized to access. He was (You were) horrified to discover that one of the highly respected teachers in his sister's elementary school was on the list. According to the record, the teacher was suspected in a rape case in the East 12 years ago. However, he was not convicted because of lack of evidence.

1. What should John (you) do?

_______ Contact the principal.
_______ Contact his parents.
_______ Do nothing.

Case 2. Chris is (you are) the chief accountant for a medium size manufacturing firm. Chris (you) completed preparation of the company's annual financial statements and delivered them to his (your) boss, the company controller. He congratulated Chris (you) on a job well done and said that he was very excited because the company's net income is higher than he thought it would be. "This is great news," he said, "because my bonus pool is based upon net income, and now I know my pool this year will be huge! This means your bonus will be a lot bigger than you ever dreamed. Isn't that great? What are you going to do with all this windfall?" After returning to the office, Chris (you) checked the financial statements more carefully and realized that ending inventory was misstated. Because of the misstatement, the net income Chris (you) reported to the boss was significantly overstated. If Chris (you) corrects the error, net income will be less than the company originally forecast and much less than the number the controller has just received. Of course, then Chris' (your) bonuses will be very small—if they even get any. If Chris doesn't (you don't) correct the error this year, next year's net income will be understated, but by next year-end, retained earnings will be ok (i.e., the inventory errors counterbalance).

1. What would Chris (you) do? (Check the appropriate line):
   ________ Let the error "correct" itself over the next year.
   ________ Correct the error this year.

Note: [1]This was varied to either indicate the observer (John) or the actor (you).

ACKNOWLEDGMENT

This paper was presented at the Ernst & Young Research on Accounting Ethics Symposium, Binghamton University, New York, June 12-14, 1994.

NOTES

1. The relevant studies analyzed by Weber (1990) include Martin (1981, 1982), Boyd (1981, 1982), and Stead and Miller (1988). In addition, Arlow and Ulrich (1983, 1985, 1988) also tested effectiveness of ethics courses on ethical reasoning and awareness skills.

2. The survey used for the attribution theory experiment varied from the one used in experiment two in only one respect. In the first experiment, the students responded to scenarios specifically formulated to test the attitudes for actors and observers. In the second experiment, the scenarios were designed to be of a general ethical nature.

REFERENCES

Accounting Education Change Commission. 1990. Objectives of education for accountants. *Accounting Education Change Commission*. Bainbridge Island, WA: AECC.

American Accounting Association, Committee on the Future Structure, Content and Scope of Accounting Education (The Bedford Committee). 1986. Future accounting education: Preparing for the expanding profession. *Issues in Accounting Education* (Spring): 168-195.

Arlow, P., and T.A. Ulrich. 1983. Can ethics be taught to business students. *The Collegiate Forum* 14: 17.

———. 1985. Business ethics and business school graduates: A longitudinal study. *Akron Business and Economic Review* (November): 13-17.

———. 1988. A longitudinal survey of business school graduates' assessments of business ethics. *Journal of Business Ethics* 7: 295-302.

Arrington, C.E., C.D. Bailey, and W.S. Hopwood. 1985. An attribution analysis of responsibility assessment for audit performance. *Journal of Accounting Research* (Spring): 1-20.

Bernard, J.L., and C.S. Jara. 1986. The failure of clinical psychology graduate students to apply understood ethical principles. *Professional Psychology: Research and Practise* 17: 313-315.

Bernard, J.L., M. Murphy, and M. Little. 1987. The failure of clinical psychologists to apply understood ethical principles. *Personal Psychology: Research and Practice* (5): 489-491.

Boyd, D.P. 1981. Improving ethical awareness through the business and society course. *Business and Society* 20: 27-31.

———. 1982. Improving ethical awareness through the business and society course. *Business and Society* 21: 27-31.

Brady, F.N. 1990. *Ethical Managing: Rules and Results*. New York: MacMillan.

Burton, S., M.W. Johnston, and E.J. Wilson. 1991. An experimental assessment of alternative teaching approaches for introducing business ethics to undergraduate business students. *Journal of Business Ethics* 10: 507-517.

Cohen, J.R., and L.W. Pant. 1989. Accounting educators' perceptions of ethics in the curriculum. *Issues in Accounting Education* (Spring): 70-80.

Cooper, D.E. 1985. Cognitive development and teaching business ethics. *Journal of Business Ethics* (4): 313-329.

Harrison, P.D., S.G. West, and J.H. Reneau. 1988. Initial attributions and information-seeking superiors and subordinates in production variance investigations. *The Accounting Review* (2): 307-320.

Heider, F. 1958. *The Psychology of Interpersonal Relations*. New York: Wiley.

Hiltebeitel, K., and S. Jones. 1991. Initial evidence on the impact of integrating ethics into accounting education. *Issues in Accounting Education* (Fall): 262-275.

Jones, E., and R. Nisbett. 1972. The actor and the observer: Divergent perceptions of the cause of behavior. In *Attribution: Perceiving the Causes of Behavior*, eds. E. Jones, D. Kanouse, H. Kelley, R. Nisbetter, S. Valins, and B. Weiner, 79-94. Morristown, NJ: General Learning Press.

Kelley, H.H. 1967. Attribution theory in social psychology. In *Nebraska Symposium on Motivation*, ed. D. Levine, 192-238. Lincoln, NE: University of Nebraska Press.

Loeb, S.E. 1988. Teaching students accounting ethics: Some crucial issues. *Issues in Accounting Education* (Fall): 316-329.

________. 1991. The evaluation of "Outcomes" of accounting ethics education. *Journal of Business Ethics* (10): 77-84.

Martin, T.R. 1981. Do courses in ethics improve ethical judgement in students? *Business and Society* 20: 17-21.

Martin, T.R. 1982. Do courses in ethics improve ethical judgement in students? *Business and Society* 21: 17-21.

McNair, F., and E.E. Milam. 1993. Ethics in accounting education: What is really being done? *Journal of Business Ethics* (12): 797-809.

Mintz, S.M. 1990. Ethics in the management accounting curriculum. *Management Accounting* (June): 51-54.

National Commission on Fraudulent Financial Reporting (The Treadway Commission). 1987. *Report of the National Commission on Fraudulent Financial Reporting.*

O'Connor, B.P. 1988. Actors and observers: Are their descriptions of behavior indications of their causal attributions? *Social Behavior and Personality* 16(2): 207-213.

Ponemon, L.A. 1992. Can ethics be taught in accounting? Proceedings of the American Accounting Association National Meeting, Sarasota, FL.

Ponemon, L.A. 1993. Fostering the ethical reasoning of accounting students. *Ethics in Accounting* (March): 15, 19.

Schlenker, B.R., J.R. Hallam, and N.E. McCown. 1983. Motives and social evaluation: Actor-observer differences in the delineation of motives for a beneficial act. *Journal of Experimental Social Psychology* 19: 254-273.

Scribner, E., and M.P. Dillaway. 1989. Strengthening the ethics content of accounting courses. *Journal of Accounting Education* (Spring): 41-55.

Shaub, M. 1991. An analysis of factors affecting the cognitive moral development of auditors and auditing students. Working paper, University of Nebraska, College of Business Administration.

Shields, M.D., J.G. Birnberg, and I.H. Frieze. 1981. Attributions, cognitive processes and control systems. *Accounting, Organizations and Society* 6(1): 69-93.

Snyder, M., and P. White. 1981. Testing hypotheses about other people: Strategies of verification and falsification. *Personality and Social Psychology Bulletin* (March): 39-43.

St. Pierre, K., E. Nelson, and A. Gabbin. 1990. A study of the ethical development of accounting majors in relation to other business and nonbusiness disciplines. *The Accounting Educators' Journal* (Summer): 23-35.

Stead, B.A., and J.J. Miller. 1988. Can social awareness be increased through business school curricula? *Journal of Business Ethics* (7): 553-560.

Watson, D. 1982. The actor and the observer: How are their perceptions of causality divergent? *Psychological Bulletin* (November): 682-700.

Weber, J. 1990. Measuring the impact of teaching ethics to future managers: A review, assessment, and recommendations. *Journal of Business Ethics* 9: 183-190.

Weiner, B. 1990. On perceiving the other as responsible. *Nebraska Symposium on Motivation*, ed. D. Levine, 165-198. Lincoln, NE: University of Nebraska Press

Wilkins, M.A., J.M. McGuire, D.W. Abbott, and B.I. Blau. 1990. Willingness to apply understood ethical principles. *Journal of Clinical Psychology* (July): 539-547.

THE IMPACT OF ETHICS EDUCATION IN ACCOUNTING CURRICULA

James Lampe

ABSTRACT

Accounting students enrolled during academic years 1990-1994 participated in a study measuring moral development using the Defining Issues Test and a series of professional accounting situation vignettes. The students were enrolled in Accounting Information Systems courses ($n = 144$) and Auditing courses ($n = 328$). The study was designed to measure the impact of ethical interventions in intermediate-level classes taken between those two classes. Conclusions are that the participating sudents did not achieve higher levels of moral reasoning following the class interventions designed for that purpose.

Research on Accounting Ethics, Volume 2, pages 187-220.

ISBN: 1-55938-997-4

INTRODUCTION

Accounting education at both the undergraduate and graduate levels provides students with much of the technical knowledge and abilities they need to provide entry level service as professional accountants. Above and beyond these technical aspects, other skills and qualities that are part of a "socialization process" are also developed during the collegiate environment in preparing students for entry into the profession. This socialization process as well as additional technical training continues at a rapid pace soon after students graduate and begin practice and subsequently slows throughout their remaining careers.

Establishment of 150-hour requirement in many states and by the American Institute of CPAs (AICPA) has placed greater emphasis on broader learning abilities and softer interpersonal skills relative to additional technical training. One of the areas that has received increased attention from practitioners, educators, and standard-setters (both for practice and education) is ethics education. Formal recommendations for increasing ethics instruction have been made by educationally associated organizations such as the AACSB, American Accounting Association (AAA), Federation of Schools of Accounting (FSA), and Accounting Education Change Commission (AECC). Accounting practitioner groups such as the American Institute of Certified Public Accountants (AICPA), Institute of Management Accountants (IMA), Data Processing Management Association (DPMA), and the National Commission on Fraudulent Reporting (the Treadway Commission), in addition to accounting firms, have similarly called for increased ethics education during the collegiate preparation of students for professional accounting service.

Different accounting curricula have responded to the call for increased ethics education in a variety of ways. Some of the commonly adopted methods of providing additional ethics education have been to: (1) add ethical decision cases, such as those made available via the AAA, accompanied by class discussion, in existing courses throughout the accounting curriculum; (2) add more code-of-conduct content to the auditing and policy courses where ethics has traditionally been covered; (3) develop a new course(s) within the accounting curriculum devoted completely to ethical development; or (4) require additional liberal arts courses in ethics.

This paper presents and analyzes objective empirical measures of moral development collected over the past four years from students at a school that has adopted the first approach mentioned above—adding ethical content, cases and discussion to intermediate-level accounting courses as well as additional cases, videos, and discussions in the principles of auditing course. The student response data collected prior to and following the intermediate-level interventions provide additional insights into some basic and interrelated questions about ethics education in accounting curricula:

1. Does this type of ethics education improve the level of students' moral development?
2. How do these educational interventions affect students' reasoning and decisions in professional dilemma situations?
3. What are the objectives of providing accounting students with additional ethics education?
4. How and when should ethics be taught in accounting curricula?

The remainder of this paper is organized as follows. In the immediately following section, an historical background of ethical components in higher education in general and the more specific status of ethics education in accounting curricula are presented. Following this background, aspects of stage-sequence theory relied upon in this study and stage-sequence measurements from prior studies of accountants are discussed. The methods of data collection and analysis are presented and followed by discussion of the results achieved. Conclusions and implications based on the study findings comprise the final section.

THE ETHICS ENVIRONMENT IN ACCOUNTING CURRICULA

The accounting firms and various business organizations that hire most accounting graduates have entered a more globally competitive environment that has forced them to provide higher quality output with reduced resources—that is, become both more effective and more efficient. Most universities are now facing similar forces where legislative and contributor support dollars are decreasing but demands are being made for more effective educational processes that generate higher quality graduates.

Within this resource constricting environment, it is logical to question if the additional resources being allocated to ethics education in accounting curricula are achieving desired results. When additional ethics cases and materials are added to intermediate-level and/or auditing courses, it often comes at the expense of other topics either omitted or reduced in scope relative to prior coverage. Instructor and student time requirements for case preparation are often increased significantly. This study provides some evidence that raises further questions concerning the effectiveness of introducing only one or two cases with associated class discussions in multiple intermediate-level classes with the pedagogical objective of improving moral reasoning by students. Before discussing and analyzing empirical data about the impact of increased ethics education interventions adopted by the participating university from 1991 to 1994, a historical background of previous approaches to ethical education at the collegiate level and a brief discussion of stage-sequence theory as a measure of moral development are needed.

The History of Moral Development in Higher Education

Since the early history of American higher education, a clearly recognized goal has been to develop individuals who would think and act morally (Rudolph 1956, 1962; Sloan 1979, 1980). In early years, moral philosophy was a major portion of coursework throughout most curricula. A capstone ethics course was often required as the culmination of the various preceding courses (McBee 1980). Many of the religiously based liberal arts colleges of the late 1800s followed Plato's adage that "education makes good men and that good men act nobly" (Adler 1952).

With the establishment of greater numbers of state-supported public institutions and large fragmented research universities during the early twentieth century, direct curricular endeavors to develop students' character and moral sensitivity were significantly reduced or abandoned. Faculties became more concerned with fragmented logic and literature within narrower and more technically specific disciplines relative to broader questions of human values and morality (Morrill 1980). Despite these obvious changes, however, the concern for developing the holistic individual still appears to be a commonly held ethos of American higher education.

There have been, and continue to be, ethical theorists who believe little or no moral development occurs during the collegiate years. Freudian doctrine that the superego provides the basic structure of morality would further contend that the superego is fully developed at an early age and would not permit significant alteration in collegiate curricula of professional coursework. This view of accountants' ethical behavior was stated in an earlier decade by the editor of the *Journal of Accountancy*:

> all the professions have attracted men and women who, for lack of background or suitable environment or proper moral fiber, have been slow to grasp the true significance of professional life. It has been said repeatedly (and the remark, we believe, was originally made by an eminent member of the accounting profession) that ethics is a state of mind and he who has it not will never acquire it (Richardson 1936, 311).

A more recent publication (Fulghum, 1986) has popularized this stream of thought with the view that "all I really need to know I learned in kindergarten." The personal virtues of professional accountants have also been recently investigated from the perspective of virtue ethics.[1]

This study, however, is premised on a substantial body of research providing evidence that a clear association exists between college curricula and substantial moral development (see, e.g., Chickering 1974; Chickering and McCormick 1973; Clark et al. 1972; Feldman and Newcomb 1969; Lehmann and Dressel 1962, 1963; Pace 1974; Spaeth and Greely 1970; Trent and Medsker 1968; Withey 1971; Clouse 1985; Czapski and Gates 1981; de Vries and Walker 1986; Fishkin, Kenistion, and MacKinnon 1973; Hogan and Dickstein 1972; Hult 1979; Liberman, Gaa, and Frankiewicz 1983; Lupfer, Cohn, and Brown 1982; Parish, Rosenblatt, and Kappes 1979; Polovy 1980; Sullivan, McCullough, and Stager 1970; as well as Rest 1986a and the remainder of the references throughout this paper). One of the theoretical frameworks that has commonly served as basis for measuring moral development has been Kohlbergian stage development theory (Kohlberg 1964, 1969, 1984). Additional works on stages of maturation (Perry 1970; Nucci and Pascarella 1987) have linked cognitive intellectual growth with moral development but are not strictly based on stage development. Before discussing how stage-sequence theory has been used to measure the impact of ethics education in accounting curricula in the 1990s, it is appropriate to more specifically describe the status of ethics education in accounting curricula during the decade of the 1980s.

Accounting Curricula in the 1980s

A large part of accountants' claims for professionalism and self-regulation have been based on a moral schema represented by rule-based codes of ethics adopted by representative professional societies such as the AICPA. The 1905 code (developed by the AICPA's predecessor, the American Association of Public Accountants) contained two rules and was written as part of the bylaws. The AICPA code as modified throughout the years primarily with the addition of more rules, interpretations, and rulings to provide greater specificity for guiding professional accounting behavior. There was, however, very little emphasis on or discussion of ethics education by either practitioners or academics prior to the 1980s. During the 1970s, described as "years of trial" for the accounting profession (Olson 1982), and the early 1980s, numerous challenges (such as the Moss and Metcalf committees) were raised against the accounting profession. During the 1980s, many practitioner (CAR, the Treadway Commission, AICPA, IMA, Big Eight White Paper) and academic (AAA, AECC, FSA) organizations encouraged more ethics education to be incorporated into accounting curricula. Despite this encouragement, the empirical evidence indicates that little ethical training was incorporated in the education of business and accounting students during the decade of the 1980s.

Two different studies (Engle and Elam 1985; Cohen and Pant 1989) indicate that auditing was the only accounting course, across both accredited and nonaccredited schools, in which consistent and significant integration of ethics education occurred. Outside of accounting curricula, 60% of colleges of business did not offer a separate business ethics course (Hoffman and Moore 1982; DeGeorge 1987; Cohen and Pant 1989). Ingram and Peterson (1989) question if most accredited schools' coverage of ethics was adequate to meet minimum AACSB requirements. In 75% of those schools that offered a business ethics course, it was not required of accounting majors. Other business courses such as "Business Law" or "Business Strategy" often contained some additional ethical modules but with lesser content coverage than that in auditing courses (Cohen and Pant

1989). For accredited institutions, the average total class time devoted to professional ethics was less than two hours throughout the entire accounting curricula (Engle and Elam 1985).

Numerous reasons have been hypothesized for the apparent lack of ethical training in collegiate-level business and accounting curricula during the 1980s. One study noted that although practitioners publicly emphasized its importance, ethics questions comprised less than 2% of the CPA exam content coverage from 1982 to 1986 (Cooke et al. 1987-1988). Ethics coverage on the Certified Management Accountant (CMA), Certified Internal Auditor (CIA), and Certified Financial Analyst (CFA) professional exams was even less. To the extent that accounting curricula were designed to teach the content of professional entrance exams, a conflicting message was being given by the profession on the amount of ethics coverage desired in college courses. Another study (Carver and King 1986) concluded that many accounting practitioners did not have confidence in accounting faculty providing moral and ethical guidance to students.

Another empirically supported reason for the paucity of ethics training in accounting curricula during the 1980s was a lack of incentives for faculty to develop and to integrate ethical materials into accounting courses (Cohen and Pant 1989). Langenderfer and Rockness (1989) proposed three dilemmas to explain the reluctance of accounting educators to incorporate ethics in their courses: (1) legal-ethical, (2) philosophical-practical, and (3) moral-amoral. In partial solution to these dilemmas, the researchers offered an eight-step approach to teaching ethical decision making. This method is closely patterned after the previously developed Arthur Andersen program materials (Cooke 1988) and also serves as the current AAA Ethics Committee recommendation for an effective approach to incorporate instruction on ethics in accounting curricula. It is also consistent with empirical investigations based on cognitive developmentalist stages of moral development (Kohlberg 1984; Rest 1986a). An additional aspect of the AAA eight-step approach is a book of case materials (AAA 1993) designed to help accounting faculty integrate ethics education in various classes. The set of 51 cases is accompanied by readings and teaching notes to assist class discussions in accordance with the recommended eight-step approach. It appears that adopting subsets of the cases and discussion materials for use in intermediate-level classes, as done by the accounting faculty participating in this study, is one of the most common methods for providing students with additional ethical training.

Several studies have provided mixed results with respect to whether students' ethical attitudes were favorably influenced by exposure to ethics training interventions in the undergraduate business curriculum during the 1980s (Arlow and Ulrich 1980, 1985, 1988; Boyd 1981-1982; Martin 1981-1982). A conclusion of the most recent Arlow and Ulrich longitudinal study is that while most recent graduates and executives favor development of business ethics courses, the impact has not been considered great. Of six factors influencing ethical conduct in business, recent graduates consistently ranked family training first, conduct of superiors second, and university training last. Another study (Stevens 1984) compared business students with business executives using two independent measures (scales) to quantify ethical standards: (1) Clark's personal ethics and social responsibility scale, and (2) the Crown-Marlowe social desirability scale. The conclusion drawn in the Stevens study was that business graduates of the early 1980s, following ethical training in their respective schools, were a source of different and lower ethical standards than more experienced business executives who had graduated in prior periods.

Studies specifically investigating ethics interventions in accounting curricula have reported similar mixed results. Some studies indicate improving or above average measures for accounting students (Armstrong 1993; Jeffrey 1993) while others have been unable to show improvements and/or have demonstrated lower-than-average measures of moral development (Ponemon 1993; Lampe and Finn 1992; Hiltebeitel and Jones 1991).

STAGE-SEQUENCE THEORY

The current study of accounting students in the 1990s is based primarily on measurements derived from stagesequence theory in order to determine the impact of introducing small sets of cases and discussions in intermediate-level accounting classes. Brief discussions of this theory development and associated measures of moral development are necessary to evaluate the approach used in this study to determine the impact of ethics interventions on accounting students in the 1990s.

Dewey (1960 [1891]) proposed three levels of intellectual and moral development. Jean Piaget (1946 [1932]) developed further theories about the cognitive development of children passing through three similar stages of reasoning: (1) the intuitive, (2) the concrete operational, and (3) the formal operational. Lawrence Kohlberg (1958, 1984) engaged in a stream of research that has resulted in proposing six discrete stages—two each within three levels of moral development.[2]

In addition to postulating the stage-sequence theory, Kohlberg and his colleagues at Harvard University have developed the Moral Judgement Interview (MJI) as a means of identifying the level of an individual's moral development according to the six stages. James Rest (1974, 1979, 1986) developed another psychometric instrument referred to as the Defining Issues Test (DIT) which is consistent with the stage-sequence theory and provides a less complex, but commonly used and validated, scoring of moral development in terms of Kohlberg's six stages.

Stage-Sequence Measurements

The most commonly referenced measure from the DIT is the "P" score, which provides a measure of "the selective importance a subject gives to principled moral considerations in making a decision about moral dilemmas" (1986b, 5.2). In other words, this is the percentage of a subject's postconventional (Stages 5 and 6) thinking about what is right or wrong when faced with an ethical decision. A point of emphasis for this study is that virtually all accountants' P scores are less than 100. This indicates that reasoning for an ethical decision in an accounting situation is influenced by different stages of development in conventional (and possibly preconventional) as well as the postconventional logic represented by the P score. The influences on an individual faced with an ethical decision are distributed across multiple stages. For example, consider the following hypothetical stage scores:

	Conventional			*Postconventional*		*P Score*
Subject	*Stage 2*	*Stage 3*	*Stage 4*	*Stage 5*	*Stage 6*	
A	25	25	35	5	0	5
B	5	15	55	15	O	15
C	0	5	55	25	5	30
D	0	2	38	38	12	50

Several observations about the above-listed stage scores augment the understanding of how different stages of moral development influence the ethical decision making of accounting students and practitioners. It should first be noted that higher scores are not equated with "better" or "right." The four hypothetical subjects range in P scores from 5 for subject A (far below college graduate norms) to 50 for subject D, which is well above the norm. Although the P scores indicate that subjects A and D will often think differently when faced with an ethical dilemma, it does not mean D is a better person or always acts more ethically. All four subjects are influenced by cognitions distributed across four different stages. No one subject thinks solely within one stage. It should also be noted that although subjects A, B, and C have widely varying P scores, all three rely most heavily on Stage 4 logic. Some observations about the differing stage scores are:

1. Subject A has developed little cognitive ability to use postconventional logic and is about equally influenced by Stage 2 (self-needs), Stage 3 (group approval), and Stage 4 (law and order) reasoning. Because Stage 2 is relatively strong, subject A is still substantially influenced by preconventional cognitions even though Stage 4 is the strongest influence.
2. Subjects B and C have developed greater postconventional cognitive ability than subject A, but both are most influenced by Stage 4 reasoning.
3. Subject D demonstrates primarily postconventional reasoning, as indicated by the P score, but is also substantially influenced by Stage 4 reasoning.

It is further emphasized that relative stage scores measured for individuals are general indicators of cognitive influences when making ethical decisions and should not be considered static. Although stage scores indicate relative amounts of reasoning influence, they do not remain constant across time and all situations. Any of the subjects could temporarily utilize primary reasoning from a lower stage in a given situation, even after higher cognitive abilities have been developed.

Other Influences

In addition to the relative and dynamic aspects of stage score measurements discussed in the preceding section, it is also important to note that the stages of cognitive development are not the sole determinant of ethical behavior. Rest (1986a) proposes a four-component model that includes: recognizing the moral issue, making a moral judgment, establishing moral intent, and following through to take action. In this context, the relative stage of moral development has primary influence on the middle two stages—making a moral judgment and establishing the moral intent. Although there is a correlation between the cognitive decision and the subsequent action taken by an individual, an alternative action different from what has been cognitively determined to be best or right is also feasible. A body of literature and substantial discussion has been developed on the role that character plays in the cognitive decision process and the follow-through to take action by professional accountants. Virtue ethics theory focusses on the character and motivations of the decision maker and his/her ability to perform with virtuous excellence (MacIntyre 1984). Adherence to virtues of character such as honesty, objectivity, fairness, integrity, perseverance, consistency, and courage are marks of achieving excellence in professional performance.

It is further recognized that many other influences on ethical decision making and behavior exist. The norms, rules, and duties assumed by accountants in a socialization process leading to their professional performance are influenced by the community (family, local, and extended) and specific job situations in which accountants operate. The previously referenced study (Lampe and Finn 1992) developed and tested an ethical decision model for accountants in which situational (Trevino 1986), issue-contingent (Jones 1991), and individual variables were all concluded to influence the decision process of accounting students and practitioners as well as the relative stages of moral development.

From an overall perspective, the stage measures of moral development as measured by the DIT are not precise, absolute, static, or the sole indicators of accountants' ethical behaviors. They do, however, provide a validated and measurably important influence on accountants' ethical decisions. The primary focus of this study is to use DIT stage scores and other compatible metrics to measure the impact of cases and discussions used as interventions in intermediate-level accounting classes.

Impact of Educational Interventions

One of numerous benefits provided by quantitative DIT measures is the ability to objectively compare levels of moral development before and after educational interventions. Results of many independent studies clearly indicate that collegiate education leads students to higher levels of moral reasoning as measured by the DIT stage scores (Rest 1979, 1986a). These studies further indicate that the level of formal education is the foremost indicator or correlate of moral development as measured by the P score. The degree of change in moral development can be computed by comparing within-group P scores before and after a specific intervention, such as a course module on ethical training. In this study, it is measured via comparisons of average stage scores between different groups of students at different stages of the college curriculum.

A second advantage of quantitative psychometric measures such as the P score is that empirical research can subsequently identify the types of educational programs and interventions that best develop moral judgement in students. Rest (1986a) concluded, following extensive review of numerous educational programs and many specific interventions, that roughly half of those reviewed were effective in promoting development of moral judgment—that is, resulted in measurably higher P scores. The programs that were most effective in raising the level of postconventional decision making were treatments that lasted longer than just a few weeks and involved participant discussion of controversial moral dilemmas. Presumably the greatest advancement is made in a classroom setting where the teacher assumes the role of discussion leader for short ethical case dilemmas which stimulate peer give-and-take discussion, and such dilemma discussion is continued throughout a 10- to 12-week segment of the course. Short-term projects (less than three weeks), those that did not include exposure to stage-sequence theory, and those that did not generate participant discussion of dilemmas had measurably weaker effect.

A separate study of numerous universities and professional schools (Penn and Collier 1985) concluded that only a small percentage of graduates have developed significant capacity for postconventional moral reasoning. Both the theoretical and empirical data reviewed in the Penn and Collier study indicate that properly designed educational interventions enable individuals to move from primarily conventional to postconventional patterns of moral reasoning. A specific example was provided of an MBA course in which dilemma discussion interventions were applied throughout the course. At the beginning of the course, most students were at the conventional level; a few were at a transition point between conventional and postconventional, but none of the students demonstrated predominately postconventional dilemma decision-making attributes. At the end of the course, 37% of the students had moved to a primarily postconventional moral reasoning basis. The interventions were designed to be a "gradual equilibration of role-taking structures and principles of justice" (p. 133)—that is, cases in small increments which emphasize the next higher stage of moral development. This study has been designed to determine if the case usage and ethics discussions integrated into intermediate-level accounting classes result in increased levels of principled reasoning by the students involved.

PRIOR STUDIES OF ACCOUNTING ETHICS

There have been several prior studies of practicing and student accountants based on DIT measures that provide a base for further comparison of moral development. General conclusions of these studies have been:

- Practicing accountants have P scores significantly lower than those of average college graduates, while those of medical and law students are significantly higher;[3]
- Accounting students have P scores significantly lower than those of average college students;[4] and
- Accounting students at the school participating in this study have lower P scores than those reported for accounting students at other schools (Lampe and Finn 1992).

The first stated conclusions may be surprising to readers who are familiar with the high ranking of ethical standards accorded accountants in the Harris Poll (1986), the Pinnacle Group Survey

(1989), and the Touche Ross (1988) surveys of business leaders and the general public. In these polls, accountants have been ranked at the top or near the top of numerous professional groups by virtually all the subgroups of survey respondents. Although P scores are not equated with morality, they are an indicator of moral development and raise the question of apparent inconsistency with the public perception of high ethical standards. The results of the studies cited at the beginning of this paper provide consistent conclusions that average practicing accountant P scores are significantly less than average college graduate scores, and relatively even lower when compared with the averages of physicians and lawyers. Possible explanations for the lower P scores by accountants include:

- Accountants' self-selection to a rule orientation results in moral development that lags behind average college graduates and other professions;
- The university training for accountants is less conducive to moral development than that of liberal arts students and other professions;
- Accountants regress in moral development once within the day-to-day practice of the profession;
- More experienced accountants in decision-making roles select and promote only persons with a similar rule orientation, so accountants with greater postconventional thinking are excluded from the practice; and
- The socialization process in both college and practice leads accountants to utilize primarily rule-based Stage 4 reasoning in professional decisions, even when postconventional cognitive skills have been developed.

The studies cited earlier indicate that accounting students experience substantial growth in postconventional reasoning from their freshman to senior years but not as much as liberal arts students or college students on average.

In response to the many different organizations' recommendations to provide increased ethics education and the below-norm P scores obtained from senior-level students in the 1990-1991 academic year, faculty at the participating university agreed to increase the ethics content in the intermediate-level accounting classes and in the auditing class. Implementation was left to the discretion of the individual instructors, but all faculty involved agreed to increase the ethical content of each respective course. The method most commonly implemented in the intermediate courses was presentation of the AAA eight-step model followed by assignment of one or two of the cases with associated class discussions. Instructors also increased the emphasis and discussion of ethical issues associated with other textbook problems assigned throughout the respective semesters. In the auditing course, a section on stage-sequence theory was added to the typical code of conduct coverage, segments of the Arthur Andersen "Business Ethics" videotapes were presented, nine smaller ethical dilemma vignettes and four larger cases were integrated, and all were accompanied by class discussion.

A survey instrument designed to measure changes in reasoning was derived from the previously referenced study. The survey designed to measure changes in moral reasoning was assigned to the classes of junior-level AIS students and to senior-level auditing students at the beginning of their respective semesters. Two or more intermediate-level classes including ethical interventions were taken following the AIS class and preceding the audit class. These intermediate classes varied in the number of ethical discussions and case assignments included. By the 1993-1994 school year, virtually all students in the auditing class had experienced presentation of the AAA eight-step model, varying numbers of ethical case assignments, and associated class discussions on ethical issues involved with accounting problem solving during the prerequisite intermediate-level classes.

METHODS AND RESULTS

The study was designed to measure and evaluate the impact of the ethics education interventions described above. Three different types of responses were obtained from the participating auditing students: (1) attitudinal responses about peer accounting students' ethical behaviors, (2) decision and reason responses to four ethical dilemma vignettes, and (3) responses to the three-story version of the DIT. These same data were already available from the 1990-1991 senior-level auditing students prior to implementation of increased ethical interventions and were collected for comparison from the 1991-1992 through 1993-1994 auditing classes. DIT responses only were obtained from junior-level AIS students during the 1991-1992 and 1992-1993 academic years.[5]

Attitudinal Data

Auditing students participating in this study responded to a total of 20 statements designed to measure their perceptions of the ethical behaviors of peer accounting students, other college students, practicing auditors, and other professionals. Students responded to the 20 statements about various ethical activities by selecting a number from a 7-point adjective scale with verbal anchors from (1) Strongly Agree to (7) Strongly disagree. The 20 statements included: seven statements about activities as a student or the students' personal activities after entering the profession, seven statements about external auditor activities such as fees and competitive bidding, and six statements about internal or governmental auditor activities. For purposes of this paper, only the seven statements about direct student activities are considered relevant and included for further analysis.

Table 1. Student Attitudes About Ethical Behaviors

	Means and (Modes) of Responses			
	1990-1991	*1991-1992*	*1992-1993*	*1993-1994*
1. Peer accounting students often engage in unethical behaviors.	4.96 (6)	5.09 (6)	5.00 (6)	4.85 (6)
2. Nonaccounting students often engage in unethical behaviors.	3.78 (3)	3.86 (3)	3.75 (3)	3.68 (2)
3. Accounting students have many opportunities for unethical activities.	3.88 (3)	3.75 (3)	3.16[a] (3)	3.57 (2)
4. Successful accounting students are more ethical than unsuccessful.	3.03 (2)	2.72 (2)	2.61 (2)	3.10 (2)
5. One must compromise his/her ethics to succeed in practice.	5.82 (7)	6.25 (7)	5.92 (7)	5.17[b] (6)
6. Personal gain is the primary reason for unethical behaviors.	2.83 (2)	3.02 (2)	2.93 (2)	3.01 (2)
7. I have experienced serious ethical dilemmas in college	4.81 (6)	4.70 (6)	4.71 (6)	4.62 (5)

Note: Data based on responses to an abjective scale from (1) Strongly Agree to (7) Strongly Disagree.
[a] Less than 1990-1991 responses at $p < .05$.
[b] Less than all prior year responses at $p < .05$.
No other differences in between-year responses significant at $P < .05$ based on ANOVA for unbalanced data per General Linear Models (GLM).

The primary concern of this study is to determine the impact of ethical interventions on students' attitudes. A comparison of student responses to statements concerning collegiate and personal behaviors over the four-year period of the study indicates whether or not student attitudes were changed by the interventions and other socialization activities during the study period. The average responses for the seven statements selected as most relevant to this study are summarized in Table 1.

Vignette Decision and Reasoning Data

A total of seven vignettes designed to obtain decisions and reasoning for accounting related ethical dilemmas were included in the original 1990-1991 study.[6] In order to conserve instrument completion time but still collect decisions and reasoning from a broad scope of situations, the surveys collected in years 1991-1994 contained only four of these vignettes:

1. A student must decide whether to keep a part-time accounting job with a small business whose owner is avoiding taxes and misstating financial statements.
2. A staff auditor for a large CPA firm is deciding whether to submit extraneous expenses to compensate for previously disallowed expenses.
3. An in-charge auditor for a large CPA firm must decide whether to reallocate time and some expenses from an over-budget client to another under-budget client.
4. An experienced internal auditor has been instructed by a company executive not to include a chemical dump, currently safe but potentially contaminous in future years, in the audit report.

Responses to each vignette included a yes/no decision on the prescribed action to be taken and a ranking of eight reasons potentially influencing the decision. The eight potentially influential reasons were designed for two each to support reasoning in four categories: (1) following promulgated rules, (2) self-gratification,(3) concern for third parties involved, and (4) rationalization for the desired decision. A decreasing scale of 16 points (7, 5, 3, 1) was assigned to the top four reasons ranked by the participating students

Table 2. Summary of Subgroup Decisions and Reasons

Vignettes	*1990-1991*	*1991-1992*	*1992-1993*	*1993-94*	*Average*
#1—Student Job					
Decision ratio*	0.33	.30	.31	.21	0.30
Code	6.58	6.74	6.69	6.81	6.50
Self	3.10	3.28	3.73	2.52	3.14
External	1.68[a]	2.48	3.22	2.68	2.40
Rational	3.99[b]	2.00	1.65	1.27	2.90
#2—Staff Expenses					
Decision ratio*	0.10	.11	.06	.06	0.08
Code	6.29	6.32	6.92	6.68	6.82
Self	5.81[b]	4.89	4.31	4.22	4.98
External	3.09	2.33[a]	3.43	3.34	3.11
Rational	0.88	1.93[b]	0.39	0.20	0.58
#3—In-Charge Spread Costs					
Decision ratio*	0.09	0.07	0.16	0.05	0.16
Code	3.72	3.73	4.41	4.20	4.02
Self	2.69	3.89	3.57	3.15	3.36
External	7.56	7.01	8.04	7.88	7.31
Rational	.78	0.44	.61	0.36	0.61
#4—Internal Audit Report					
Decision ratio*	0.89	0.85	0.76	0.84	0.84
Code	5.05	5.18	5.55	5.86	5.45
Self	3.71	2.80[c]	3.51	2.97	3.30
External	5.45	4.10[a]	5.47	5.59	5.33
Rational	1.40	1.75	2.43	1.67	1.97

Notes: * The decision ratio is the proportion of students who would decide contrary to the implied decision rule.

[a] Significantly lower than other years at $p < .05$ level

[b] Significantly higher than other years at $p < .05$ level

[c] Significantly less than 1990-1991 responses at $p < .05$ level (Based on GLM ANOVA)

Overall reason category averages:		
	Code	5.70
	Self	3.70
	External	4.29
	Rational	1.52

because about 75% of the subjects ranked four or more reasons across all four vignettes. Fewer than 50% of the students assigned importance to and ranked five or more reasons across all vignettes.

If 100% of the students had rated four or more of the eight listed reasons, the overall average per category would be 4.0, based on dividing 16 points by four different reason categories. Because about 25% of the subjects assigned important influence to only three or fewer reasons, the overall average for categories of influence was 3.6. Therefore, when average student responses in a category are above 3.6, it is an indicator of relatively greater influence on the decision-making process, while an average score of less than 3.6 indicates relatively less influence. The average student decision and reasoning responses to each of the four vignettes over the four academic years are presented in Table 2.

DIT Response Data

***Table* 3.** Dit Results for Auditing and AIS Students

	Conventional			*Postconventional*		
Sample Group	*P-Score*	*Stage 2*	*Stage 3*	*Stage 4*	*Stage 5*	*Stage 6*
Audit Students:						
1990-91 (*n* = 112)	34.49	6.41	15.71	36.08	30.10	4.38
1991-92 (*n*=44)	32.35	6.74	13.64	39.92	27.35	5.00
1992-93 (*n*=83)	36.55	7.33	13.49	35.74	30.77	5.78
1993-94 (*n*=90)	31.44[a]	7.37	16.44	37.33[b]	26.78[a]	4.67
(No other significant differences between years based on GLM ANOVA)						
AIS Students:						
1991-92 (*n*=73)	33.52	7.81	18.13	32.97	28.45	5.07
1992-93 (*n*=71)	35.05	6.71	19.17	30.09	31.25	3.80
(No significant differences between years based on GLM ANOVA)						
DIT Indixes for Comparisons (Based on standardizing sample)[1]						
High School Juniors	20.00	10.34	25.00	33.73	17.65	2.35
High School Seniors	31.03	19.48	19.73	31.95	28.33	4.03
College Students	43.19[c]	5.08	14.33	28.35[d]	35.01[c]	8.15[c]
College Graduates	44.85	28.26	13.26	29.95	33.92	10.93
(Based on *t* test of population means). (No other significant differences)						

Notes: A large sample of 1080 subjects (270 in each of the four listed groups) have been used for standardizing computations (Rest, 1979). The raw scores have been converted to percentages for comparison with current study DIT results.

[a] Less than 1992-93 AIS student scores at .01 level.
[b] Greater than 1992-93 AIS student scores at .01 level.
[c] Greater than all Audit and AIS student scores at .01 level.
[d] Less than all Audit Student Stage 4 scores at .01 level.

The third group of data collected from the participating auditing students (the only data collected from AIS students) were responses to the three-story version of the DIT. The previous study (Lampe and Finn 1992) reported lower-than-college-norm P scores for the auditing students from the 1990-1991 school year. In order to investigate these differences more thoroughly, the current study extends analyses of students' development in conventional (Stages 3 and 4) as well as the postconventional (Stages 5 and 6) reasoning through the 1993-1994 school year. Table 3 reports the stage-score data for previously reported auditing students collected in 1990-1991 and the additional data collected from 1991-1994 AIS and Audit classes. These data allow comparison of DIT results obtained from participating auditing (primarily senior-level) across the four-year period and against the AIS (primarily junior-level) students.

Subjects in the Study

A total of 482 usable[7] DIT responses were obtained from students in AIS and Auditing courses at the participating university. The numbers of participating students, by academic year, are as follows:

Year	*Audit Students*			*AIS Students*		
	Female	*Male*	*Total*	*Female*	*Male*	*Total*
1990-1991	52	60	112			
1991-1992	21	23	44	38	35	73
1992-1993	47	45	92	33	38	71
1993-1994	44	46	90			
Total:	164	174	338	71	73	144

The Auditing students completed all three sections of the previously described research instrument—attitudes, vignettes, and DIT—while the AIS students responded to the DIT only. There is substantial overlap in the responses because many of the 1992-1993 and 1993-1994 Audit students had previously completed the DIT instrument in the AIS course in a preceding semester. There is a minimum of a one semester, and typically two or three semesters, delay between the AIS course and the Auditing course. Most students take an intermediate-level course concurrently with the AIS course in the first semester of their junior year, additional intermediate-level classes in the second semester, and the Auditing course in the senior year. Student responses were collected near the beginning of each respective semester for the participating AIS and Auditing classes. This means that at the time of completing the research instrument, students in the AIS classes had not yet experienced any of the ethics education interventions designed for the intermediate-level classes. The participating students who completed the instrument at the beginning of the Auditing class, by prerequisite requirement, would have experienced the interventions included in the intermediate-level classes but would not have yet experienced any interventions from the auditing class. Comparisons of senior-level auditing student measures across the four years of study will indicate if there have been changes in overall moral development, decisions on identical vignette situations, or reasoning for those decisions. The differences between the AIS and Audit class stage scores serve as measures of impact from the intermediate-level class interventions and the other socialization aspects of college life experienced between the two times of measurement.[8]

DISCUSSION OF RESULTS

Overall results indicate that senior-level Audit students' measures of moral development, reasoning in ethical dilemma situations, decisions, and attitudes toward ethical behaviors have remained basically unchanged and strongly oriented to code-implied rules. These results are disappointing to the faculty who invested development time and reallocated class resources with the primary objective of raising students' levels of principled reasoning. It was expected that normal collegiate activities (without any specific ethics education interventions) would have resulted in cognitive moral development and that the case-oriented ethics interventions in intermediate-level classes would have further augmented this growth. Instead, principled reasoning, as measured by the P score, remained relatively constant over the first three years and declined for the senior-level auditing students during the most recent period of this study. More detailed analyses of the research data collected provide the bases for these conclusions.

DIT Stage Scores (Table 3)

From an overall perspective, it was expected that the ethical education interventions would have resulted in measurable increases in the auditing students principled reasoning, as measured by the DIT P scores reported in Table 3. Instead, the results indicate no significant change in the P scores over the four years of Audit student comparisons. Although not statistically significant, there is a noticeable decline in the most recent year. When comparing the 1991-1992 junior-level AIS students (P score = 33.52) with the 1992-1993 senior-level Auditing students (P score = 36.55), there was an expected increase, but the difference was not considered significant at the $p < .01$ level. In the following year, the 1993-1994 Audit students (31.44) generated significantly lower P scores than the 1992-1993 AIS students (35.05). The unexpected decline is associated with a similar decrease in the Stage 5 scores—1993-1994 Audit students have significantly lower scores than the AIS students from the preceding year. Contrary to expectations, these data lead to a conclusion that the ethical interventions and other aspects of socialization have not resulted in higher levels of principled reasoning by the student groups involved. Instead, the case and discussion interventions in intermediate-level classes in 1992-1993 (plus the influences from other class and collegiate activities) are associated with a significant decrease in average P scores measured in the auditing classes the following year.

Attitudinal Responses (Table 1)

The mean data responses reported in Table 1 are generally consistent within each of the seven attitudinal statements about ethical activities. There are very few statistically significant differences in the mean auditing-student responses across the four years included in this study. The statements with which students strongly disagree are:

1. Peer accounting students often engage in unethical behavior.
5. One must compromise his/her ethics to succeed in practice.
7. I have experienced serious ethical dilemmas in college.

The single attitudinal measure that was significantly different (decrease from 6.5 in 1992-1993 to 4.3 in 1993-1994) from other years was statement 5—one must compromise his/her ethics to succeed in practice. The decrease in the modal response coupled with the significant difference between mean responses indicate that the 1993-1994 students still disagree, but do not disagree with the statement as strongly as the prior year students. The mean responses are much lower than the modal responses for each of these statements, which indicates that there were a smaller number of students who agreed with these statements although the majority were in strong disagreement.

The statements with which most students indicated strong agreement were:

4. Successful accounting students are more ethical than less successful ones.
6. Personal gain is the primary reason for unethical behavior.

The attitude that personal gain is the primary motivation for unethical behavior is indicative of conventional and preconventional reasoning. It is also interesting to note that the students' attitudes are in contrast to the Treadaway Commission study conclusion that most known frauds are the result of management manipulation of financial statements (87%), with only indirect personal benefits versus employee embezzlement (13%) or other direct personal-gain-oriented behaviors. It also should be noted that the means of these responses are greater than the modes, which indicates that a smaller number of students were at the other end of the spectrum—that is, in disagreement with this statement. When analysis is limited to the modal responses, it can be observed that there were no changes across the first three years of this study. In the most recent year (1993-1994), there was a decline in the amount of disagreement with three of the seven attitudinal statements—that is, a trend toward greater ambivalence.

Vignette Decision Data (Table 2)

The decisions made by the auditing students in this study are exceptionally consistent across the four years of data collection. There were no significant differences between years for any of the four vignettes. This finding is more meaningful in the context of the previous study (Lampe and Finn 1992) in which the 1990-1991 group of student decisions for the first three vignettes were found to differ significantly from both staff and manager levels of practicing auditors.

In vignettes 2 and 3, students responded very conservatively and indicated that only a small percentage would either submit extraneous charges on an expense report or spread costs between under- and over-budget engagements. Although there are no significant differences between the four groups of auditing students responding to either of these questions, it can be noted there is a trend toward fewer students deciding in favor of these actions. The lack of significant change and trend toward greater conservatism are made more important in comparison with the prior study results, indicating that significantly greater proportions of practicing auditors would engage in these activities.

Although the differences between years are not significant, the responses to vignette 1 also indicate more conservative decision making by the participating Audit students. The group of 1993-1994 auditing students decided in greater proportions that it was inappropriate for a student to continue a much-needed part-time job with an unethical small businessman. The decision ratio for the group of 1990-1991 students was 0.33 and was higher than for practicing audit managers at 0.26. The 1993-1994 auditing student average group response declined to 0.21.

Student decision responses to vignette 4 were consistently in favor of reporting the situation of a chemical dump that is currently safe but potentially hazardous in the future, even though an executive-level manager strongly objects to this being included in the internal audit report. These responses are consistent between years and with the previously reported group of practicing auditors.

Vignette Decision Reasoning (Table 2)

The most dominant reason category across all years and vignette situations is compliance with code-implied decision rules. It is the highest-rated reason category in all vignettes except vignette 3, where an in-charge auditor must decide whether to spread time and costs between over- and under-budget jobs. In this vignette (#3), concern for external parties (the client and future auditors) was the highest-ranked category across all four years. Code-implied rules were, however, the second-highest-ranked reason category in this vignette with an above average importance weighting. The overall high ranking accorded rule-oriented reasoning across all four years is consistent with the above-average Stage 4 scores from the DIT by the same students in the same time periods.

Beyond rule-oriented reasoning being ranked the most influential on vignette decisions, there is general consistency within each of the four reason categories across all four years of this study. Although there are several significant differences in numeric reasoning values between years for given reason categories, the reasons ranked of above-average importance for a given vignette remain above average across all years. Similarly, those reasons ranked of below-average importance are consistently ranked below average. Student reasoning on ethical dilemmas changed very little over the years of this study.

CONCLUSIONS AND IMPLICATIONS

A summary of the findings made or confirmed in this research are:

- Accounting students participating in this study have below-norm P scores;
- Accounting students participating in this study have above-norm Stage 4 scores;
- There are no significant differences in the P, Stage 4, and Stage 5 scores of senior-level auditing students across the first three years of this study;
- The P scores and Stage 5 scores of the 1993-1994 group of auditing students are significantly lower than those of the junior-level AIS students in the preceding year;
- The Stage 4 scores of the 1993-1994 group of auditing students are significantly higher than those of the junior-level AIS students in the preceding year;
- There are no significant changes in the attitudes of auditing students toward the measured ethical behaviors across the four years of this study;
- There are no significant changes in decision ratios on professional dilemma vignettes across the four years of this study;
- There is a noticeable, but not significant, trend toward greater decision conservatism in the most recent (1993-1994) year of study;
- Auditing students consistently ranked Code-implied decision rules as the most important influence on ethical dilemma decisions across all four situations and in all four years of this study; and

- The general ranking of degree of relative influence exerted by each of the four consistent reason categories did not change across the four years of this study.

The overall conclusion based on the previously listed findings is that the educational interventions designed to further develop accounting students' level of principled moral reasoning have not accomplished the desired objective. The increased emphasis on cases and class discussions in the intermediate-level accounting classes (plus the other class and collegiate activities) have resulted in lower P scores and more conservative decision making, although not all of the measures are statistically significant. This finding is disappointing to the faculty who designed and implemented curriculum changes with the objective of raising students' ethical sensitivity and principled reasoning. These results are, however, consistent with prior single-period studies of accounting students that concluded no significant changes occurred in the moral development of accounting students following ethics education interventions designed with the specific objective of raising levels of principled reasoning (Ponemon 1993; Hiltebeitel and Jones 1991).

These findings and conclusions permit partial answers to the research questions raised in the introduction of this paper:

1. Do these interventions change the level of moral development?

   The interventions used by the faculty in this study are similar to those adopted by numerous other schools and have not done so with the students participating in this study. If there is a direction of change, the case intervention plus other socialization factors have resulted in reduced levels of moral development.
2. How do ethical cases and class discussions affect ethical decisions?

   They have not had significant measurable impact in this study. If there was a change, it was in the opposite-to-intended direction, to more conservative rule-based decisions and reasoning.
3. What are the objectives of ethical education?

   The objective of raising students' level of moral development is questionable. It appears that from the perspective of total socialization through collegiate years, the majority of students, faculty, and future employers all prefer rule-oriented conventional reasoning from accounting graduates.

4. How and when should ethics be taught?

   Introduction of the AAA eight-step model coupled with assignments of one or two cases with associated class discussions in two or three intermediate-level accounting classes do not appear to significantly improve the ethical decisions or moral reasoning of students. More indepth coverage, such as the course developed by Armstrong (1993), appears more effective for the purpose of significantly altering students' moral reasoning.

Although these partial answers are available, the data collected and analyses performed raise additional substantive questions:

- Whether the objective of ethics education in accounting curricula should be to raise students' levels of postconventional reasoning?
- Whether accounting students have a self-selection bias toward a law-and-order (or rule-based) orientation in ethical reasoning not easily extended to postconventional logic?
- Whether a greater number of cases, accompanied by more extensive class discussion, would be more effective in intermediate-level accounting classes?
- Whether accounting faculty and/or practitioners are providing subtle, but strong, signals that technical skills and following promulgated rules are more important than development of postconventional moral reasoning?
- Whether primarily rule-oriented education on GAAP, GAAS, and other accounting standards overrides interventions designed to develop principled reasoning?
- Whether time and other scarce class resources should continue to be allocated to these types of ethical interventions?

The results further imply that the accountants' socialization process encourages utilization of primarily Stage 4 conventional reasoning even when higher stages of cognitive development have been achieved. The lower-than-normal and declining trends for P scores generated by professional accountants may be due to a socialization process in both collegiate and on-the-job training activities that encourage and reward a rule orientation in professional decision making.

The research design of this study does not provide an objective basis for concluding the cause, or causes, of the unexpected results. There are, however, several potential reasons that have been anecdotally associated with the students' greater decision conservatism and lower P scores observed in this study:

- Inadequate interventions—the number of cases, amount of class discussion, the amount of time, and/or the orientation of material were inadequate to achieve desired improvements in students' moral development.
- Student perceptions—the self-selection of rule oriented students in upper division accounting classes was also used as a screen so that regardless of the content of ethical presentations, the interpretation was that more strict adherence to promulgated rules and policies is equivalent to higher ethical standards.
- Conflicting pedagogical messages—an objective sensing approach of cognitive style for problem solution (objective data collection followed by analysis in accordance with generally accepted principles) is strongly recommended for virtually all other accounting problems, but when applied to ethical dilemmas is equated with adherence to promulgated rules.
- Conflicting job market messages—recent graduates, speakers at accounting society meetings, and recruiters all provide a subtle, but strong, message that technical excellence and strict obedience to firm or company policies are the most important determinants of being hired and promoted.

Several options follow the overall conclusion reached and questions raised concerning the effectiveness of ethical case interventions in accounting classes: (1) change intermediate accounting class content back to the exclusion of ethical cases, (2) expand the number of ethical cases and content in more accounting classes throughout the curriculum, (3) develop a new ethics course within the accounting curriculum required of all accounting majors, (4) require more liberal arts classes on ethics prior to or concurrent with accounting classes, or (5) continue the status quo under the assumption that positive changes not measured by the methodology of this study have resulted.

A logical implication, in an environment of shrinking resources for higher education, is that reduction or omission of ethical education interventions that appear to lack effectiveness is a likely course of action. This would not, however, meet the wants and needs of the many academic and practitioner groups seeking improved ethics education for future graduates who will be facing more complex ethical dilemmas with increasing frequency. Additional research and insight into the previously raised questions are necessary to best determine the objectives and methods of ethics education most appropriate for accounting students.

NOTES

1. From an ethicist's perspective, MacIntyre (1984) posits that virtue theory provides an alternative to other theories or codes based on justice, rules, or principles. Specific applications of virtue theory to accountants' professional behavior have been presented by Doucet and Ruland (1994) and Armstrong (1994).
2. The six stages of development proposed by Kohlberg have been used by numerous researchers in many different disciplines. They have been summarized in several recent studies of accountants' moral development, including Armstrong (1987, 1993), Ponemon (1990, 1991, 1993), Shaub (1991), and Lampe and Finn (1992).
3. For example, the DIT manual (Rest 1986b, iii) provides several different student group P score averages for comparison with 44.9 for average college graduates:

65.2 Moral philosophy and political science doctoral students
59.8 Seminarians in a liberal Protestant seminary

53.7 Medical students	52.2 Law students
48.1 Nursing students	44.9 Average college graduates

Comparative studies for practitioners, with scores, are:

Armstrong (1987) 38.5	Ponemon (1988) 38.1
Shaub (1989) 41.3	Lampe and Finn (1992) 39.8

4. Comparative P scores for business or accounting college seniors from previous studies are: 37.28 (Ponemon and Glazer 1990), 41.32 (Shaub 1989), 37.26 (Jeffrey 1993), and 34.49 (Lampe and Finn 1992).
5. Because all DIT responses are completely anonymous, it is not possible to match specific student responses between the two groups.
6. A discussion of design objectives, description of all seven vignettes, and complete text example of one vignette are available in the previous study report (Lampe and Finn 1992). Copies of the total instrument are available on request.
7. Two checks were made on the internal validity of the DIT responses by students. First, an "M" score was computed to determine if a subject checked items

according to perceived complexity or pretentiousness rather than according to the meaningfulness of the items. Second, a consistency check was performed to compare the subjects' evaluations of 12 reasons influencing their decisions, with a separate ranking of the four most important reasons. Inconsistencies on more than two stories or more than eight ratings or "M" scores greater than 14% resulted in elimination of the given subject's response. An average of three or four (range from two to nine) student responses were eliminated from analysis each semester as a result of these internal reliability checks. Additionally, one or two were excluded each semester due to incomplete responses in one or more of the three sections of the total instrument.

8. Because all DIT responses are completely anonymous, it is not possible to match specific student responses between the two time periods.

REFERENCES

Adler, M. 1952. *The Great Ideas: A Syntopican of Great Books of the Western World.* Vol. 1. Chicago: Encyclopedia Britannica.

American Accounting Association 1993. *Ethics in the Accounting Curriculum: Cases & Readings,* ed. W.W. May, Cases C1-C38. Sarasota, FL: AAA.

Arlow, P., and T. Ulrich, 1980. Business ethics, social responsibility and business students: An empirical comparison of Clark's study. *Akron Business and Economic Review* (November): 17-22.

————. 1985. Business ethics, social responsibility and business students: An empirical comparison of Clark's study. *Akron Business and Economic Review* (November): 13-17.

————. 1988. A longitudinal survey of business school graduates' assessments of business ethics. *Journal of Business Ethics* (July): 295-302.

Armstrong, M.B. 1987. Moral development and accounting education. *Journal of Accounting Education* (Spring): 27-43.

————. 1993. Ethics and professionalism in accounting education: A sample course. *Journal of Accounting Education* (Spring): 77-92.

————. 1994. Application of virtue ethics theory: A lesson from architecture. Presented at Research on Accounting Ethics Symposium, Binghamton University, Binghamton, NY.

Boyd, D.P. 1981-1982. Improving ethical awareness through the business and society course. *Business and Society* (Winter/Spring): 20-31.

Carver, R.M., Jr., and T.E. King. 1986. Attitudes of accounting practitioners towards accounting faculty and accounting education. *Journal of Accounting Education* (Spring): 31-43.

Cavanaugh, G.F., and D.J. Fritzsche. 1985. Using vignettes in business ethics research. *Research in Corporate Social Performance and Policy,* Vol. 7, ed. L. Preston, 279-293. Greenwich, CT: JAI Press.

Chickering, A. 1974. The impact of various college environments on personalty development. *Journal of the American College Health Association* 23: 82-93.

Chickering, A., and J. McCormick. 1993. Personality development and the college experience. *Research in Higher Education* 1: 43-70.

Clark, B., P. Heist, M. McConnell, M. Trow, and G. Yonge. 1972. *Students and Colleges: Interacting and Change.* Berkeley: University of California

Clouse, B. 1985. Moral reasoning and Christian faith. *Journal of Psychology and Theology* 13: 190-198.

Cohen, J.R., and L. Pant 1989. Accounting educators' perceptions of ethics in the curriculum. *Issues in Accounting Education* (Spring): 70-81.

Cooke, R.A. 1988. *Ethics in Business: A Perspective.* St. Charles, IL: Arthur Andersen & Co. Center for Education.

Cooke, R., H. Kanter, and S. Martens. 1987-1988. The importance of ethical training in an accounting education. *Association of Government Accountants Journal* (Winter): 44-67.

Czapski, D., and L. Gates. 1981. Love and justice: An examination of effective and cognitive aspects of moral judgment development. *Educational and Psychological Research* 1: 215-221.

DeGeorge, R. 1987. The status of business ethics: past and future. *Journal of Business Ethics* 6: 201-211.

deVries, B., and L. Walker. 1986. Moral reasoning and attitudes toward capital punishment. *Development Psychology* 22: 509-513.

Dewey, J. 1960. *Theory of the Moral Life.* New York: Holt, Rinehart & Winston.

Dobson, J., and M.B. Armstrong. 1994. Application of virtue ethics theory: A lesson from architecture. Paper presented at the Ernst & Young Research on Accounting Ethics Symposium, Binghamton, NY.

Doucet, M., and R. Ruland. 1994. An exploration of the professional role: Necessary virtues for the public accountant. *Ethics in Accounting: A Special Issue.* Sarasota, FL: American Accounting Association.

Engle, T.J., and R. Elam. 1985. The status of collegiate auditing education. *Issues in Accounting Education* (Spring): 97-108.

Feldman, K., and T. Newcomb. 1969. *The Impact of College on Students.* San Francisco: Jossey-Bass.

Fishkin, J., K. Kenistion, and C. MacKinnon. 1973. Moral reasoning and political ideology. *Journal of Personality and Social Psychology* 27: 109-119.

Fulghum, R. 1986. *All I Really Need to Know I Learned in Kindergarten.* New York: Ivy Books

Harris, L. 1986. How the public sees CPAs. *Journal of Accountancy* (December): 92-104.

Hiltebeitel, K.M., and S.K. Jones. 1991. Initial evidence on the impact of integrating ethics into accounting eduction. *Issues in American Education* (Fall): 262-275.

Hoffman, W.M., and J. Moore. 1982. Results of business ethics curriculum survey conducted by the center for business ethics. *Journal of Business Ethics* (January): 17-23.

Hogan, R., and F. Dickstein. 1972. A measure of moral values. *Journal of Consulting and Clinical Psychology* 39: 210-214.

Hult, R. 1979. The relationship between ego identity status and moral reasoning in university women. *Journal of Psychology* 103: 203-207.

Ingram, R., and R. Peterson. 1989. Ethics education in accounting: Rhetoric or reality. Paper presented at the Ohio Regional Meeting, American Accounting Association.

Jeffrey, C. 1993. Ethical development of accounting students, non-accounting business students, and liberal arts students. *Issues in Accounting Education* 8(Spring): 86-96.

Jones, T. 1991. Ethical decision making by individuals in organizations: An issue contingent model. *Academy of Management Review* 16: 366-395.

Kohlberg, L. 1958. *The development of modes of moral thinking and choice in the years ten to sixteen.* Unpublished Ph.D. dissertation, University of Chicago.

________. 1964. The development of moral character and moral ideology. In *Review of Child Development Research*, Vol. 1, ed. M. Hoffman. New York: Russell Sage Foundation.

________. 1969. Stage and sequence: The cognitive-developmental approach to socialization. In *Handbook of Socialization Theory and Research*, ed. D. Goslin, 347-480. Chicago, IL: Rand McNally.

________. 1984. *Essays on Moral Development.* Vol. 2: *The Psychology of Moral Development*. New York: Harper and Row.

Lampe, J.C., and D.W. Finn. 1992. A model of auditors' ethical decision processes. *Auditing: A Journal of Practice & Theory* 11(Supplement): 33-73.

Langendefer, M., and J. Rockness. 1989. Integrating ethics into the accounting curriculum: issues, problems, and solutions. *Issues in Accounting Education* 4: 58-69.

Lehmann, I., and P. Dressel. 1962. *Changes in Critical Thinking, Attitudes, and Values from Freshman to Senior Years.* East Lansing: Michigan State University.

Liberman, D., J. Gaa, and R. Fran Kiewicz. 1983. Ego and moral development in an adult population. *Journal of Genetic Psychology* 142: 61-65.

Lupfer, M., B. Cohn, and L. Brown. 1982. *Jury Decisions as a Function of Level of Moral Reasoning*. Memphis, TN: Memphis State University

MacIntyre, A. 1984. *After Virtue*. 2nd ed. Notre Dame, IN: University of Notre Dame Press.

Martin, T.R. 1981-1982. Do courses in ethics improve the ethical judgments of students? *Business and Society* (Winter/Spring): 17-26.

McBee, M. 1980. The values development dilemma. In *Rethinking College Responsibilities for Values*, ed. M. McBee. San Francisco: Jossey-Bass.

Morrill, R. 1980. *Teaching Values in College: Facilitating Development and Ethical, Moral, and Value Awareness in Students*. San Francisco: Jossey-Bass.

Nucci L., and E. Pascarrella. 1987. The influence of college on moral development. In *Higher Education: Handbook of Theory and Research*, Vol. 3, ed. J. Smarta. New York: Agathon.

Olson, W.E. 1982. *The Accounting Profession: Years of Trial: 1969-1980*. New York: AICPA.

Pace, C. 1974. Evaluating higher education. Topical Paper No. 1, University of Arizona, College of Education.

Parish, T., R. Rosenblatt, and B. Kappes. 1979. The relationship between human values and moral judgment. *Psychology* 16: 1-5.

Penn, W.Y., Jr., and B.D. Collier. 1985. Current research in moral development as a decision support system. *Journal of Business Ethics* 4: 131-136.

Perry, W. 1970. *Forms of Intellectual and Ethical Development in the College Years: A Scheme*. New York: Holt, Rinehart, & Winston.

Piaget, J. 1946. *The Moral Judgment of the Child.* Trans. M. Gabain. New York: Free Press.

Pinnacle Group. 1989. Ethics survey compares various professions. *PR Reporter* (August 14): 5.

Polovy, P. 1980. A study of moral development and personality relationships in adolescents and young adults. *Journal of Clinical Psychology* 36: 752-757.

Ponemon, L. 1988. A cognitive-developmental approach to the analysis of certified public accountants' ethical judgments. Unpublished Ph.D. dissertation, Union College of Union University.

________. 1990. Ethical judgments in accounting: a cognitive-developmental perspective. *Critical Perspectives on Accounting* (1): 191-215.

________. 1991. Ethical reasoning and selection-socialization in accounting. Presented at American Accounting Association Annual Meeting, Nashville, TN.

________. 1993. Can ethics be taught in accounting? *Journal of Accounting Education* (Fall)2: 185-210.

Ponemon, L., and A. Glazer. 1990. Accounting education and ethical development: The influence of liberal learning on students and alumni in accounting practice. *Issues in Accounting Education* (5): 195-208.

Rest, J. R. 1974. Longitudinal study of the defining issues test. *Developmental Psychology*, 11: 738-748.

________. 1979. *Development in Judging Moral Issues*. Minneapolis, MN: University of Minnesota Press.

________. 1986a. *Moral Development: Advances in Research and Theory*. New York: Praeger.

________. 1986b. *DIT Manual for the Defining Issues Test*. Minneapolis: University of Minnesota Center for the Study of Ethical Development.

Richardson, A.P. 1936. Ethics in retrospect. *Journal of Accounting* (November): 5-6.

Shaub, M.K. 1989 An empirical examination of the determinants of auditors' ethical sensitivity. Unpublished Ph.D. dissertation, Texas Tech University.

________. 1991 Trends in the cognitive moral development of auditors and auditing students. Paper presented at Critical Perspectives Symposium, New York, New York.

Spaeth, J., and A. Greely. 1970. *Recent Alumni and Higher Education: A Survey of College Graduates*. New York: McGraw-Hill.

Stevens, G. 1984. Business ethics and social responsibility: The responses of present and future managers. *Akron Business and Economic Review* 15: 1-17.

Sullivan, E., G. McCullough, and M. Stager. 1970. A developmental study of the relationship between conceptual, ego, and moral development. *Child Development* 41: 399-411.

Touche Ross. 1988. *Ethics in American Business: An Opinion Survey of Key Business Leaders on Ethical Standards and Behavior*. New York: Touche Ross & Co.

Trent, J., and L. Medsker. 1968. *Beyond High School: A Psychology Study of 10,000 High School Graduates*. San Francisco: Jossey-Bass.

Trevino, L. 1986. Ethical decision making in organizations: A person-situation interactionist model. *Academy of Management Review* 2: 601-617.

Withey, S. 1971. *A Degree and What Else*. San Francisco: Jossey-Bass.

COMMENTARY ON "INTEGRATING ETHICS EXERCISES INTO INTERMEDIATE ACCOUNTING" AND "THE IMPACT OF ETHICS EDUCATION IN ACCOUNTING CURRICULA"

Bruce L. Oliver

INTRODUCTION

There are several similarities between the Kenny and Eining paper, "Integrating Ethics Exercises Into Intermediate Accounting," and the Lampe paper, "The Impact of Ethics Education in Accounting Curricula." Both deal with "ethical interventions" within the structure of accounting/auditing classes. Both are also empirical and designed to measure selected aspects of the impact of the intervention. The Kenny and Eining paper develops from mini-cases created to measure

Research on Accounting Ethics, Volume 2, pages 221-226.

ISBN: 1-55938-997-4

effects on the subjects, while the Lampe paper develops from the Kolbergian stage development hierarchy and Rest's DIT "P" scores over a period of time. Finally, both papers report a lack of success with their particular interventions.[1] The former paper detects "actor-observer" effects and suggests that this requires different teaching strategies for financial accounting and auditing courses.[2] The latter finds constant or declining DIT P scores. One should remember, however, that moral reasoning (à la P scores) can change without any change in decisions or vice versa.

INTERPRETING THE RESULTS

Taken together and viewed from a broad perspective, what conditions might have lead to these results. Two hypotheses immediately emerge:

- The particular interventions were unsuccessful in enhancing the studies' subjects' ethical decision-making abilities and the research designs captured those failures.
- The interventions were successful and the research designs were unsuccessful in capturing those successes.

One cannot, at this point at least, empirically or even intuitively refute either hypothesis. If one assumes the correctness of the second, there is little left of interest except to criticize the experimental design, also known as "the-research-project-the-authors-should-have-conducted" gambit. This being a frequent and easy target, let us leave it aside. So, let us assume the first hypothesis.

If the interventions were in fact unsuccessful, this raises a number of interesting questions about the authors' outcomes, some of which are discussed and some of which are not mentioned. First, as a group, accounting students possess an ethical decision-making framework that is immutable, or at least rigidly formed, strongly held, and highly difficult to alter. Most interventions are, thus, subject to failure.

Second, the quality of the interventions themselves was insufficient to alter subject responses, independent of the subject group. The presumed new information, or uniqueness of the material, simply was not present.

Third, the quantity of interventions was insufficient to alter responses, independent of the subject group. There were not enough interventions to make a measurable difference.

Fourth, the individual instructors providing the interventions were unable to adequately convey the intended meaning or importance of the prescribed "ethical" material.

In considering the first question, not only may there be some preselection process which brings certain types of students into accounting, as was suggested, but there is also an indoctrination process that occurs during the students' progress through the accounting curriculum, as was also suggested.

This consideration raises a precondition question: what is the impact of this indoctrination process on the types of academics who become accounting instructors? If, as suggested, rule-driven (or dogma-loving) individuals succeed as accounting undergraduates, who succeeds as accounting professors? There may be a double impact present. Not only are "rule-driven" individuals initially attracted to accounting curricula, but we accounting academics, being similarly inclined, may reinforce and reward students with this predisposition. We likely do this not only through our evaluation processes but through our daily behaviors as well.

The second and third questions are related and deserve considerable comment, for it is the context of these study interventions, coupled in part with the first question above, that may be of utmost importance in explaining these studies results. The interventions are few in number and apparently comprise only a minor portion of the entire undergraduate curriculum. Given the subjects' limited exposure, we should not be especially surprised by the findings.

Moral codes and ethical behaviors are usually formed at very early ages and for most individuals, absent some catastrophic event, are gradually reinforced or modified over the remainder of their lifetime. Modification often requires some degree of effort, repetition, and reinforcement. A few interventions embedded in a single accounting course seem predestined to be insufficient. Perhaps this is the most important outcome to be derived from these two projects.

COMMENTS TOWARD A FRAMEWORK FOR INSTILLING ACCOUNTING ETHICS

How, then, might positive change be accomplished with a greater likelihood of some modicum of lasting success? Is it reasonable to assume that a sense of the key role of "accounting ethics" can be instilled when there is little, if any, exposure to "professional ethics?" Can "professional ethics" be understood and internalized if there is little, if any, exposure to "ethics?"

It can be, and has been, argued that there are necessary building blocks prior to any teaching of accounting ethics. What can be understood about the small, focused domain of accounting ethics when at the most basic level, the typical accounting student:

- Has no exposure to Plato ("the unexamined life is not worth living"), his concept of eternal truths/innate ideas, and the "Myth of the Cave" and all of its meaning; or to Aristotle's counter-insistence on examining the results of actual human behaviors to determine ethical standards.
- Has not questioned, along with historical great minds (such as Machiavelli, Hobbs, Locke, Voltaire, Rousseau, Hume, Kant, and Mill, to name but a few), whether humanity's essential nature is for the achievement of good (à la Rousseau) or for evil (à la Hobbs, "the life of man is solitary, poor, nasty, brutish, and short"). This is a basic starting point for *any* discussion of ethics or moral reasoning.
- Has not discussed different ideas about how and why human beings create and maintain a social structure.
- Has no reasoned concept of what comprises a "social contract," what is the nature of the forces that lead to individuals forming a social contract, or what its advantages and disadvantages are?
- Has had no academic inquiry into what attributes we are born with and what attributes we acquire. Is all that we are there at birth and discovered through education, as Plato espoused? Or, are we initially a tabula rasa, a clean slate, as argued by John Locke?
- Does not recognize the difference between an ethical dilemma and a false dilemma.[3]

What can be comprehended about "accounting ethics" when accounting students have no prior education about "professional" ethics?

- What forces create the social contract that creates and differentiates professions?
- What are the rights and responsibilities of professions? Why are there privileges for professionals? How do the provisions of "special status" for professionals fit into a sense of fairness or justice? With other ethical values?

The granting of a professional monopoly is an act of faith and trust by a society. Do we provide our prospective entrants with a sufficient sense of the depth or importance of this act? The monopoly is a moral transaction between the society and the individuals who accept the profession. Do we convey this transaction as strongly as we convey the contractual transaction with other accounting entities or with audit clients? Do we instruct that society may, and is indeed entitled to, because of the privileges granted to the profession, assess performance on criteria *not* appropriate for assessing nonprofessionals. A failure to meet societal demands is most problematic for a profession. Society creates professions and can be justified in reversing that creation.

What is the actual role of a professional code of ethics or conduct? It has been argued that the existence of a legalized code is simply a precursor to the end of effective ethical professional behavior as it acts as a static substitute for what was, should, or even must be a moral commitment to ethical behavior. Ethical behavior comes from an internal commitment, not from an outside, imposed prescription for behavior, which raises the most interesting question: is "doing the right thing" ethical if the internal inclination or desire is to "not do the right thing"? This, in turn, can lead to consideration of Pascal's Wager about whether or not it is rational to believe in God and whether or not that rationality is moral.

In today's society, are the motivations of accountants, lawyers, and physicians to engage or not engage in any particular behaviors any different from those of butchers, bakers, or candlestick makers? More and more professionals are salaried members of one or another large, impersonal, profit-oriented organization. Therefore, it may be difficult to visualize oneself as an autonomous professional exercising ethical judgments. This may be so in light of the freedoms that salary, as opposed to fee-for-service, provides. On the other hand, the person will now have two parties evaluating such judgments: the client and his or her supervisor.

And, what about distributive justice? Accounting is intimately involved in the allocation of economic resources, so this should be a key area of discussion. What is fair or equitable? For instance, how do Nozick and Rawls, two contemporaries, approach questions of distributive justice?

And finally, one should ask: is the difficulty in perceiving what is appropriate ethical behavior rooted in the perceived difficulty in performing the technical dimension of accounting? This is possible, but to date there appears to be no measured decline in the technical competency of accounting students (or practicing CPAs). Actually, it may be that as the need for and the existence of technical skills have increased, there have grown increased expectations about ethical performance as well.

ACKNOWLEDGMENT

This paper was presented at the Ernst & Young Research on Accounting Ethics Symposium at Binghamton University, New York, June 12-14, 1994.

NOTES

1. In the Kenny and Eining paper, both scenarios presented involve "whistle blowing," which represents a certain type of ethical dilemma with some of its own characteristics. Also, it is difficult to create *really* controversial ethical dilemmas within accounting scenarios.

2. One can question whether teaching financial accounting and auditing is as different as the practice of each. Intermediate accounting is often taught with an auditing perspective, and auditing builds upon intermediate accounting.

A necessary question to address is: what are the appropriate points in the curriculum to address the charge of the AECC (that majors should be able to "identify ethical issues and apply a value-based reasoning system to ethical questions") and how much effort is needed to achieve success? While well beyond the scope of either paper, it is relevant to their outcomes.

3. An ethical dilemma involves choosing between two moral principles where the choice of one causes harm under the other. A false dilemma occurs when a choice does not create harms under a moral principle. This raises the question of what constitutes a moral principle? Does one, for example, adopt Kant's "categorical imperative," which holds that only rational acts are moral acts and for an act to be rational, it must be universally acceptable?

ETHICS FOR BUSINESS SCHOOL FACULTY

Raef A. Lawson

ABSTRACT

Accountants in academia face a variety of ethical issues. This paper presents the results of a survey of business faculty at five schools regarding their beliefs as to what constitutes ethical behavior by faculty members and the frequency with which unethical behavior occurs. Significant differences were found in the beliefs of faculty members at teaching-oriented schools and those at research-oriented schools. Few differences were found between faculty at liberal arts and technically oriented institutions.

Factor analysis identified three factors as being significant. These include faculty meeting classroom responsibilities, overall faculty ethical conduct, and faculty respect for the rights of students. Identification of these factors can be useful when establishing faculty standards of conduct, and enhance the likelihood that such standards will reinforce ethical behavior by faculty members.

Research on Accounting Ethics, Volume 2, pages 227-241.

ISBN: 1-55938-997-4

INTRODUCTION

The issue of ethical behavior is of increasing importance in the accounting profession. This is true in all areas of accounting, including public accounting, management accounting, government accounting, and academia. While the ethical issues confronting the first three of these areas have received attention, this has not been the case for academia.

Examining the ethical issues faced by accounting academics in business schools or departments is important for several reasons. First, as Robert Sweeny (1993, 14) noted, "a critical element in the mission of colleges and universities is the promotion of an environment for intellectual, cultural, and ethical development.... This may be accomplished only if these institutions require standards of conduct that include integrity, honesty, trustworthiness, loyalty, and avoidance of conflicts of interest from members of the university community, particularly faculty." However, before standards of conduct can be prescribed, a consensus needs to be reached as to what constitutes unethical behavior in an academic setting. While this can be done on a campus-by-campus or system-wide basis, knowledge of how faculty members at other institutions feel about these issues and identification of the key elements of such standards may assist these efforts.

Additionally, study of faculty attitude toward ethical issues is important because faculty attitudes and beliefs greatly influence the moral atmosphere of an institution. As Jeffrey (1993) notes, the moral atmosphere at a private liberal arts college may be significantly different than at a public research institution. A finding of significant differences in faculty attitudes among different types of institutions could indicate differences in moral atmosphere and, thus, provide added insight into the results obtained in studies such as Poneman and Glazer (1990), which found that the rate of ethical development is greater for accounting students in a liberal arts college than for those from a state university with a more traditional curriculum. Furthermore, it would raise questions regarding the generalizability of the results obtained by administering surveys to a single school's faculty, students or alumni.

METHOD

In order to examine faculty beliefs regarding what constituted ethical behavior in an academic setting, business faculty members were sent a survey and asked to express their opinion regarding nine situations which could be viewed as having the potential for unethical behavior. Faculty members in all functional areas were surveyed and no attempt was made to differentiate between responses by area. This was done for a variety of reasons. First, prior studies have generally found no significant differences in the attitude of faculty across functional areas (Harris 1988). Second, from the perspective of establishing standards of conduct, these criteria are generally set at a school-wide level and would reflect the ethical beliefs of faculty in all areas. Thus, the beliefs of faculty from all functional areas would be relevant. Third, due to the small size of some of the schools surveyed, insufficient data would have been collected by further restricting the sample. Finally, identification of functional area affiliation by the respondents on the survey would have, in many cases, breached the confidentiality of the survey respondents' identities.

For each of the nine situations presented, faculty members were asked to rate the situation on two dimensions using a five-point Likert scale. The first dimension was the potential of the situation for unethical behavior (or "degree of severity"). A ranking of 5 indicated an extremely high potential; a ranking of 1 indicated no potential for unethical behavior. The second dimension was the frequency of occurrence. A ranking of 5 represented a situation which occurs extremely frequently; a ranking of 1 indicated a situation which does not occur. In addition to these rankings, faculty members were asked to provide their rank and the number of years of nonacademic work experience.

For this study, the faculty at five colleges and universities in New York were surveyed. The institutions included (1) a large state university with a traditional accounting program, (2) a large private university with a traditional accounting program, (3) a medium-size private college with a traditional accounting program, (4) a medium-size college with a liberal arts orientation, and (5) a small state college with a technically oriented program. The first two of these institutions can be described as having research as an important part of their mission; the latter three are primarily teaching-oriented. The number of faculty responding from each institution is presented in Table 1. The overall response rate was 50%, which compares favorably with rates achieved for other surveys of this type.[1]

Table 1. Description of Faculty Responding to Survey

College/ University	Description	Number of Questionnaires Sent Out	Number of Responses Received	Response Rate
1	Large, research-oriented, liberal arts oriented, state university	76	34	44.7
2	Large, research-oriented, private university specializing in technical education	15	11	73.3
3	Small, private, teaching oriented liberal arts college	17	11	64.7
4	Medium-size, teaching-oriented, private liberal arts college	13	53	8.5
5	Small, teaching-oriented, state college specializing in technical education	6	3	50.0
Total		127	64	50.4

The situations selected for this survey were chosen after extensive discussions with other faculty members regarding possible situations which could arise in academia which contained a need for an ethical judgement. The relevance of these situations may help explain the relatively high response rate to the survey. The situations were selected so as to present a wide range of situations, ranging from the fairly benign to those in which there is general concern regarding the possibility for unethical behavior.

In addition to the above questions, faculty members were asked whether they agreed with the statement that "ethical standards have declined over the last 10 years for faculty." Responses were obtained using a five-point Likert scale, with 1 representing "strongly agree" and 5 representing "strongly disagree." Finally, faculty members were asked where ethics should be taught. Provided responses included "school of business," "some other unit of the university," "joint venture of schools and business," and "should not be taught."

HYPOTHESES

As previously noted, research in the field of business ethics (Ponemon and Glazer 1990) with accounting students has provided evidence that students and alumni from institutions with a liberal arts oriented curriculum rank higher in terms of ethical development than those from schools with a more traditional accounting program. Other studies (e.g., Harris 1988) have indicated that the ethical values of faculty at business schools in general, and in accounting departments specifically, are not much different from those of students. If ethical development and ethical values are related, it may follow that faculty ethical values as well vary depending on the type of educational institution. Thus:

Hypothesis 1. The ethical values of faculty members at institutions with liberal arts oriented curriculum will differ, on average, from those at institutions with more technically oriented curriculums.

While the liberal arts orientation of a school is one way to group higher educational institutions, clearly there are many others. Another way to divide these schools is by examining their teaching versus research orientation. The need to publish at a research-oriented institution could influence faculty attitude by either (1) attracting faculty with a set of ethical attitudes different from those possessed by faculty attracted to teaching-oriented institutions, or (2) influencing faculty values once they arrived at the school. Thus:

Hypothesis 2. The ethical values of faculty members at institutions with research oriented curriculum will differ, on average, from those at institutions with teaching-oriented curriculums.

Another factor which could potentially influence faculty responses is the number of years of nonacademic work experience. This type of experience could alter the way in which faculty members approach situations requiring an ethical decision or influence what they considered ethical and unethical behavior. Thus:

Table 2. Means and Standard Deviations for Each of the Nine Situations

Label	*Situation*	*Degree of Severity*	*Frequency of Occurrence*
Textbooks	Faculty members resell textbooks and other materials received without cost for review purposes.	2.536 (1.159)	3.558 (1.211)
Students	Faculty members fail to respect the confidentiality of student information.	4.018 (0.952)	2.157 (0.857)
Department	Faculty members fail to maintain confidentiality with regard to privileged departmental and/or university matters.	3.732 (1.000)	2.712 (1.054)
Colleagues	Faculty members criticize colleagues or the administration in their classes.	3.018 (1.258)	2.654 (1.046)
Classes	Faculty members fail to personally meet all their scheduled classes.	3.429 (1.291)	2.538 (1.179)
Relationships	Faculty members engage in romantic or sexual relationships with their students.	4.127 (1.139)	1.784 (0.730)
External	Faculty members permit external professional endeavors to interfere with their teaching assignments.	3.661 (0.996)	2.846 (1.036)
Research	Faculty members compel students too select research topics that assist the faculty member's research.	3.107 (1.260)	2.706 (1.119)
Current	Faculty members fail to keep current with developments in their field.	3.018 (1.243)	3.039 (0.979)

Note: Standard deviations shown in parentheses.

Hypothesis 3. The ethical values of faculty members with extensive nonacademic work experience will differ from those with little nonacademic work experience.

RESULTS

Table 2 presents the nine situations with the mean and standard deviations of each situation's rating along the degree of severity and frequency of occurrence dimensions. The greatest potential for unethical behavior was the degree to which faculty members engage in romantic or sexual relationships with their students. Conversely, the lowest potential for unethical behavior was a situation in which faculty members resell textbooks and other materials received without cost for review purposes. In terms of frequency of occurrence, the overall rankings were generally reversed. The romantic/sexual relationship situation was ranked as occurring least frequently, while the reselling of review textbooks occurred most frequently. This inverse relationship between the degree of potential for unethical behavior and frequency of occurrence was expected: faculty members were less likely to engage in situations with a high potential for unethical behavior than those with a lesser potential for such behavior. The situation for which this inverse relationship held the most weakly was the one involving faculty members criticizing colleagues or the administration in their classes. One explanation for this may be that respondents simply did not see this situation as involving any ethical problem at all. An indication of this was one faulty member's response of "so what?" to this question.

Differences Between Teaching and Research-oriented Institutions

In analyzing the influence of the type of educational institution on faculty beliefs, the schools were divided into two groups. The first group consisted of the two large, research-oriented universities. The second group contained the three other schools which, as previously noted, generally view their missions as more teaching oriented.

The use of a *t*-test in comparing the means of these two samples was rejected due to the small sample size and the nonnormal distribution of the responses. Instead, Kendall's tau-B statistic was used, with the null hypothesis being independence of type of school with each of the other variables. From Table 3, it can be seen that five of the severity and three of the frequency measures were significant at normal levels.

Faculty at teaching-oriented institutions were more likely to believe that there was a high or extremely high potential for unethical behavior when faculty members had sexual or romantic relationships with students. A similar situation held for the situation regarding faculty failing to keep current in their field: faculty at teaching-oriented institutions were more likely to believe that there existed a high or very high potential of unethical behavior resulting from this situation. One possible explanation of this may be that faculty members at research-oriented institutions may need to keep current

Table 3. Significance Test of Situations by Type of Institution

	Research versus Teaching Orientation		*Liberal Arts versus Technical Orientation*	
Label	*Severity*	*Frequency*	*Severity*	*Frequency*
Textbooks	.1716 (0.081)	.0168 (n.s.)	.0339 (n.s.)	-.0154 (n.s.)
Students	.1522 (n.s.)	.0537 (n.s.)	.2641 (0.018)	-.1098 (n.s.)
Department	.1616 (0.099)	-.1269 (n.s.)	-.1216 (n.s.)	-.0964 (n.s.)
Colleagues	.1793 (0.070)	.0948 (n.s.)	-.0897 (n.s.)	-.0802 (n.s.)
Classes	.0400 (n.s.)	-.2623 (0.020)	-.0177 (n.s.)	-.1992 (0.059)
Relationships	.1951 (0.062)	.0592 (n.s.)	-.0186 (n.s.)	-.0737 (n.s.)
External	-.0294 (n.s.)	-.0652 (n.s.)	-.1473 (n.s.)	-.0805 (n.s.)
Research	.1065 (n.s.)	-.1810 (0.080)	-.0324 (n.s.)	-.0493 (n.s.)
Current	.3035 (0.006)	-.2120 (0.052)	-.0461 (n.s.)	-.0118 (n.s.)

Notes: Significance levels in parentheses.
n.s. = Nonsignificant at .10 level.

in their field in order to publish research; therefore, the perceived severity of this behavior is less. In addition, faculty at teaching-oriented institutions tended to view as more serious the sale of complimentary teaching materials, the failure to maintain confidentiality regarding privileged departmental matters, and the criticizing of colleagues or administrators in class.

With regard to the frequency with which the various situations occur, three significant differences existed between the two groups of schools. These include the situations in which faculty members (1) fail to personally meet all their scheduled classes, (2) permit external professional endeavors to interfere with their teaching assignments, and (3) compel students to select research topics that assist the faculty member's research. In each case, faculty members at research-oriented institutions believed that these situations occurred more frequently than faculty members from the teaching-oriented institutions. This is as expected given the orientation of these institutions.

In total, a significant difference between the beliefs of the two groups of faculty was found in eight of 18 cases. It can, thus, be concluded that there is some support for Hypothesis 1.

Differences Between Liberal Arts and Technically Oriented Institutions

The schools were next divided into two groups based on their liberal arts or technical orientation. In the first group were the large, private, research-oriented technical university and the small, state, teaching-oriented technical college. The remaining three schools were included in the second group.

As before, Kendall's tau-B statistic was computed in order to determine whether the various variables considered were statistically independent of school grouping. The result of these analyses generally indicated that there were no significant differences between the technically-oriented and liberal arts-oriented groups. The sole exception for the "severity" variables was for the severity of faculty failing to respect the confidentiality of student information variable. Here, the technically oriented group ranked this situation as being a more severe problem than did the liberal-arts oriented institutions' faculty (with a group mean of 4.429 versus 3.878).

In addition, the two groups of faculty differed with regard to the perceived frequency of faculty failing to meet all classes. The faculty from the liberal arts schools viewed this as occurring more frequently than those at the technically oriented schools.

In summary, of the 18 cases examined, only two had a statistically significant relationship with type of school when the institutions were divided into liberal arts and technically-oriented groups. It can, thus, be concluded that Hypothesis 2 is not supported.

Effect of Nonacademic Work Experience

The relationship between the number of years of nonacademic work experience and the situation variables was examined in a manner similar to the one described in the previous section. From Table 4, it can be seen that only three (out of nine) of the "severity" variables and three of the "frequency" variables were significantly related to the number of years of experience. It can, thus, be concluded that Hypothesis 3 is not supported.

Table 4. Significance Test of Situations: Additional Analyses

	Years of Nonacademic Work Experience		Decline in Faculty Ethical Standards	
Label	*Severity*	*Frequency*	*Severity*	*Frequency*
Textbooks	.1047 (n.s.)	-.1329 (n.s.)	-.1061 (n.s.)	-.0967 (n.s.)
Students	.2273 (0.018)	.1677 (0.070)	.0256 (n.s.)	-.2721 (0.012)
Department	-.0077 (n.s.)	.0314 (n.s.)	-.0566 (n.s.)	-.1260 (n.s.)
Colleagues	.0380 (n.s.)	.2224 (0.022)	-.0792 (n.s.)	-.1539 (0.093)
Classes	.0097 (n.s.)	-.1337 (n.s.)	.0693 (n.s.)	-.3104 (0.004)
Relationships	.0815 (n.s.)	.0480 (n.s.)	.1340 (n.s.)	-.0715 (n.s.)
External	.0865 (n.s.)	-.0737 (n.s.)	-.2851 (0.006)	-.1432 (0.000)
Research	.1536 (0.072)	-.0212 (n.s.)	-.1239 (n.s.)	-.1653 (n.s.)
Current	.1014 (0.062)	-2266 (0.021)	-.0326 (n.s.)	-.3070 (0.005)

Notes: Significance levels in parentheses.
n.s. = non-significant at .10.

Further Analyses

As previously mentioned, faculty members were asked to respond to the statement that "ethical standards have declined over the last ten years for faculty" on a five-point Likert scale, with 1 representing "strongly agree" and 5 representing "strongly disagree." The average response was 2.78, indicating some degree of agreement, on average, with this statement. The question then arises as to the manner in which these standards have declined. In order to examine this issue, the cross-classifications of the responses to this question with each of the "situation" variables were examined, with the null hypothesis of independence being tested, again, with Kendall's tau-B statistic.

The right-hand side of Table 4 presents the results of this analysis. It can be seen that only one of the "severity" variables is statistically significantly related to faculty beliefs regarding the change in standards over time. On the other hand, five—more than half—of the "frequency" variables are significantly related. The implication of this is that the perceived decline in ethical standards results not from the perceived seriousness of the situations increasing over time but rather from an increase in their occurrence.

Regarding the previous analyses of type of institution on faculty ethical beliefs, it may be argued that the teaching/research or the technical/liberal arts dichotomy is not the most important criteria in differentiating these schools. In order to determine the characteristics of schools that differentiate their faculties' beliefs from those of other institutions, a discriminate analysis was performed on the data. The discriminant variables included the nine "severity" ratings, the nine "frequency" ratings, and the "level" and "where" variables. These were entered stepwise according to the Wilks' lambda criterion. Stepwise analysis was used because the discriminant variables were not known from previous research to be related to the school variable. The discriminant functions were rotated using varimax rotation in order to assist interpretation of the functions' meanings.

The discriminant analysis revealed that the Wilks' lambdas for the four discriminant functions were 0.202, 0.458, 0.655, and 0.841, respectively. The first lambda had a level of significance of .0013; the second, a level of .1086. The remaining two functions had lambdas that were not significant at normal levels.

The first discriminant function had an eigenvalue of 1.263, accounting for 58.31% of the variance, with a canonical correlation of 0.747. The eigenvalue for the second function was 0.430; its percentage of explained variance was 19.84, and its canonical correlations was 0.548.

Results of the rotation of the discriminant functions are reported in Table 5. The first discriminant function places the greatest weight (with a negative coefficient) on the variable related to frequency of faculty failing to maintain confidentiality with regard to department and/or university matters. The next highest weighting is applied to the variable dealing with the severity of failing to meet scheduled classes. The second function most highly weights (with a negative coefficient) the variable regarding the severity of failing to maintain the confidentiality of student information. Next most highly weighted is the variable regarding the severity (as opposed to frequency in the previous factor) of the failure to maintain confidentiality with regard

Table 5. Results of Discriminant Analysis

	Function 1	*Function 2*
Canonical Discriminant Functions Evaluated at Group Means (Centroids)		
School 1	-0.357	0.475
School 2	-0.206	-1.108
School 3	1.548	-0.357
School 4	-1.372	1.054
School 5	1.065	-0.934
Rotated Standardized Discriminant Function Coefficients		
Department (frequency)	-0.784	0.290
Textbooks (frequency)	0.653	0.024
Students (severity)	0.340	-1.151
Department (severity)	0.189	0.936
Classes (frequency)	-0.194	0.020
Current (severity)	0.004	0.436
Classes (severity)	0.706	-0.071
Where	-0.012	-0.021
Colleagues (frequency)	0.352	-0.077

to departmental matters. While interpretation of these functions may be subject to dispute, they appear to represent two aspects of a dichotomy based on student versus school orientation.

Table 6 contains the *F*-statistics and level of significances between each pair of schools in this study based on this discriminant analysis. From the table, it can be seen that the schools can be divided into two groups. The first of these contains schools 1 and 4; the other contains schools 2, 3, and 5. With the exception of one of the schools, the dichotomy lends some support to the idea that a liberal arts versus technical orientation is an important distinction with regard to faculty ethical values.

Factor Analysis

While the nine scenarios represent a wide diversity of situations, there may be similarities between many of them in terms of the underlying ethical principles involved. This idea is supported by the fact that the ratings for many of the situations were moderately to highly correlated. It, thus, appeared that these situations could be represented by a smaller number of underlying factors. An understanding of these factors would be useful in designing future studies and also would aid schools which attempted to establish faculty codes of conduct.

Table 6. F-statistics and Significances Between Pairs of Schools (Each F has 9, 37 degrees of freedom)

	School 1	School 2	School 3	School 4
School 2	2.0330 (0.063)			
School 3	4.0847 (0.001)	2.0428 (0.062)		
School 4	1.4041 (0.222)	2.2608 (0.039)	3.1659 (0.006)	
School 5	1.9249 (0.079)	1.2194 (0.313)	0.82441 (0.598)	1.8957 (0.083)

Note: Significance levels are in parentheses.

Two-factor analyses were performed using (1) the rating of the situations on the degree of severity, and (2) the frequency of occurrence ratings. Factors were identified using principle-component analysis. In both cases, three factors were identified as being significant (using the criteria that factors account for variances greater than one). To increase interpretability of the factors, a rotation using a varimax criteria was performed. The results of this analysis for the degree of severity ratings is presented in Table 7.

The situations with the highest loading for the first factor were (in order): failing to meet class, failing to keep current with developments in the field, and criticism of colleagues or administrators in class. This factor, which accounts for 43% of the variability in the data, could be interpreted as representing faculty meeting their classroom responsibilities. It is interesting to note that the three situations with the highest loadings were among those indicated in Table 4 as being related to the decline in faculty standards in the last decade.

Table 7. Factor Analysis of Degree of Potential for Unethical Behavior Ratings: Factor Loadings

Identifier	Factor 1	Factor 2	Factor 3
Textbooks	-.01847	.86923	.01876
Students	.27397	.60715	.44809
Department	.42079	.64397	.16827
Colleagues	.69122	.03099	.32276
Classes	.85821	.05103	.06370
Relationships	.45304	-.00276	.65631
External	.58289	.32588	.28993
Research	.03457	.17354	.90387
Current	.74941	.37150	.04150

The second factor, which explained an additional 13% of the variability in the data, had high loading for the review textbook resale, student confidentiality, and department/university confidentiality situations. The interpretation of this factor could be a faculty member's overall ethical conduct. For the final factor, the situations with the highest loading were faculty using students to assist their own research and faculty members engaging in romantic or sexual relationships with students. This factor could be interpreted as faculty members' respect for the rights of students. It accounted for an additional 11.4% of the variability in the data; the three factors, thus, explained a total of 67.4% of the variability in the data. The analysis of the frequency of occurrence data yielded factors that were similar to those just described.

LIMITATIONS

Several limitations in the present study can be identified. The first is that the relatively small samples somewhat limit the power of the statistical tests utilized here. Second, the schools selected for this study were all located in one state and the generalizability of the results of this study to other regions of the United States may be limited.

Finally, further research is needed on the relationships between ethical beliefs and ethical development and the relationship between these constructs and actions taken by faculty members.

IMPLICATIONS AND CONCLUSION

Despite these limitations, this study provides support for the proposition that the ethical values of faculty at teaching-oriented institutions differ from those at research-oriented schools. It also generally failed to support the proposition that the ethical beliefs of faculty at liberal arts-oriented schools differ significantly from those at technically oriented schools. An implication of these findings is the need for selecting samples across a variety of institutions when examining the ethical beliefs of students, faculty, or alumni, in order to be able to generalize the results to other schools.

This study also identified areas that a faculty code of conduct needs to address. These areas include faculty meeting classroom responsibilities, overall faculty ethical conduct, and faculty respect for the rights of students. Consideration of these areas when establishing faculty standards of conduct may enhance the likelihood that such standards will lead to the desired results.

NOTE

1. The questions analyzed in this paper were part of a larger survey. The numbers presented in Table 1 indicate the number of surveys returned. However, eight of the faculty members from the first institution failed to respond to any of the questions analyzed here. This was probably due to the location of the questions on the back side of one of the pages of the questionnaire.

REFERENCES

Harris, J.R. 1988. A comparison of the ethical values of business faculty and students: How different are they? *Business & Professional Ethics* 7(1): 27-49.

Jeffrey, C. 1993. Ethical development of accounting students, non-accounting business students, and liberal arts students. *Issues in Accounting Education* 8: 86-96.

Ponemon, L., and Glazer, A. 1990. Accounting education and ethical development: The influence of liberal learning on students and alumni in accounting practice. *Issues in Accounting Education* 5(2, Fall): 195-208.

Sweeny, R. 1993. Ethics for academics. *Management Accounting* (February): 14.

ETHICS VIOLATIONS IN THE ACCOUNTING PROFESSION:

AN EMPIRICAL INVESTIGATION

C. William Thomas and Samuel L. Seaman

ABSTRACT

In the present study, we explored the associations between certain demographic variables and the propensity to commit accounting ethics violations. The demographic variables were recorded for individuals found guilty of 805 violations of the Code of Professional Conduct of the Texas State Board of Public Accountancy for the period January 1985 through May 1991. A total of 404 individual cases (189 one-time violators and 215 multiple violators) were documented. Almost all of the violators were employed in public practice. For comparative purposes, a sample of 59 public practitioner licensees who had not been found guilty of ethics violations was selected at random from the remaining population of Texas' licensees. The same demographic information was obtained for each of these individuals.

Research on Accounting Ethics, Volume 2, pages 243-263.

ISBN: 1-55938-997-4

Descriptive measures for each of the samples indicate possible differences between the nonviolator and the violator groups. Recommendations are made for future research efforts.

INTRODUCTION

In its first 100 years, the accounting profession achieved an enviable reputation for ethical behavior. A 1988 survey of key business leaders, deans of business schools, and members of Congress revealed that certified public accountants (CPAs) ranked second only to members of the clergy in practicing high standards of ethical conduct (Touche Ross & Co. 1988). Recently, however, an avalanche of litigation resulting in massive court judgments against CPAs and the attendant negative publicity has eroded the profession's public image (AICPA 1993). It is quite possible that some of the pressures of litigation facing the accounting profession are unjustifiable and are the result of frivolous claims aggravated by a plaintiff-oriented legal system (Arthur Andersen & Co. et al. 1992). Nevertheless, an examination of the burgeoning backlog of ethics enforcement dockets of various state boards of accountancy suggests that there is a high incidence of substandard audit and tax work on the part of some CPAs in public practice, indicating a possible breakdown in adherence to technical ethical standards.

In 1988, the American Institute of Certified Public Accountants (AICPA) overwhelmingly adopted a revised Code of Professional Conduct that includes mandatory continuing education and quality review for all members. In addition, the Institute has mandated post-baccalaureate education for all persons applying for membership (to take effect in the year 2000). By the end of 1993, over half of all states had revised public accountancy laws to require post-baccalaureate education for licensees. Colleges and universities across the country are presently designing and implementing extensive post-baccalaureate educational programs for entry level accountants that in many cases include increased general education requirements as well as requirements for ethics education.

Conjecture about the possible impact of certain personal characteristics on the ethical behavior of CPAs remains largely untested in the literature. The purpose of this study is to begin that testing in a somewhat informal way by examining certain traits of

CPAs who have engaged in unethical practices and by comparing them with others chosen at random from the general population of CPAs who have not been charged with an ethics violations. In this study, unethical practices are defined as deviations from codified ethical standards contained in the Code of Professional Conduct of the Texas State Board of Public Accountancy. An empirical look at the associations between potentially significant demographic factors and the professional conduct of CPAs may prove useful to the AICPA and to various state boards of accountancy as they seek to refine rules of ethical conduct and enforcement policies as well. The data may also prove valuable to accounting educators who are considering modifications to curricula and instructional methodologies in order to accomplish identified goals in their educational programs. In addition, the study provides baseline data for state boards of accountancy which, when compared to similar data in later time periods, may be helpful in determining whether revised policies and enforcement practices have had the desired effect on the professional conduct of CPAs.

PRIOR RESEARCH

Theories of Moral Development and Moral Expertise

A body of theoretical literature is beginning to develop around the concepts of moral judgment and moral expertise that is useful in defining the context within which to study actual behavior of CPAs in public practice. To date, theories of moral judgment and moral expertise have been used in a number of studies regarding judgments of those engaged in the practice of auditing. Results of some of these studies indicate that demographic factors such as age, gender, and education appear at least to be indirectly related to some aspects of individuals' moral development.

Gaa (1992) presents the outlines of a normative theory of the auditor's role as a moral and professional expert, based on the philosophical literature dealing with moral judgment and action. In this context, expertise is defined as "the ability, acquired by practice, to perform qualitatively well in a particular task domain" (Frensch and Sternberg 1989, 158). Gaa draws on the theory of moral development advanced by Rest (1986) and the theory of moral judgment developed by Kohlberg (1984) and Rest (1986). The theory of moral development asserts that moral behavior has four components: (1) the ability to recognize ethical issues within various situations, (2) the judgment of an action that is considered morally correct, (3) the commitment to giving priority to ethical principles over personal gain, and (4) the perseverance and strength of character to carry out the decision consistent with the morally correct choice. The first, second, and fourth of these components of moral development involve some form of skill or expertise that may be possessed by individuals in varying degrees. In addition, it is generally perceived that those skills may be developed (Gaa 1992, 26). However, the exercise of those skills in a real-life setting has not been measured.

Kohlberg's theory of moral judgment asserts that human moral reasoning progresses through a series of developmental stages (preconventional, conventional, and postconventional) as persons learn to deal with ethical issues in increasingly sophisticated ways. Each of these three stages is again broken into two substages. At preconventional Stage 1, the person decides how he or she should act purely in terms of whether the action would cause the person to be punished. At Stage 2, the correct action is defined as that which is in the person's best interest without considering the interests of others. At the conventional stage, the person takes into account the interests of others in deciding how to act but in an indirect way—that is, through the impact of his or her actions on others with whom the person seeks approval (Stage 3) or through impact of the perceived action on the norms ("law and order") set forth by the social institutions to which the person belongs (Stage 4). At the postconventional stage, the person has developed a set of basic principles which sometimes may override the dictates of the established social institutions. Within this framework, persons exercising conventional moral judgment would define right and wrong primarily by standards set forth in a code of conduct or in law. In contrast, persons exercising postconventional moral judgment, while recognizing the importance of codes of conduct or law, would sometimes find it necessary to violate the code in order to do the right thing. Kohlberg posits that, beginning in early childhood, all persons move through these stages from lower to higher. At some point (presumably different for all persons and dependent on such things as cognitive abilities, level of education, and the nature of their experience), development ceases. Not all persons progress all the way to the postconventional stage. It is important to note that *higher stages of sophistication in moral judgment do not necessarily make a person more ethical in terms of compliance with predetermined norms, such as those set forth in codes of professional conduct or in law.*

The ability of accountants to recognize issues (the first component of Rest's model) has been studied by Shaub, Finn, and Munter (1992). The ability of accountants to make moral judgments (the second element of Rest's model) has been studied by Ponemon and Glazer (1990), Ponemon (1992), Shaub (1992), Lampe and Finn (1992), and Armstrong (1987). These researchers assessed the ability of various subjects to exercise more sophisticated postconventional reasoning skills in various situations. Among their findings were the following:

1. As a group, CPAs appear to be predominantly Stage 3 or Stage 4 conventional moral reasoners (e.g., either seekers of approval or "law and order" types).
2. Females appear to have more postconventional reasoning skills in recognizing ethical issues than men.
3. Postconventional reasoning skills among CPA firm employees increase from staff level to senior to supervisor but decline at the manager level and still more at the partner level.

Gaa (1992, 36) infers, therefore, that accountants tend to be Stage 4 conventional moral reasoners (e.g., that they tend to use "law and order" set forth in codes of conduct as criteria for ethical behavior). Gaa further points out that Stage 4 conventional reasoning may be a sufficiently high level of reasoning for accountants, as long as the rules that they follow are in accordance with the "moral point of view" expected of them by society. In rule-based theories of morality, individual actions, in order to be judged as ethical, should be chosen in accordance with the rules.

Prior Studies on Impact of Demographic Characteristics

Schaefer and Welker (1994) investigated the characteristics of CPAs disciplined by six state boards of accountancy which distinguish them from a control group of practicing CPAs. The study included 208 CPAs disciplined for three categories of work-related ethics violations: due-care violations, violations of state regulation, and criminal violations. Competency violations were not specifically investigated. The control group for the study consisted of 271 CPAs randomly selected from the general population of CPAs in the six states. Independent variables studied included gender, years of experience, firm size, membership in a state CPA society, and population of the locality of practice. Data for the disciplined group were obtained from the public record rather than individual enforcement files as in the present study. Data for the control group were obtained by questionnaire. LOGIT results revealed that CPAs disciplined for these types of ethical violations were likely to be experienced males practicing in small firms. Because of interactions with other variables, experience was dropped as a significant predictor of unprofessional conduct. Formal education was not included in the set of independent variables.

Table 1. Summary of Relevant Prior Research

	Demographic Variable Influencing Behavior			
Name of Study	*Level*	*Age*	*Gender*	*Education*
Kohlberg (1969)	N/A	No	N/A	Yes
Hodgkinson (1971)	Yes	No	No	N/A
Broverman et al. (1972)	N/A	Yes	Yes	Yes
Freeman and Giebink (1979)	N/A	Yes	Yes	Yes
Johnson et al. (1986)	Yes	N/A	N/A	N/A
Kidwell et al. (1987)	N/A	N/A	No	N/A
Barnett and Karson (1989)	No	Yes	Yes	N/A
Longeneecker et al. (1989)	N/A	Yes	N/A	N/A
Harris (1990)	No	N/A	No	No
Bonner and Pennington (1991)	N/A	N/A	N/A	Yes
Schaefer and Welker (1994)	Yes	No	Yes	No

Aside from the Schaefer and Welker study, most of the previous research regarding impact of these demographic variables on ethical behavior in general has relied upon survey data or laboratory experiments that measure respondents' perceptions in the context of various hypothetical situations. In Table 1, we cite examples of this research. As shown therein, results from such research are neither conclusive nor consistent. In the sections that follow, we discuss results of pertinent studies by demographic variable.

Age

According to Kohlberg (1969), most empirical studies of socialization do not reveal clear association between age development per se and the ability to make incrementally better ethical decisions. Kohlberg maintains, in fact, that development of personality traits such as honesty and integrity are seldom either age-developmental or longitudinally stable. Rather, they result from the differential balancing of conflicting forces that vary over time (such as the time spanned by one's career) and that may change whenever new developmental tasks (such as the issuance of a new technical pronouncement) are introduced. Persons who subscribe to this theory, for example, would reject the notion that a CPA who is 50 years of age would be more prone to read, understand, and follow a new technical pronouncement than one who is 30 years of age, merely due to the difference in the chronological maturity of the two professionals.

Several studies have focused on the impact that age has upon ethical behavior—again, with mixed results. England (1978) found that younger managers tend to assign less importance to trust and honor and more importance to money and advancement than older executives. Broverman et al. (1972), Freeman and Giebink (1979), and Longenecker et al. (1989) concluded that age appears to have a positive impact on certain ethical behaviors. In contrast, Hodgkinson (1970) found no relationship between age and the development of values.

Career stage is sometimes used as a surrogate for age in ethical studies. Barnett and Karson (1989), for example, have observed that females in both the early and late stages of their careers are more likely to be ethical, while males in the early stages are more likely to make decisions based purely upon economic factors. In contrast, males in the middle stages of their careers are more likely than females to be ethical. In other words, career stage (a surrogate for age) has an important effect on male versus female orientation. Stake and Oliver (1991), in a study of sexual misconduct among psychologists and their clients, found that professionals with more years of practical experience showed somewhat less sensitivity to issues of sexual misconduct than psychologists with fewer years of practical experience. Schaefer and Welker (1994) found no support for the hypothesis of a positive relationship between experience of CPAs and the propensity to commit an ethics violation. Three cross-sectional studies concerning moral judgment of auditors (Ponemon 1990, 1992; Shaub 1992) revealed a link between moral expertise and rank (career stage) in public accounting firms. Specifically, the ability to apply postconventional reasoning in moral judgment increases from the staff level to senior and supervisor. However, rather than continuing to increase at higher levels, postconventional reasoning declines from supervisor to manager and partner levels. Assuming that rank (career stage) and age are positively correlated, we may infer that age has a positive correlation with the level of sophistication used by certified public accountants through the supervisor level and a negative correlation from supervisor through partner. It must be remembered, however, that demonstration of higher levels of sophistication in reasoning does not necessarily make a person more ethical.

Gender

A sizable body of literature suggests that women are more sensitive to the impact of their decisions on relationships than are men (Chodorow 1974; Erickson 1968; Carlson 1971; Miller 1976; Kanter 1977, 1987; Hodgson and Watson 1987). Other research (Sargent 1981) suggests that women are more concerned with means to achieve an end (methods) than are men, who are more task-oriented and focused on the "bottom line." Some studies (Broverman et al. 1972; Freeman and Giebink 1979; Barnett and Karson 1989) have shown that, in certain hypothetical situations, females tend to make more ethical decisions than their male counterparts. Stake and Oliver (1991) found that women psychololgists demonstrated more sensitivity to issues involving sexual misconduct than men psychologists. In contrast, Hodgkinson (1971), Kidwell et al. (1987), and Harris (1990) found that gender did not appear to have a significant impact upon ethical decisions. Barnett and Karson (1989) warned that researchers should be careful to avoid gender sterotypes and, as indicated above, found much interaction between career stage (age) and gender as determinants of respondents' ethical or unethical responses to various hypothetical situations.

Shaub (1992) found that female accountants possess higher levels of moral expertise (evidenced by higher levels of postconventional reasoning skills) in making ethical judgments than their male counterparts. However, as emphasized previously, the employment of higher-order judgment skills does not necessarily make one a more ethical person.

Schaefer and Welker (1994) found position correlation between gender and the propensity of CPAs to commit ethics violations. Specifically, they found that males are more likely to commit due care and criminal violations, as well as violations of state regulations.

Education

Behavioral experiments conducted by Kohlberg (1969) demonstrate that "resistance to temptation" to deviate from group norms is positively correlated with a person's intelligence quotient (IQ). To the extent that education enhances cognition, it can be argued that individuals with greater levels of education should demonstrate the ability to make more informed and, thus, better ethical choices. Bonner and Pennington (1991, 27) found a "strong relation between the learning environment and performance, which suggests that performance is probably poor in some tasks because auditors have not had good opportunities to acquire knowledge." Conversely, we may expect that performance will be improved in tasks in which auditors have been exposed to the proper amount and quality of knowledge. If performance is defined in terms of adherence to the technical standards of a code of professional conduct, we may infer that the more knowledge acquired by a person regarding the subject matter of the technical standard, the more compliant he or she will be with the technical standard in practice.

Survey and experimental research is effective in measuring individuals' ethical perceptions, but it fails to document the behavior of individuals as they make real-world decisions. Responses to a survey and behavioral experiments carry no loss function or immediate consequence for a wrong decision or an unethical act. Such studies have not answered the question of whether the respondent actually would have behaved in the same manner as he or she responded in the questionnaire or lab experiment had a real-life process been substituted for the hypothetical.

POSSIBLE ASSOCIATIONS

It is quite possible that certain personal characteristics of persons who are indicted for ethics violations might be markedly different from those of nonoffenders. If, for example, older persons tend to be more ethical than younger ones, as implied in the Longenecker et al. (1989) study, one might expect that more violators would be found within the ranks of younger practitioners than among older practitioners. If education has a positive impact on actual ethical conduct, as suggested by Bonner and Pennington (1991), one might also conjecture that violators would have less formal and/or professional education and weaker scholastic performances (grade point averages) than nonviolators. To address questions like these, we identified CPAs who are violators (a further distinction is made between first-time violators and multiple violators) from those who have not been charged with an ethics violation. Given the many inconsistencies found in the literature, it was difficult to develop any specific expectations regarding the nature of these associations. Instead, we simply chose to use descriptive measures and contingency tables to locate and document potentially important relationships. It is not unlikely that the demographic characteristics of violators could differ depending on the particular type of violation. Thus, as shown in Table 2, we divided the Code of Professional Conduct into four major categories, where each category contains rules of a similar conceptual nature: 11, independence; 21-24, competency and adherence to technical standards; 31, 32, 41, violations of confidentiality and acts discreditable; and 42-50, other responsibilities and practices. The number of violations for Code section 11 is small and we have not examined the characteristics of these violators as a separate group.

METHODOLOGY

We used the variable "violator" (yes or no) as a surrogate for the actual ethical decisions of approximately 500 certified public accountants over a five-and-one-half year period. We were given permission by the Texas State Board of Public Accountancy to examine actual enforcement files between January 1985 and May 1991. For this period, we examined every violation of the Code of Professional Conduct that resulted in punitive action against the practitioner. The consequences for unethical behavior in our study range from private reprimand to revocation of the practitioner's license. Pertinent demographic data for each person identified as a violator was gathered and, using the demographic data, separate profiles for one-time violators and for multiple violators were constructed. For comparative purposes, a smaller sample of nonviolators of the Code was selected at random from the remaining population of approximately 58,500 licensees in Texas. Similar profiles were constructed for this group of nonviolators. Demographic profiles were constructed using the following information:

- Date of birth;
- Age at date of infraction (for violators);
- Gender; and
- Formal education (including grade point average, number of semester hours of accounting, ethics education, and number of sittings required to pass various sections of the CPA examination, as well as scores on those portions of the exam.

Table 2. Ethics Violations By Code Section for Which Punitive Action was Taken By the Texas State Board of Public Accountancy, January 1985 to May 1991

Code Section	*Number of Violations*	*Repeat Offenders*	*Number of Persons*	*Multiple Violations*	*Exclusive Violations*
11	21	2	19	15	4
21, 22, 23, 24	480	256	224	19	205
31, 32, 41	145	12	133	53	80
42-50	159	5	154	39	115
Total	805	275	530	126	404

Notes: Code Section Legend:

11: Independence.
21, 22, 23, 24: Competence and compliance with technical standards.
31, 32, 41: Confidentiality and acts discreditable.
42-50: Advertising, solicitation, form of practice, and other responsibilities.

Table 2 summarizes the 805 violations by Code section: 11, independence; 21, competency; 22, compliance with auditing standards; 23, adherence to generally accepted accounting principles; 24, adherence to other professional standards; 31, confidentiality with client; 32, retention of records; 41, acts discreditable to the profession; 42, acting through others; 43, advertising; 44, solicitation; 45, competitive bidding; and 46, form of practice and name. Repeat offenders accounted for 275 of the violator cases. In addition, 126 cases involved multiple rule violations by an individual within a single case. To avoid including demographic data for these individuals more than once, such violations were eliminated, leaving a total of 404 independent observations, each representing an individual case violation committed by a single individual.

Of the 404 independent cases listed in Table 2, we found that the number of CPAs who had committed single violations (189) was about the same as the number of CPAs who had committed multiple violations (215). Information concerning the nature of the ethics violation as well as dates of birth and certification, firm affiliation, and gender were obtained from computer data files. Information regarding college or university educational background was obtained from microfiche records kept on file at the Board's offices.

Contingency tables were constructed in an effort to view the relationship, if any, between various demographic factors and unethical conduct (violators versus nonviolators), as well as any differences that might exist between violators and nonviolators of the Code with regard to factors of age, gender, and education. Again, however, we have chosen to report only descriptive measures, avoiding inferential techniques since we have been unable to use a formal experimental design. Therefore, the contingency tables and related chi-square analysis are not included.

Comparisons with the sample of nonviolators have been made both on an overall basis and for each individual code section. Ages of practitioners were categorized in 10-year increments (20-30, 31-40, 41-50, 51-60, over 60). Measurements of educational achievement and categories include grade point averages (below 2.0, 2.0-3.0, 3.1-4.0); number of accounting hours (less than 20, 20-30, 31); presence of an ethics course in educational background (yes/no); and number of attempts necessary to pass the CPA examination (1, 2, 3, 4, 5, 6, or more).

RESULTS

Table 3 presents the demographic profile of the nonviolating control group. Table 4 presents the demographic profiles of single and multiple violators of the Code of Professional Conduct. While we did not look for statistically significant results, practically important differences in the frequencies in given groups are highlighted.

Age

Table 3 shows that the average age for a certified public accountant in Texas in 1992 was 41.98 years. Looking at Table 4, one can see that the average age at date of violation was 40.6 years for single violators and 47.23 years for multiple violators of the Code of Professional Conduct. Age appears to have been associated with the propensity for multiple offenders to commit an ethics violation. Thirty-four percent of multiple violators were 50 years of age or older, as compared with only 25% of the control group of nonviolators. The association may be better understood by looking at age and the propensity to commit a violation of the technical standards rules (requirements for competency, compliance with accounting and auditing standards, and compliance with other standards). Thirty-five percent of these violators were age 50 or above, as compared to 25% of the control group of nonviolators. We infer from these results that multiple offenders appear to be significantly older than the average population and that most of the offenses for these persons tend

Table 3. Profile of Nonviolating CPA

	Average	*Median*	*Range*	*Number*
Age	41.98	41	73-26	59
Gender				
Male				39 (66.1%)
Female				20 (33.9%)
Education				
Grade point	3.12/4.0	3.17/4.0	3.996-1.2/4.0	59
Acconting hours	28.15	30	48-6	59
Attempts at CPA exam	3.73	3	9-1	59

to be violations of the technical standards. Age did not appear to be associated with any of the other outcomes that we have examined.

The majority of the ethics violations included in our database during the five-and-one-half year study period are violations of technical standards (see Table 2). When these results were presented to the Texas State Board of Public Accountancy, knowledgeable members confirmed that many of the practitioners who had been found guilty of technical standards violations have been over age 50. The Board inferred that these CPAs may not have been keeping pace with the proliferation of new accounting and auditing pronouncements that were promulgated over the time period included in the study.

Gender

Without exception, all associations based on gender appear to be practically important. Examination of Tables 3 and 4 reveals that male/female ratios are noticeably larger in the populations of both single and repeat violators for all code sections than in the sample of nonviolators. Frequency distributions show that approximately 88.4% of one-time violators were male and 11.6% were female. An even larger percentage of multiple violators were male (92.6%) versus female (7.4%). These proportions differ greatly from the 66% male/34% female breakdown for the sample of nonviolators. These results appear to substantiate findings of studies cited earlier suggesting that females tend to be less prone to unethical behavior than their male counterparts.

It is important to note that a potentially confounding factor is the age of reported violators. We have demonstrated that multiple violators tend to be older than the average population and, since the older practitioners in the profession tend to be mostly males, we might expect that the multiple violators would be mostly males. The fact that our study reveals fewer female than male violators may be more reflective of the relatively recent emergence of females into the accounting profession than of a lower propensity to commit ethical violations on the part of females. It may be that, as time passes, allowing females to achieve higher levels of employment and maturity in organizations than they presently hold, gender differences in ethical conduct may fade or disappear altogether. Replication of this study

Table 4. Profile of Violating CPAs

	Average	*Median*	*Range*	*Number*
Age at violation				
One-time	40.61	39	71-45	189
Repeat	47.23	44	82-28	215
Years experince at violation				
One-time	10.25	9	35-0	189
Repeat	15.6	14	45-0	215
Gender		*One time*	*Repeat*	
Male		167 (88.4%)	199 (92.6%)	
Female		22 (11.6%)	16 (7.4%)	
Education				
Grade point				
One time	2.94	3.0	3.9-1.9	189
Repeat	2.78	2.7	3.9-1.2	215
Hours of accounting				
One time	28.17	27	61-3	189
Repeat	26.23	27	51-0	215
CPA Examination attempts				
One time	4.66	4	21-1	189
Repeat	5.42	5	27-1	215

after a period of three to five years may provide further evidence of an association (or lack of association) with regard to this issue.

Education

Several different variables are indicative of educational attainments among the population of violators and nonviolators. These variables include grade point averages, number of hours of accounting, and number of attempts before successful completion of the Uniform CPA Examination. We present the results of our examination for each of these factors.

Grade Point Averages

Without exception, grade point average tended to be associated with unethical behavior. Tables 3 and 4 reveal that college grade point averages for both single and multiple violators are markedly different from those of the nonviolating group. The average college grade point for nonviolators is 3.12/4.0. This contrasts with a grade point average of 2.94/4.0 for one-time violators and 2.78/4.0 for multiple violators. Additionally, persons violating specific Code sections 21-24 (technical standards), 41 (acts discreditable and related sections), and 44 (advertising and solicitation) have considerably lower grade point averages than the nonviolating group. These findings support Bonner and Pennington's (1991) finding of a "strong relation between the learning environment and performance, suggesting that performance is probably poor in some tasks because auditors have not had good opportunities to acquire knowledge."

Hours of Accounting

Tables 3 and 4 reveal that there is a possible association between propensity to violate the code and number of accounting hours obtained in college. Possible differences also were noted for multiple violators versus nonviolators, technical standards violators versus nonviolators, and violators of other standards versus nonviolators. The average number of semester hours of accounting for a nonviolating CPA is 28.15. This compares with an average of 28.17 hours of accounting for one-time violators and 26.23 hours of accounting for multiple violators. Of the nonviolating group, 44% had fewer than 30 semester hours on a college transcript, while 56% had 30 semester hours or more. In contrast, 58.3% of all violators had fewer than 30 semester hours of accounting on their college transcripts while only 41.7% had 30 hours or more. For multiple violators, 60.4% had fewer than 30 hours on a transcript, and 39.6% had 30 or more. For technical standards violators, the contrast was a little greater (61.4% versus 44.3%). As with gender, these findings are correlated with the fact that the multiple violating population is older than both the nonviolating group and single violator group on the average.

Educational requirements for various state boards have been steadily increasing over the past two decades, denying the opportunity for certification to persons having fewer than 30 semester hours of accounting at the college or university level. The trend in these findings is also consistent with Bonner and Pennington's findings that an increased opportunity for education improves performance. We would particularly expect this to be the case as performance relates to compliance with technical standards.

Attempts at CPA Examination

Results show that multiple violators (who also tended to violate Code sections 21-24 with greater frequency than single violators) required more attempts to pass the Uniform CPA Examination than the nonviolating group. Multiple violators required an average of 5.4 times to pass all four parts of the examination, compared with 3.7 times for nonviolators. Some licensees in the multiple violator group required as many as 27 times to pass the complete examination. Sixty-seven percent of multiple violators required four or more times to pass the CPA examination: 68 percent of the violators of technical standards required four or more times to pass the CPA examination.

SOME FINAL COMMENTS AND RECOMMENDATIONS FOR FUTURE RESEARCH

In this study, we have documented some possible associations between age, gender, and education and the propensity to engage in unethical conduct in the accounting profession. Specifically, persons in older age categories (for whatever reason) tend to commit a greater number of technical ethics violations than their younger counterparts. Additionally, male CPAs tend to be implicated in unethical behavior more frequently than their female counterpart. Finally, multiple violators of the Code tend to have lower grade point averages and tend to sit for the CPA examination more often than the control sample of nonviolators.

The greater incidence of technical violations among the senior ranks of the profession may be changing as policymakers take steps to improve technical competency by requiring more continuing professional education (CPE). For example, newly enacted rules require at least 40 hours of CPE per year, of which 50% or more must be of a "technical" nature. However, it is apparent from studying a sample of license notices reporting CPE hours that the Board has neither clearly defined nor enforced the distinction between "technical" and "nontechnical" CPE. As a result, courses that were listed as "nontechnical" on the license notices of some CPAs were listed as "technical" on the notices of other CPAs. It is important that boards of accountancy reach definitive conclusions regarding the definition of "technical" (vis-à-vis "nontechnical") continuing professional education and that they take steps to carefully monitor the reporting of such courses. Boards may find it useful to outline strict enforcement guidelines for technical continuing education and require significant portions of technical continuing education for those in accounting, auditing, and tax practice. In addition, state boards may need to begin to require technical education in specialty fields (e.g., audits of school districts, taxation, SEC practice) as indicated by the practitioner's stated specialty area. Periodic competency examinations might also be needed throughout a CPA's career in order to assure continued competency in highly technical areas of accounting practice.

Our findings related to gender suggest that it is desirable from an ethical standpoint to attract and retain females in the profession of accountancy. In order to do so, it may be necessary to encourage policies that are proactive toward retention of women in the ranks of public accounting. For example, policies that support balancing of family and career for women might be expanded and improved. It should be remembered, however, that our findings suggest that there may be an interaction between age and gender. The fact that our study reveals fewer female than male violators may be more reflective of the relatively recent emergence of females into the accounting profession than a lower propensity to commit ethical violations on the part of females. Replication of this study in a few years would be most beneficial in this regard.

Our findings regarding association of educational background with ethical violations indicate that it may be beneficial to implement 150-hour degree programs in accounting. For many educational institutions, post-baccalaureate education will require admission to graduate school. In order to be admitted to graduate school, most universities have rather stringent grade point requirements. By strict enforcement of those standards, persons with relatively low grades will be prevented from going to graduate school and, thus, may be prevented from entering the profession. Using this information as baseline data for purposes of longitudinal analysis in future years will help to clarify this issue.

In light of our findings regarding the association between violators of the Code and number of attempts at the CPA examination it appears that recent actions by various state boards of accountancy to limit the number of sittings for the CPA examination and to require certain scores on all parts in order to retain credit for any part were wise decisions. We recommend that state boards of accountancy consider further restrictions in this area. For example, they might set a certain limit for the lifetime number of sittings available to an individual.

LIMITATIONS OF THIS STUDY

It is assumed that the individuals in the "control" sample were nonviolators of the Code of Professional Conduct. Since, by definition, a CPA is a violator of the Code only if reported, it is, in fact, uncertain whether any individuals in the control sample had or had not violated the Code during the period of study. The only thing that is known is that these individuals had not been reported as violators.

Limitations on time and the expense involved in accessing information restricted the collection of data for violators (we could only access records for the five-and-one-half year time period between January 1985 and May 1991). Additionally, the CPAs who were included in the study were licensees from the State of Texas (although a number of them were residents of other states). The generalizability of any results to time periods and populations other than those studied, therefore, may be questionable. Nevertheless, it may be argued that, due to the size and diversity of the population of CPAs in Texas, our samples may be representative of a valid cross section of CPAs across the United States. Replication of this study using data from other state boards of accountancy would further provide evidence of the validity of our conjectures regarding possible associations. Additionally, the time period chosen is relevant for such a study, since it includes the period in which much adverse media publicity and criticism has been leveled against the accounting profession. The use of a five-and-one-half year time period has facilitated one of the primary objectives of the study—namely, to provide baseline demographic data on both the general population of CPAs as well as ethics violators for the purpose of making future comparisons.

REFERENCES

American Institute of Certified Public Accountants. 1988. *Restructuring Professional Standards to Achieve Professional Excellence in a Changing*

Environment. Report of the Special Committee on Standards of Professional Conduct for Certified Public Accountants. New York: AICPA.

———. 1993. *Meeting the Financial Reporting Needs of the Future: A Public Commitment From the Public Accounting Profession.* New York: AICPA.

Armstrong, M.B. 1987. Moral development and accounting education. *Journal of Accounting Education* (Spring): 27-34.

Arthur Andersen & Co., Coopers & Lybrand, Deloitte & Touche, Ernst & Young, KPMG Peat Marwick, and Price Waterhouse. 1992. *The Liability Crisis in the United States: Impact on the Accounting Profession* (Statement of Position), August 6.

Barnett, J., and M. Karson. 1989. Managers, values, and executive decisions: An exploration of the role of gender, career stage, organizational level, function, and the importance of ethics, relationships and results in managerial decision-making. *Journal of Business Ethics* 8: 747-771.

Bonner, S.E., and N. Pennington. 1991. Cognitive processes and knowledge as determinants of auditor expertise. *Journal of Accounting Literature* X: 1-50.

Broverman, I., S. Vogel, D. Broverman, F. Clarkston, and P. Rosenkranz. 1972. Sex-role types: A current appraisal. *Journal of Social Issues* 28: 58-78.

Carlson, R. 1971. Sex differences in ego functioning: Exploratory studies of agency and communion. *Journal of Consulting and Clinical Psychology* 37: 261-77.

Chodorow, N. 1974. Family structure and feminine personality. In *Women, Culture, and Society,* eds. M.Z. Rosaldo and L. Lamphere. Stanford, CA: Stanford University Press.

England, G.W. 1978. Managers and their value systems: A five-country comparative study. *Columbia Journal of World Business* 13(2): 35-44.

Erickson, E.H. 1968. *Identity, Youth and Crisis.* New York: W.W. Norton.

Freeman, S.J.M., and J.W. Giebink. 1979. Moral judgment as a function of age, sex, and stimulus. *Journal of Psychology* 102: 43-47.

Frensch, P.A., and R.J. Sternberg. 1989. Expertise and intelligent thinking: When is it worse to know better? In *Advances in Psychology of Human Intelligence,* Vol. 5, ed. R.J. Sternberg, 157-188. Hillsdale, NJ: Lawrence Erlbaum.

Gaa, J.C. 1992. The auditor's role: The philosophy and psychology of independence and objectivity. *Auditing Symposium XI. Proceedings of the 1992 Deloitte & Touche/University of Kansas Symposium on Auditing Problems,* ed. R.P. Srivastava, Lawrence, KS.

Harris, J. 1989. Ethical values and decision processes of business practitioners: A review and extension. Unpublished manuscript Department of Marketing and Transportation, College of Business, Auburn University, Auburn, AL.

———. 1990. Ethical values of individuals at different levels in the organizational hierarchy of a single firm. *Journal of Business Ethics* 9: 742-750.

Hodgkinson, C. 1971. Organizational influence on value systems. *Educational Administration Quarterly* 7(Autumn): 46-55.

Hodgson, R.C., and E.D. Watson. 1987. Gender-integrated management teams. *Business Quarterly* 52: 68-72.

Johnson, R.A., J.P. Neelankavil, and A. Jadhav. 1986. Developing the executive resource. *Business Horizons* (November/December): 29-33.

Kanter, R.M. 1977. *Men and Women of the Corporation.* New York: Basic Books.
________. 1987. Men and women of the corporation revisited. *Management Review* 76(March): 14-16.

Kidwell, J.M., R.E. Stevens, and A.L. Bethke. 1987. Differences in ethical perceptions between male and female managers. *Journal of Business Ethics* 6: 489-493.

Kohlberg, L. 1969. Stage and sequence: The cognitive developmental approach to socialization. In *Handbook of Socialization Theory and Research,* ed. D. Grosling, 347-388. Chicago, IL: Rand-McNally.

________. 1984. *Essays in Moral Development,* Vol. II: *The Psychology of Moral Development.* San Francisco: Harper & Row.

Lampe, J.C., and D.W. Finn. 1992. A model of auditors' ethical decision processes. *Auditing: A Journal of Practice and Theory* 11(Supplement): 33-59.

Longenecker, J.G., J.A. McKinney, and C.W. Moore. 1989. The generation gap in business ethics. *Business Horizons* 32: 9-14.

Miller, J.B. 1976, *Toward a New Psychology of Women.* Boston, MA: Beacon Press.

Ponemon, L. 1990. Ethical judgments in accounting: A cognitive-developmental perspective. *Critical Perspectives in Accounting* I(June): 191-215.

Ponemon, L.A., and A. Glazer. 1990. Accounting education and ethical development: The influence of liberal learning on students and alumni in accounting practice. *Issues in Accounting Education* (Fall): 195-208.

Rest, J.R., 1986. *Moral Development: Advances in Research and Theory.* New York: Praeger.

Sargeant, A. 1981. *The Androgymous Manager.* New York: AMACOM.

Schaefer, J., and B. Welker. 1994. Distinguishing characteristics of certified public accountants disciplined for unprofessional behavior. *Journal of Accounting and Public Policy* 13(2): 97-119.

Shaub, M.K. 1992. An analysis of factors affecting the moral reasoning of auditors and auditing students. Unpublished report, The University of Nebraska.

Shaub, M.K., D.W. Finn, and P. Munter. 1992. The effects of auditors' ethical orientation on commitment and ethical sensitivity. Unpublished report, The University of Nebraska.

Stake, J.E., and J. Oliver. 1991. Sexual contact and touching between therapist and client: A survey of psychologists' attitudes and behavior. *Professional Psychology: Research and Practice* 22(4): 297-307.

Touche Ross & Co. 1988. *Ethics in American Business: An Opinion Survey of Key Business Leaders on Ethical Standards and Behavior.* New York: Touche Ross & Co.

ON SERVING THE PUBLIC'S EXPECTATIONS:

THE ETHICAL IMPLICATIONS OF SAS 59, GOING-CONCERN REPORT MODIFICATIONS

Marshall A. Geiger, K. Raghunandan, and D.V. Rama

ABSTRACT

Statement on Auditing Standards No. 59 was issued as an "expectations gap" auditing standard to "better serve the public" (Ellingsen, Pany, and Fagan 1989). The results in this paper suggest that a substantial proportion of bankrupt companies did not receive a going-concern modified opinion prior to bankruptcy. Given continuing congressional concerns over the lack of adequate warning before client failures and the ongoing efforts to legislate auditing requirements in this area, the evidence suggests that the accounting profession may need to further increase auditor responsibility regarding going-concern evaluations. Enhanced efforts appear

---

Research on Accounting Ethics, Volume 2, pages 265-279.

ISBN: 1-55938-997-4

necessary in order to mitigate the expectations gap by providing a more reliable reporting mechanism to the financial statement users from auditors that possess a considerable amount of nonpublic information regarding these eventually failed clients. Steps toward this end are the responsibility of the public accounting profession and would not only aid in the prevention of future governmental regulation but also bolster the profession's credibility to the financial community and society in general.

INTRODUCTION

> *SAS No. 59 increases auditors' responsibility vis-à-vis going concern.... The ASB issued SAS No. 59 to better serve financial statement users.... The new standard demonstrates the ASB's belief that auditors can and should take more responsibility for assessing the ability of their clients to continue as going concerns.*
>
> —Ellingsen et al. (1989)

> *If an audit cannot provide an early warning of impending business failure, what good is it?*
>
> —Carmichael and Pany (1993)

The public accounting profession has historically been the target of criticism from the public and legislators for not having provided early warning disclosures about impending client failures (Carmichael 1978). In the mid 1970s, the Moss/Metcalf congressional hearings soundly criticized all aspects of the accounting profession in the United States (see, e.g., U.S. Congress 1977). Beginning in 1985, the House Committee on Energy and Commerce of the U.S. Congress has held numerous hearings concerning the role and performance of the public accounting profession (U.S. Congress 1985, 1987, 1990). A recurring theme in these hearings has been: where were the auditors, and why was there no earlier warning of a client failure?

Carmichael and Pany (1993, 38) note that "in the mid-1980's, the auditors faced a 'political' situation in which at least two key representatives believed that not only were going-concern report modifications necessary, but that auditor performance in issuing them needed to be improved." In response to such criticisms, the AICPA issued a series of nine "expectations gap" auditing standards in early 1988. These expectations gap standards can be thought of as political standards issued to head off further congressional criticism and, perhaps, subsequent public regulation of the auditing profession.

Statement on Auditing Standards (SAS) No. 59, "The Auditor's Consideration of an Entity's Ability to Continue as a Going Concern" (AICPA 1988) was issued as one of the nine auditing standards. Under SAS 59, an auditor must issue a going-concern modified opinion if there is "substantial doubt" about the ability of an entity to continue as a going-concern over the ensuing fiscal year. "Substantial doubt," however, is a subjective phrase that is not specifically defined in the literature. Accordingly, this paper provides some evidence regarding how auditors actually interpret and report on substantial doubt. Specifically, this issue is addressed by comparing the proportion of bankrupt companies receiving a SAS 59 going-concern report to results of earlier research on SAS 34 going-concern reports.

This issue of early warning for client failures continues to be of interest to legislators. Recently, Congress passed the Private Securities Litigation Reform Act, which mandates that every audit of an SEC registrants' financial statements by an independent public accountant include, "in accordance with methods prescribed by the Commission (SEC) ... an evaluation of whether there is substantial doubt about the ability of the issuer to continue as a going concern during the ensuing fiscal year" (U.S. Congress, 1995, sec. 301).

Given the extensive discussions about the public's expectations gap and the assertion that the AICPA has not adequately responded to such public needs, it is important to assess the extent to which SAS 59 has been successful in terms of improving auditor's early warning for client bankruptcies. Additionally, since SAS 59 changed the reporting requirements to reflect the auditor's substantial doubt about a client's continued viability, is there a need for the early warning requirement to be enacted by Congress into law? Does it mean that the current system of private sector regulation and standard setting (including SAS 59) is (or is perceived as) not functioning as well as it should? The evidence in this paper is a first step in answering these and other relevant questions.

The next section of the paper discusses the recent developments behind the SAS 59 going-concern audit opinion and presents a summary of the research on SAS 34 reports. A method section is then presented, followed by a discussion of the results. A summary and conclusions are presented in the last section.

GOING-CONCERN AUDIT OPINIONS

The audit opinion is only one source of information in evaluating the financial status of a company. Other information about the company available in financial statements, annual reports, news releases, and elsewhere can be helpful in predicting client bankruptcies. However, the audit opinion can still be useful in predicting or foretelling probable client failure. This is because the auditor has a more thorough knowledge of the client's activities and future plans than most financial statement users. The information set of the auditor includes a considerable amount of information not available to the public or other interested outsiders. Arguably, access to such information, coupled with the auditor's incentives to avoid potential litigation following a client failure without prior warning, provide the ability and sufficient incentive to make reporting decisions with relative precision. Hence, the audit opinion can be useful to financial statement users (see also Menon and Schwartz 1987; Mutchler 1985).

However, the AICPA's Commission on Auditors' Responsibilities (1978) viewed accounting and auditing requirements differently and did not fully embraced the above premise. Instead, since under existing accounting standards uncertainties need to be disclosed in the financial statements, the Commission recommended that the AICPA remove the "redundant" going-concern qualified audit report requirement. Following the Commission's report, there were three attempts to remove the required going-concern "red flag" in the audit report. These attempts failed, however, in the face of strong opposition from users and the belief on the part of the Auditing Standards Board (ASB) that the redundancy was acceptable ("Late Developments" 1982; "News Report" 1978; "News Report" 1982; Geiger 1993).

However, as part of the recent expectations gap effort, the ASB issued SAS 59, which is effective for audits of financial statements for periods beginning on or after January 1, 1989. It requires the auditor to specifically evaluate whether there is substantial doubt about the client's ability to continue as a going concern in every audit.

Prior standards under SAS 34 (AICPA 1981) regarded the client's ability to continue as a going concern to be assumed, unless the auditor encountered information to the contrary during the audit. Thus, SAS 59 increases the auditor's responsibility and requires an *active* affirmation of a client's ability to continue. Thus, by raising audit requirements for going concern, SAS 59 has been considered to be the most controversial of the expectations gap auditing standards (Guy and Sullivan 1988).

Prior Research

Prior research on auditors' ability to correctly report on troubled clients under the former requirements of SAS 34 reveals that relatively few bankrupt firms received properly qualified going-concern audit reports just prior to bankruptcy—referred to as Type II errors. Likewise, a substantial portion of firms receiving going-concern reports remained viable into the future—referred to as Type I errors.[1] As noted by Hopwood, McKeown, and Mutchler (1994), the relative cost in terms of potential law suits and reputational damage to the auditor for Type II errors is generally believed to be considerably greater than for Type I errors. Accordingly, a considerable amount of research has been directed toward examining bankrupt firms in an attempt to assess whether there was a proper early warning provided by the auditor's report just prior to bankruptcy. As indicated in Raghunandan and Rama (1995), Table 1 presents the results of these SAS 34 studies.

Table 1. SAS 34 Research on the Association Between Bankruptcy and Prior Going-Concern Opinion

Study	*Time Period of Sample*	*Proportion with Prior Going-Concern Modified Audit Opinions*
Altman and McGough (1974)	1970-1973	0.45
Altman (1982)	1970-1982	0.48
Menon and Schwartz (1987)	1974-1980	0.42
Hopwood et al. (1989)	1974-1981	0.39
McKeown et al. (1991a)	1974-1985	0.40
Chen and Church (1992)	1983-1987	0.42
Average		0.42

Source: Taken from Raghunandan and Rama (1995).

As reflected in Table 1, only 39% to 48% (average of 42%) of failed firms received a going-concern modified opinion under SAS 34 just prior to bankruptcy. This study examines whether SAS 59 improved auditors' reporting compared to the results presented in Table 1 for companies that have more recently filed for bankruptcy.

SAS 59 specifically states that even if a business fails shortly after receiving a clean audit opinion, that does not, of itself, indicate an audit failure. Yet, financial statement users *expect* the auditor "to issue a warning signal, regardless of auditing standards, and accordingly, they might consider absence of any warning signal to be an error" (McKeown, Mutchler, and Hopwood 1991b). Thus, since SAS 59 was issued "to better serve financial statement users" (Ellingsen et al. 1989), the focus of this study is on what would be considered an "error" by financial statement users.

METHOD

Sample

As noted by Hopwood, McKeown, and Mutchler (1989), instances where a company has gone bankrupt without a prior going-concern modified opinion are of particular interest to the public. Consequently, this paper focuses on clients filing for bankruptcy and their prior audit opinions.

Initially, a list of bankrupt firms was obtained from New Generation Research's *Database of Bankrupt/Distressed Securities* for the years 1991-1994. This database utilizes several information sources and includes all publicly disclosed bankruptcy filings. The last audit report and financial information prior to bankruptcy was obtained from *Compact Disclosure–SEC* and/or *Laser Disclosure*.

Only those companies which filed for bankruptcy within one year (i.e., 370 days) from the end of the last published financial statements were included. We also eliminated companies that filed for bankruptcy within 90 days of the annual report date due to the fact that the audit report may not have been issued as of the date of bankruptcy filing. We also eliminated additional companies where the audit report date was found to be subsequent to the bankruptcy filing date. This conservative approach follows SAS 59's

Table 2. Sample Selection

Sample Details	*Number of Companies*
Filed for bankruptcy during 1991-1994	373
Deleted for	
Lack of financial or audit report data	89
Filed for bankruptcy <90 or >370 days from the financial statement date	98
Type of industry	34
Final Sample	152

requirements and ensures that bankruptcy filings were made after the auditor's report on the financial statements just prior to bankruptcy. Finally, we also eliminated companies in the banking, other financial, real estate, and utilities sectors because such companies have unique financial characteristics.

The number of companies in our sample for which all information was available was 152. Table 2 presents the sampling frame used to arrive at the final sample.

Financial Stress

Zmijewski's (1984) PROBF score was used as the measure of the bankrupt company's relative level of financial stress. The PROBF model includes the current ratio, return on assets, and leverage ratio to estimate a firm's probability of bankruptcy. Zmijewski's bankruptcy prediction model has received wide use and has been argued to be relatively free of the problems associated with choice based dependent variable sampling approaches as well as being a parsimonious model (Bamber, Bamber, and Schoderbek 1993; Chen and Wei 1993; Wheeler, Pany, and Chewning 1993). This bankruptcy probability estimate was then used as the relative indication of the level of financial stress reflected in the financial statements for each of the 152 firms just prior to bankruptcy.

The predicted probability of bankruptcy (i.e., failure) is calculated as follows:

$$PROBF = -4.803 - 3.599(PRFT) + 5.406(LVRG) - 0.100(LIQ)$$

where: $PROBF$ = a standard normal variable,
$PRFT$ = net income/total assets,
$LVRG$ = total debt/total assets,
LIQ = current assets/current liabilities.

Substantial Doubt

Additionally, the U.S. Congress has considered legislation that would mandate the SEC to specify audit procedures to be performed when there is "substantial doubt" about the ability of a public company to continue as a going concern. Ponemon and Raghunandan (1994) found, upon interviewing key legislative counsel/staff involved in drafting the legislation, that substantial doubt was interpreted by them to be a probability of failure greater than 0.33.

Accordingly, this study uses the threshold probability of bankruptcy of .33 to create a subset of the full sample. Specifically, we separately analyze only those firms with PROBF scores greater than .33 prior to bankruptcy. These appear to be the specific types of firms that Congress is looking for better reporting on (that is, a going-concern warning) prior to bankruptcy. These are also the types of firms that SAS 59 was intended to better report on (Ellingsen et al. 1989).

Client Size

Prior research has indicated that client size is negatively correlated with the issuance of a going-concern modified report, even after controlling for financial factors (see McKeown, Mutchler, and Hopwood 1991a). Hence, our analysis also attempts to discern whether client size had an effect on the issuance of SAS 59 going-concern modifications for the bankrupt firms in our sample.

Audit Firm

We also analyze whether audit firms differ in their tendency to issue prior going-concern audit reports. Accordingly, we identify the audit firm in the year preceeding bankruptcy for each of the companies in our sample. Seven categories of audit firms were established for analysis—one for each of the Big 6 and a seventh for all other audit firms.

Table 3. SAS No. 59 Period (1991-1994) Association Between Bankruptcy and Prior Going-Concern Opinion

	Number	*Percentage*
Panel A: All Companies (n = 152)		
Received prior going-concern report	89	58.6%
Did not receive prior going-concern report	63	41.4%
Total	152	100.0%
Panel B: Companies with PROBF Scores over .33 (n = 116)		
Received prior going-concern report	80	69.0%
Did not receive prior going-concern report	36	31.0%
Total	116	100.0%

RESULTS

The sample of bankrupt firms ranged in size from $42,000 to over $6.6 billion in sales (mean = $324 million), and roughly 84% of the companies were audited by Big 6 audit firms. The average PROBF score for the group, as would be expected, was relatively high at 0.68.

The results of the examination of audit reports issued just prior to bankrupttcy filing are summarized in Table 3. Panel A of Table 3 presents the number and percentage of the firms that received a SAS 59 going-concern modified report. Compared to the research findings on SAS 34 reports presented in Table 1, the SAS 59 results represent an improvement in reporting on these bankrupt firms. Prior research found an average of 42% received a prior SAS 34 modified going-concern report, while our sample reflects roughly 59%. A binomial test indicates the post-SAS 59 proportion is significantly higher ($p < .01$)

While this is an improvement, Type II errors (i.e., bankrupt firms without prior going-concern reports), in our sample remain relatively high at 41%. Although, auditors are not expected to be predictors of future events—including bankruptcy—this persistent Type II error rate is, nonetheless, troubling.

Next, we analyzed only those firms which had a PROBF score of .33 or higher based on the financial statements just prior to bankruptcy. This restriction eliminated 36 firms from the sample,

Table 4. Analysis of Prior Going-Concern Opinions by Size of Firm (Sales Quartiles)

Quartile Rank[a]	*n*	*Received Going-Concern Reports*	*Did Not Receive Going-Concern Reports*
Panel A: All Companies (n = 152)			
1	38	23 (60.5%)	15 (39.5%)
2	38	25 (65.8%)	13 (34.2%)
3	38	22 (57.9%)	16 (42.1%)
4	38	19 (50.0%)	19 (50.0%)
Panel B: Companies with PROBF Scores over .33 (n = 116)			
1	29	24 (82.8%)	5 (17.2%)
2	29	22 (75.9%)	7 (24.1%)
3	29	20 (69.0%)	9 (31.0%)
4	29	14 (48.3%)	15 (51.7%)

Note: [a]Quartile rank = 1 represents the smallest firms.

leaving 116 for analysis. Panel B of Table 3 indicates that the accuracy rate on these more financially stressed firms increases from 58.6% to 69.0%. Thus, almost one-third of the companies in financial stress filed for bankruptcy without receiving a prior going-concern modified opinion under SAS 59.

In order to see if the size of the bankrupt company had any effect on whether or not the auditor modified the opinion prior to bankruptcy, the sample was divided in quartiles based on level of sales.[2] Table 4 presents the results of reporting on these firms by quartile.

The results presented in Table 4 are generally in the expected direction. Specifically, smaller firms receive proportionately more going-concern reports. A chi-square test indicates that the differences between the quartile groups are not significant (chi-square = 2.33; p-value = .57) for the entire sample. However, a similar analysis on the 116 highly stressed (PROBF $>$ .33) companies reveals that the pattern of going-concern modifications and firm size is significant (chi-square = 9.02; p-value = .03). Larger companies in financial stress were much less likely to receive a prior going-concern modified report in comparison to smaller similarly stressed companies.

Last, we performed an additional test to see if going-concern reporting frequency varied by auditor across the bankrupt sample. We identified each of the auditors for the bankrupt firms and coded them 1 through 6 for each of the Big 6 firms and 7 if not a Big 6 firm. A chi-square analysis indicates a significant difference across these auditor groups regarding tendency to issue a going-concern report to a subsequently bankrupt company (chi-square = 13.60; *p*-value = .04). Thus, reporting on these bankrupt firms does not appear uniform across Big 6 firms and the non-Big 6 firms.[3]

SUMMARY AND CONCLUSIONS

The issue of auditors providing early warnings about client bankruptcies continues to be of interest to the public, legislators, and the accounting profession. In response to recent pressures from the public and legislators, SAS 59 was issued as an expectations gap auditing standard. This, and the other expectations gap standards, were intended to meet the public's outcry for increased auditor responsibility and more reliable reporting on business failures.

This study found some enhanced reporting accuracy after SAS 59, but that a significant proportion of client bankruptcies still occurred without a prior going-concern modified opinion (Type II reporting errors). The proportion of Type II reporting errors decreases somewhat but is nonetheless high when only companies that experienced some financial stress (i.e., PROBF $>$ .33) before bankruptcy are considered. Overall, Type II error percentages reported in this study ranged from 34% to 52% with generally smaller percentages for the highly stressed companies. Thus, the results suggest that although gains have been made, auditors may still have to do more to mitigate the continuing expectations gap problem.

The AICPA has sought to head off governmental regulation by suggesting that the public accounting profession can effectively self-regulate. SAS 59, therefore, has been promoted as an effort toward that end and has been touted as an effort to narrow the expectations gap. However, these results suggest that the public and legislators may still have cause for criticism of the public accounting profession, which persists regarding reporting on all bankrupt firms.

In a related context, Rep. Wyden (1993) has accused the accounting profession of moving at too slow a pace in its self-regulatory process in trying to comply with its mandate to serve the public. Rep. Wyden noted that "in that case, it is up to the Congress to enact it [regulation of the public accounting profession] through legislation." Despite the issuance of SAS 59, the Private Securities Litigation Reform Act has a "substantial doubt" requirement. Does this suggest that at least some legislators are not happy about the adequacy of early warnings of failures?

Bankruptcy prediction models (see Altman 1982; Mutchler 1985; McKeown et al. 1991a) have consistently outperformed auditors' reporting on subsequently bankrupt firms.[4] While auditors appear to be able to identify troubled firms similar to the models (Kida 1980), auditors then use additional information to assist in their reporting decision.

Accordingly, there may be many reasons why auditors did not issue going-concern modified reports (see Kida 1980; Mutchler 1984) for a sizeable proportion of the bankrupt companies examined in this study. SAS 59 requires that if, as a result of procedures performed in the normal course of every audit, the auditor has substantial doubt about the client's ability to stay in business for a reasonable period of time, he/she is required to obtain and assess management's plans. If the auditor believes such plans can be effectively implemented and, thus, enable the client to mitigate or reverse the adverse conditions within a reasonable period, no going-concern modification is necessary to the audit report.

The persistence of Type II "errors" being observed could be due to the auditor's evaluations of the mitigating effects of management's plans. The empirical results are consistent with the position that auditors may not be sufficiently skeptical in evaluating the adequacy and sufficiency of management's plans for the future, and particularly those of larger companies. If such considerations are causing auditors to delay or not to issue "red flag" going-concern modified opinions, then a change in professional practices and standards might be warranted. The public accounting profession has the ethical responsibility to financial statement users and providers of capital to objectively report the findings of their audit. This overriding responsibility cannot succumb to pressures from the client to issue an unmodified opinion.

There are also direct costs to the financial markets and to society for an incomplete signal of impending business failure. Without a reliable early warning signal of business cessation, the efficient allocation of capital is impeded and/or disrupted. Such unforeseen aberrations cost society and investors needlessly due to lack of useable and credible information. The financial and reputational costs to specific auditors (see Sullivan 1992; Carcello and Palmose 1994) for failing to properly modify their opinions on bankrupt companies also can be substantial. Such ineffective reporting, in turn, reflects poorly on the standards and the self-regulatory practices established by the profession. Hence, auditors and the *public* accounting profession have an ethical and financial responsibility to report more effectively, and to the best of their professional ability, regarding issues of going concern.

ACKNOWLEDGMENTS

The authors gratefully acknowledge useful comments from the editor, Lawrence Ponemon. We thank Stephen Griffin for his able research assistance.

NOTES

1. See Altman (1982), Mutchler and Williams (1990), and Garsombke and Choi (1992) for studies examining Type I errors.
2. In order to assess the equivalence of the sales quartile group's probability of getting a going-concern report, a one-way analysis of variance was run on PROBF scores. The results indicate no difference in PROBF scores across all sales quartile groups ($p = .94$).
3. This reporting difference, however, is not driven by audit firm structure, as found in Carcello, Hermanson, and Huss (1995). Of the Big 6 firms in our sample, highly structured firms had Type II error rates ranging from 28% to 52% and less structured firms had error rates ranging from 28% to 64%. Non-Big 6 firms had a combined Type II error rate of 60%.
4. For a discussion and contrary view, see Hopwood et al. (1994).

REFERENCES

Altman, E.I. 1982. Accounting implications of failure prediction models. *Journal of Accounting Auditing and Finance* (Fall): 4-19.

Altman, E.I., and T. McGough. 1974. Evaluation of a company as a going concern. *Journal of Accountancy* (December): 50-57.

American Institute of Certified Public Accountants AICPA, Commission on Auditors' Responsibilities. 1978. *Report of the Commission on Auditors' Responsibilities.* New York: AICPA.

American Institute of Certified Public Accountants. 1981. *Statement on Auditing Standards No. 34: The Auditor's Considerations When a Question Arises About an Entity's Continued Existence.* New York: AICPA.

———. 1988. *Statement on Auditing Standards No. 59: The Auditor's Consideration of an Entity's Ability to Continue as a Going Concern.* New York: AICPA.

Bamber, M., L. Bamber, and M. Schoderbek. 1993. Audit structure and other determinants of audit report lag: An empirical analysis. *Auditing: A Journal of Practice and Theory* (Spring): 1-23.

Carcello, J.V., D.R. Hermanson, and H.F. Huss. 1995. The relationship between audit structure and public responsibility: Audit firms' propensity to qualify bankruptcy-related opinions. *Research on Accounting Ethics* (Volume 1): 21-42.

Carcello, J.V., and Z. Palmrose. 1994. Auditor litigation and modified reporting on bankrupt clients. *Journal of Accounting Research* (Supplement): 1-30.

Carmichael, D.R. 1978. *The Auditor's Reporting Obligation.* 2nd edition. New York: AICPA.

Carmichael, D.R., and K. Pany. 1993. Reporting on uncertainties, including going concern. In *The Expectation Gap Standards: Process, Implementation Issues, and Research Opportunities*, eds. Guy and Winters, 35-58. Jersey City, NJ: AICPA.

Chen, K.C.W., and B.K. Church. 1992. Default on debt obligations and the issuance of going-concern opinions. *Auditing: A Journal of Practice and Theory* (Fall): 30-49.

Chen, K.C.W., and K.C.J. Wei. 1993. Creditors' Decisions to Waive Violations of Accounting-Based Debt Covenants. *The Accounting Review* (April): 218-232.

Ellingsen, J.E., K. Pany, and P. Fagan. 1989. SAS no. 59: How to evaluate going concern. *Journal of Accountancy* (January): 24-31.

Garsombke, P.H., and S. Choi. 1992. The association between auditors' uncertainty opinions and business failure. In *Advances in Accounting*, Vol. 10, ed. B.N. Schwartz, 45-60. Greenwich, CT: JAI Press.

Geiger, M.A. 1993. *Studies in Managerial and Financial Accounting*, Vol. 1: *Setting the Standard for the New Auditor's Report: An Analysis of Attempts to Influence the Auditing Standards Board.* Greenwich, CT: JAI Press.

Guy, D.M., and J.D. Sullivan. 1988. The expectation gap auditing standards. *Journal of Accountancy* (April): 36-46.

Hopwood, W., J. McKeown, and J. Mutchler. 1989. A test of the incremental explanatory power of opinions qualified for consistency and uncertainty. *The Accounting Review* (January): 28-48.

———. 1994. A reexamination of auditor versus model accuracy within the context of the going-concern opinion decision. *Contemporary Accounting Research* (Spring): 409-431.

Kida, T. 1980. An investigation into auditors' continuity and related qualification judgements. *Journal of Accounting Research* (Autumn): 506-523.

Late developments. 1982. *Journal of Accountancy* (April): 31.

McKeown, J.C., J.F. Mutchler, and W. Hopwood. 1991a. Towards an explanation of auditor failure to modify the audit opinion of bankrupt companies. *Auditing: A Journal of Practice and Theory* (Supplement): 1-13.

———. 1991b. Reply. *Auditing: A Journal of Practice and Theory* (Supplement): 21-24.

Menon, K., and K. Schwartz. 1987. An empirical investigation of audit qualification decisions in the presence of going concern uncertainties. *Contemporary Accounting Research* (Spring): 302-315.

Mutchler, J.F. 1984. Auditors' perceptions of the going-concern opinion decision. *Auditing: A Journal of Practice and Theory* (Spring): 17-30.

———. 1985. A multivariate analysis of the auditor's going-concern opinion decision. *Journal of Accounting Research* (Autumn): 668-682.

Mutchler, J.F., and D.D. Williams. 1990. The relationship between audit technology, client risk profiles, and the going-concern opinion decision. *Auditing: A Journal of Practice and Theory* (Fall): 39-54.

News report. 1978. *Journal of Accountancy* (September): 24-26.

News report. 1982. *Journal of Accountancy* (August): 10-14.

Ponemon, J.F., and K. Raghunandan. 1994. What is substantial doubt? *Accounting Horizons* (June): 44-54).

Raghunandan, K., and D.V. Rama. 1995. Audit reports for companies in financial distress: Before and after SAS no. 59. *Auditing: A Journal of Practice and Theory* (Spring): 50-63.

Sullivan, J. 1992. Litigation risk broadly considered. In *Auditing Symposium XI: Proceedings of the 1992 Deloitte & Touche/University of Kansas Symposium on Auditing*, ed. R.P. Srivastava, 84-92. Lawrence, KS: School of Business, University of Kansas.

U.S. Congress. Subcommittee on Reports, Accounting, and Management of the Senate Committee on Government Operations. 1977. *The Accounting Establishment.* Washington, DC: U.S. Government Printing Office.

———. 1985. *Hearings Before the Subcommittee on Oversight and Investigations* of the House Committee on Energy and Commerce, No. 99-17, "SEC and Corporate Audits." Washington, DC: U.S. Government Printing Office.

———. 1987. *Hearings Before the Subcommittee on Oversight and Investigations* of the House Committee on Energy and Commerce, No. 100-83, "Financial Reporting Priorities." Washington, DC: U.S. Government Printing Office.

———. 1990. *Hearings Before the Subcommittee on Telecommunications and Finance* of the House Committee on Energy and Commerce, No.101-196, "Expanding Auditor Responsibility." Washington, DC: U.S. Government Printing Office.

———. 1995. Private Securities Litigation Reform Act. Public Law 104-67 (H.R. 1058). Washington, DC: U.S. Government Printing Office.

Wheeler, S., K. Pany, and E. Chewning. 1993. Inter-firm differences in propensities to modify audit opinions for pre-SAS no. 58 accounting principles changes. *Accounting Horizons* (September): 46-54.

Wyden, R. 1993. Testimony before the U.S. House of Representatives, January 26. Washington, DC: U.S. Government Printing Office.

Zmijewski, M.E. 1984. Methodological issues related to the estimation of financial distress prediction models. *Journal of Accounting Research* (Supplement): 59-82.

J A I P R E S S

Research on Accounting Ethics

Managing Editor: **Lawrence A. Ponemon,** *Center for the Study of Ethics and Behavior in Accounting, School of Management, State University of New York at Binghamton.*

Volume 1, 1995, 361 pp. $73.25
ISBN 1-55938-753-X

CONTENTS: Editors Note: On Ethics Research in Accounting, Lawrence A. Ponemon. The Concept of Trust and Institutional Development in Auditing, *Steven E. Kaplan and Robert G. Ruland.* The Relation Between Audit Structure and Public Responsibility: Audit Firms Propensity to Qualify Bankruptcy-Related Opinions, *Joseph V. Carcello, Dana R. Hermanson, and H. Fenwick Huss.* Commentary on Auditors' Public Responsibility, *Jack C. Robertson.* The Relation Between Audit Structure and Public Responsibility: Audit Firms Propensity to Qualify Bankruptcy-Related Opinions: A Comment, *J. Edward Ketz.* Toward an Understanding of the Philosophical Foundations for Ethical Development of Audit Expert Systems, *Steve G. Sutton, Vicky Arnold, and Thomas D. Arnold.* Comments on "Toward an Understanding of the Philosophical Foundations for Ethical Development of Audit Expert Systems", *Jagdish S. Gangolly.* Further Toward an Understanding of the Philosophical Foundations for Ethical Development of Audit Expert Systems, *Jesse F. Dillard.* On Ethical Behavior in Social, Political, and Legal Environments, *Steve G. Sutton, Vicky Arnold, and Thomas D. Arnold.* An International Comparison of Moral Constructs Underlying Auditors' Ethical Judgments, *Jeffrey Cohen, Laurie Pant, and David Sharp.* An Analysis of International Comparison of Moral Constructs Underlying Auditors' Ethical Judgments, *Joseph J. Schultz, Jr.* Comments on an International Comparison of Moral Constructs Underlying Auditors' Ethical Judgments, *W. Morley Lemon.* Do Expected Audit Procedures Prompt More Ethical Behavior? Evidence on Tax Compliance Rates, *Wanda A. Wallace and Christopher Wolfe.* Discussion Comments on "Do Expected Audit Procedures Prompt More Ethical Behavior? Evidence on Tax Compliance Rates", *Mary S. Doucet.* Commentary on the Ethics of Compliance with Tax Laws and Regulations, *Andrew Baily.* Application of Virtue Ethics Theory: A Lesson from Architecture, *John Dobson and Mary Beth Armstrong.* Professional Services and Ethical Behavior, *Haim Falk.* The Moral Expertise of Auditors: An Exploratory Analysis, *John T. Sweeney.* Ethical Development of Accountants: The Case of Canadian CMAS, *Lois Deane Etherington and Leah Schulting.* Moral Judgment and Moral Cognition: A Comment, *James Gaa.* Gender Diversity Driven Changes in the Public Accounting Workplace: A Moral Intensity Analysis, *Karen Hooks and Thomas Tyson.* Ethical Decision Making in Organizations: A Management-Employee Whistle Blowing *Model, Don W. Finn.* An Exploratory Study of Accounting Students' Professional Attitudes: Implications for Accounting Education, *Patricia Casey Douglas, Randoph T. Barker, and Bill N. Schwartz.* Perceptions of Senior Auditors: Ethical Issues and Factors Affecting Actions, *Elizabeth M. Dreike and Cindy Moeckel.* Misleading Annual Report Presentation: Ethical and Financial Considerations, *Timothy J. Louwers and Robin R. Radtke.*